Felix the Railway Cat

Felix the Railway Cat

TRANSPENNINE EXPRESS
AND
KATE MOORE

MICHAEL JOSEPH
an imprint of
PENGUIN BOOKS

MICHAEL JOSEPH

UK | USA | Canada | Ireland | Australia
India | New Zealand | South Africa

Michael Joseph is part of the Penguin Random House group of companies
whose addresses can be found at global.penguinrandomhouse.com

First published 2017
001

Text copyright © First TransPennine Express Limited, 2017
Written by Kate Moore www.kate-moore.com

The moral right of the author has been asserted

To protect the privacy of certain individuals, some names, events and
identifying details have been changed

Set in 13.5/16 pt Garamond MT Std
Typeset by Jouve (UK), Milton Keynes
Printed in Great Britain by Clays Ltd, St Ives plc

A CIP catalogue record for this book is available from the British Library

Royalties from the sale of this book will be donated to
Prostate Cancer UK (registered charity 1005541)

ISBN: 978–0–718–18543–5

www.greenpenguin.co.uk

Contents

Introduction

If you go down to Huddersfield station in Yorkshire, you may be in for a big surprise . . . For greeting you at the 'Customer Information and Assistance' point, waiting patiently to attend to customer enquiries, might not be a bright young woman or a helpful old man dressed in the purple-and-navy uniform of TransPennine Express.

Instead, the team member on duty may be Felix, the Huddersfield station cat.

She sits proudly at the desk, her ears attuned to the familiar cacophony of station sounds, her green eyes alert and intelligent as you approach. Her fluffy black tail – tipped with a dash of white – flicks back and forth rhythmically, almost wagging, as though she is delighted to see you.

But Felix is a working pest controller, not a house cat, and years of being patted and prodded by customers have made her, at times, wary of strangers. Yet when she knows you, whether you're a colleague or a commuter, her affection knows no bounds.

With a single, graceful leap, she dives from the desk to the floor and winds her way around your legs, her long white whiskers twitching as she investigates the possibility of you being in possession of a treat. Felix lives for treats and, despite her initial grumpiness, the most unfamiliar of strangers can soon become a lifelong friend in the right circumstances.

Yet a cat cannot live on treats alone; and for Felix adventure gives just as much sustenance. So although Felix can be found most days at the station – on duty at her desk, patrolling the platforms, or helping to check tickets at the gateline – she also explores far beyond the station's borders. Watch her as she goes: passing the bronze statue in St George's Square outside with a friendly flick of her swishing tail; bypassing the beflowered garden on Platform 4; or disappearing into the darkness of the railway tunnels, on her way to who-knows-where. She crosses the train tracks with a certain cockiness: a swagger to her swaying walk. Things weren't always this way but, just as Felix has grown on the job, so, too, have her confidence and courage.

Much as Felix relishes her role in charge of the station – and make no mistake, this cat is most *definitely* the Boss – it's fair to say that she does have a rather regular habit of falling asleep on the job, for she's just as likely to be found curled up in a colleague's jacket in the locker room as meeting and greeting customers on the concourse. If she's not on duty when you call by, hoping for a few words with Huddersfield's most famous railway star, forgive her absence, for she's probably catching up on a few 'zzz's . . . before trying to catch some more mice, a key part of her official role as senior pest controller.

For now, though, we leave her sitting at the customer service desk, those sharp emerald eyes missing nothing as she surveys her kingdom, her glitzy purple collar shining brightly in the morning sun. A slim gold disc dangles from it, bearing her name and her home address:

FELIX, PLATFORM 1.

This is the story of the Huddersfield station cat.

1. A Madcap Idea

'What this station needs,' announced Gareth Hope one morning in the summer of 2008, 'is a station cat.'

His colleague, Andy Croughan, laughed out loud. When the two mates got together – as they did most days, after the morning rush hour was over, to kick about some conversation during the quiet phases of their shift – they were always coming up with daft ideas, but this one had to take the biscuit. A station cat? Oh, it was a good bit of mischief, but nothing that would happen in a million years.

They knew that there was a historic tradition of railway cats – back in the days of British Rail, many signalmen used to have them, and Gareth, who was relatively new to the industry, was forever being told stories by old-timers about how there used to be cats at every depot and how they'd all get wage slips every month – but as far as Gareth and Andy knew, the tradition was now history, lost in the railway's unstoppable modernisation. Winston Churchill had once been pictured fussing over the Liverpool Street station cat, and the idea of Huddersfield getting its own moggy seemed as much a part of the past as that venerated former prime minister.

Yet despite – or perhaps because of – its far-fetched nature, the fantasy of a station cat became a favourite topic of conversation for Gareth and Andy over the next few months, especially during those shifts when the station clock ticked by agonisingly slowly, and discussing daft ideas seemed the only way to make it speed up.

Working on the railway hadn't been Gareth's original career plan. He'd attended university to study computer programming, but two years into his course he'd decided he hated it and couldn't do it for a living. Needing a job, he'd joined the barrier team at Huddersfield station towards the end of 2006 – but soon found that wasn't for him either. There were no actual ticketing gates when he'd joined the station, so at that time the gateline team themselves formed the only physical barrier stopping fare-dodgers from travelling without tickets. More times than he cared to remember, Gareth, who was slim, willowy and non-confrontational, had found himself on the wrong end of an altercation with an aggressive customer who had pushed him to the ground. He'd been relieved, after just over a year in the job, to get off the frontline and become an announcer (based safely in the office, behind a glass window), but working at the station still felt like a stopgap: something to do while he worked out what he *really* wanted to do with his life. But he didn't worry too much about it; he was only twenty-one, so there was plenty of time for figuring it out.

In the meantime, he really enjoyed working at the railway station. Amongst colleagues, it had a family feel; an atmosphere that in truth went beyond the barriers of Huddersfield and spread across the entire railway network. People who worked on the railway would do anything for each other: it was that kind of industry. Once, Gareth had got stuck down south, but a flash of his rail ID card had had the team at the station there going the extra mile to help him get safely back home. At Huddersfield specifically, many of the twenty-six-strong team had worked there for more than twenty years; they knew each other better than most brothers and sisters. In fact, if you'd been clocking in for less than a decade you were known as a 'young un'.

Gareth and Andy both fell into that category. Andy was a duty manager, also in his early twenties, who'd been at the station since 2006. He was a dynamic, mischievous man with a rangy figure and heaps of energy. Given the team spent more time with each other than they did with their families — sometimes working nights, as Huddersfield was staffed twenty-four hours a day — it was perhaps no surprise that many colleagues became close friends. Andy and Gareth had hit it off immediately, and their very favourite way of entertaining each other was to embark on flights of fancy with their conversation; they had a bit of a reputation for it. The station cat was just one of their crazy ideas; another was that TransPennine Express (TPE), the company which ran the station, should employ Mr T from *The A-Team* to do the safety announcements ('Keep behind the yellow line, fool'), while Gareth was also an enthusiastic advocate of changing all the stairs in the station to slides and pulleys, to minimise slips, trips and falls.

The station manager, Paul, a rather by-the-book sort of boss, was by now used to their ridiculous suggestions, which always came thick and fast. He was a young, good-looking man who didn't give away a lot verbally, but his eyebrows could speak volumes. Up they would go whenever Gareth put another wacky idea to him, his dismissal and disbelief writ plain across his disapproving face.

Throughout the autumn of 2008, in their natters during painfully slow shifts, Gareth and Andy kept coming back to the suggestion of a station cat — playing with the idea as a kitten does a mouse on a string, batting it back and forth between them and getting more and more excited as they came up with ever more elaborate reasons why the station *needed* a cat. Gareth was particularly enamoured of the idea that a station feline might calm down irate customers.

3

'A cat would make *everybody* happy – whenever someone was complaining, you could present the cat and they'd calm down!' he enthused with feeling, his memories of his time on the gateline still fresh. 'And just think how amazing it would be to have this cat wandering around and being in charge of everything, causing trouble and getting in everyone's way, as cats do!'

They were like kids, egging each other on. 'You should ask Paul!' Andy would say, joking about it.

And then, one day, as the manager walked through the announcer's office, where the mischievous pair were chatting, Gareth seized his moment.

'Paul, any chance we could get a station cat?' he casually asked. He tucked his straight, shoulder-length brown hair behind his ears a little nervously, awaiting his boss's verdict.

He didn't have to wait long: the station manager didn't miss a beat.

'No, absolutely not,' Paul said flatly, without breaking his stride for an instant.

Gareth sank back into his chair, deflated.

But not for long. Another of his off-the-wall ideas was that the station should replace all the concrete on the platforms with the spongy tarmac used on kids' playgrounds (to prevent injuries), and Gareth now bounced back as surely as if his chair was made of that very material. Plan A – asking Paul outright – had not worked, but Gareth was becoming far too keen on the idea of a station cat to give up that easily. His campaign to get a station pet now needed to move up a gear.

It was time for Plan B.

'OUR STATION CAT IS MISSING' read the handmade poster on Paul's official noticeboard. He unpinned it with a wry smile, and cast his eyes around the office, where further copies of the same poster adorned the walls. All Gareth's handiwork, of course. Paul balled up the poster and threw it in the recycling bin with a weary shake of his head.

The young announcer was certainly dedicated to his crazy cause. If Paul left the formal noticeboard unexamined for more than a week, distracted by more pressing issues elsewhere in the station, when he returned it would be plastered all over with notices about this fantasy cat, so that his original, official signs would be completely covered by Gareth's campaign posters. Some of these had really bad, hand-drawn sketches of cats on them; others were more text-based. Just recently, in this summer of 2009, Paul had asked the team to come up with suggestions for preventing trips, slips and falls on the station concourse, which was one of his biggest concerns as manager and something he was keen to address. Perhaps inevitably, Gareth had submitted his own unique list of suggestions.

'Provide all customers with a harness connected to a network of zip wires,' his submission had read. And continued:

- Install lots of Travellators so customers don't have to walk anywhere.
- Put a large sign outside the station saying 'ENTER AT YOUR OWN RISK' (possibly accompanied by a skull-and-crossbones image?).
- Cover the floor in a six-inch shag-pile.
- Put trampolines in falling-over hotspots, so customers would instantly be returned to their feet.
- Employ a station cat . . .

Always the station cat. No matter what the problem, a station cat, according to Gareth, was the answer. In Gareth's defence, he was able to cite countless examples of cat success stories: such as Stubbs, who had been mayor of Talkeetna,

Alaska, for over a decade, or the famous Japanese station cat, Tama, who had transformed the fortunes of her ailing railway line, bringing in 1.1 billion yen ($10.44 million) a year.

No, Gareth's campaign for the station cat showed no signs of abating. The man was obsessed! And what was more, somewhat to Paul's chagrin, he was no longer alone.

For Gareth's handmade posters weren't his only method of attack as he continued Operation 'Station Cat'. Gareth's job – much to his delight – saw him located in the announcer's office. Not only was this a coup in terms of getting him off the gateline, but it just happened to be the most sociable place in the station. The team were always walking through the announcer's office. It was a large, communal-type room, home to basic office equipment like the photocopier that everyone used, but it also provided the throughway to the booking office. Everybody on shift was in the announcer's office at some point during their working day, so there was always some chatter going on. Perhaps partly because of that, it had a very homely atmosphere, emphasised by a reddish-pink carpet that softened people's steps as they came and went throughout the day.

Inevitably, as Gareth had regularly sat and chatted with Andy at his desk about their shared enthusiasm for a station cat, the passing colleagues had listened and chipped in. It had now been over a year since Gareth had first suggested it, and during the past twelve months everybody who worked at the station had heard them talking about it – and loads of the team had come on board with the idea. Huddersfield had long been an animal-friendly station – the team had a pet-pictures noticeboard, where they stuck up snapshots of their cats and dogs in the mess room – and by now the majority of the team were behind the campaign. They even added to the banter: a new gag was that the cat could be employed as a pest controller, to tackle the station's non-existent 'mouse problem'. But everybody knew the truth: mice had nothing to do with it; they wanted a cat because it would be fun, and a real pleasure to come to work and share a shift with a furry friend.

Even the team leaders supported the idea. Although they reported to Paul, it didn't necessarily mean that he was always in charge; many of the team leaders had worked at the station for decades and had the wisdom and experience to prove it. In fact, their affectionate nickname for the manager was 'Babyface' because Paul was still relatively young, especially in comparison to them.

Perhaps the most influential of these team leaders was the inimitable Angie Hunte. A warm, outgoing black woman with an infectious laugh and a larger-than-life character, Angie had given more than twenty years' service to the station, and over that time she had proved herself to be a powerful matriarchal figure within it. Even Paul had learned that it was to his benefit to get Angie on side with new ideas, for she had huge influence at the station owing to the high esteem in which she was held. When she'd first chatted with Gareth and Andy about the station cat, Gareth had felt extremely apprehensive. *If she hates it*, he'd thought with trepidation, even as he extolled the virtues of his pet idea, *it will never happen.*

But a beaming smile had spread across Angie's face as the idea took hold. It was more than Gareth could have hoped for. 'Angie being enthusiastic about the cat idea was like a green light,' he recalled. 'I remember thinking: *it might go somewhere now.*'

But Angie wasn't the only one with influence. Huddersfield had six team leaders, who each worked in shifts, taking full responsibility for the station and team when on duty. And another of these was a chap called Billy, who'd worked alongside Angie for decades. He'd worked his whole life on the railway, first as a conductor and latterly as a team leader.

In his late fifties, he was the elder statesman of the station –
and known for being grumpy in a granddad kind of way.
Angie had known him so long, and got on with him so well,
that she had teasingly nicknamed him 'Mr Grumpy'. He was
short and balding, and his years of professed misery had
etched that expression into his lined face.

Billy was known for telling things straight. If he didn't
agree with you, he would come right out and say you were
talking a lot of rubbish. If he thought you were being a fool,
he told you as much, and he wouldn't do it in a nice PC way.

When Billy first heard about the campaign to get a station
cat, he thought it was silly. He was dismissive; and it seems
the manager, Paul, still felt the same way. Despite Angie's
enthusiasm and Gareth's creative poster campaign, the manager remained unmoved.

Undaunted, as the months passed and the idea took even
deeper hold, Gareth tried to appeal directly to Paul's business brain. Knowing his manager was a man for facts, figures
and charts, Gareth took the time to produce a summary of
the pros and cons of getting a station cat:

Pros	Cons
Happy customers	
Happy team	
Historic tradition	
Pest control	
Our NPS (national passenger survey) scores will undoubtedly go through the roof . . .	
Good PR	

Obviously, there were no cons . . .

But the chart went the way of all the posters before it. As 2009 turned into 2010, and then into 2011, Gareth was still no closer to realising his dream – nor to moving on from the station, as he'd said he would do . . . one day.

It was in the spring of 2011 that some intriguing news reached him on the office grapevine, borne to him via the passing footsteps of his colleagues journeying through the announcer's office. Paul, so rumour had it, was being seconded to a job elsewhere in the business. So someone else would be taking charge of the station in his absence – and that someone else would have the power to veto or green-light the idea of the station cat.

When he heard who'd got the job, Gareth couldn't repress the grin that stretched across his face. He ran to meet Andy, his long-time partner in crime – and the man who had just been appointed acting station manager. Andy's wide smile matched Gareth's own.

'This is it!' the announcer cried in excitement, his eyes shining with glee. 'This is our opportunity. *Let's get the cat!*'

2. A 'Mouse' in the House

Angie Hunte adjusted her yellow hi-vis jacket and cast her eyes along the commuters bustling through the gateline, stifling a yawn. It was now April, which meant that at last the mornings were lighter and brighter, but getting up at a quarter to five for an early shift was still a struggle, even after all these years. Much as she liked working at the station, some shifts you felt you just plodded your way through.

That morning, though, she felt an unfamiliar fizz of excited anticipation in her stomach as she scanned the faces of the customers coming through the station. She was looking for one face in particular: that of Belinda Graham.

Belinda was a TPE manager who worked at the company headquarters in Manchester, but commuted through Huddersfield every day. It was fortunate she did, for Angie had a very important question to ask her – about a certain station cat. With Andy Croughan, the acting station manager, having at last given the nod to the idea, all the Huddersfield team needed now was for HQ to say yes. But, Angie knew, getting that yes might be easier said than done.

There was no question of skipping this step, though, or of welcoming a cat through the back door. They all wanted it to be above board and proper. Although it had started out as a joke, the Huddersfield team were cat lovers, many of them cat owners themselves, and they took the responsibility of owning a pet seriously. Angie, Gareth, Andy and the others had already decided that, if they got the approval they were hoping for, the cat would be cared for equally by the team. Even Billy had given an – admittedly typically taciturn – acquiescence that he, too, would chip in and help out.

As the cat campaign had gone on, Billy – perhaps worn down by his friend Gareth's unfailingly upbeat enthusiasm – had come around to the idea. Over time, he'd become quite keen on the concept and would even break into a smile every now and then when Gareth raised the fantasy cat in conversation, and a smile was a rarity with Billy.

'All right, lad, all right,' he'd concede, his lips curving unnaturally upwards, as he headed outside for a smoking break, clutching his favourite cigarillos. 'I agree: a station cat would be grand.'

Billy had cats of his own, including a ginger queen called Jaffa. A railway man to his very bones, he and his wife lived in some old station buildings, and his cats would often hold up the trains as they weaved their way across the rails. Their shared love of cats was another thing that he and Gareth had bonded over, for Gareth was the proud owner of Cosmo, a fluffy black-and-white moggy with a massive tail. But one cat was not enough for Gareth – and, at last, the station cat seemed within his reach.

But first Angie had to work her magic. Angie was a brilliant people person – part of her expertise as a team leader was in managing others, and she always seemed to know exactly who to speak to and more importantly *how* to speak to them to resolve any issues or to get things done. It was Angie who'd suggested they approach Belinda for permission. Angie knew her of old, and she knew Belinda was a doer: someone who meant business and was willing to roll her sleeves up and make things happen. Nothing was ever too much trouble for Belinda. Angie gave another glance at the commuters, but it was still a little early, and there was no sign of Belinda's distinctive short blonde hair amidst the trickle of customers coming through the gates.

Angie rehearsed in her head what she was going to say, and couldn't help the almost guilty smile that twitched at her lips as she did so. For the team had decided they couldn't leave things to chance, but instead were going to pull out all the stops to bring this cat home. And so the conversation Angie was about to have was in some ways just as creative as the hand-drawn posters that Gareth had been mocking up for the past three years.

Another surge of customers swelled through the concourse, and Angie suddenly recognised the tiny figure of Belinda weaving among them.

'Belinda!' she called out urgently, bustling over to her with a practised air, neatly avoiding the steady stream of commuters.

'All right, Angie?' The manager greeted her warmly.

'Have you heard what's happened here?' Angie began, lowering her voice discreetly, as though she didn't want the customers passing by to overhear.

Belinda's brow creased in concern. 'No, what?' she asked, expecting any manner of emergency. Angie was a very experienced team leader – if she needed to call on head office for support, it must be serious.

'Do you know, we've got a mouse in the mess room?' Angie whispered theatrically, as though aghast, acting her shock and horror at this supposed 'pest invasion' perfectly. 'Sharon, one of the girls in the office, she says she's seen a mouse.'

Belinda shook her head in sympathy, completely understanding Angie's worry.

'Well, we can't be having that!' Angie continued, switching from shock to indignation with the smooth ease of an Oscar-winner. 'We eat in there!' She took a deep breath and said, more lightly than she felt, 'Belinda, could we not get a cat?'

Belinda paused for a moment before replying, coolly assessing this formal request from her colleague. Then she bobbed her head decisively. 'Yes, I dare say we can sort something out,' she said. 'We can put the cost under pest control or something like that. I think Windermere have a cat, too, and we pay for its food. Don't worry: we'll get it sorted.'

Angie listened in amazement. Though it was well-known on the railway network that the former British Rail had given their station cats joke wage slips, she had never heard of the privatised companies doing it, of covering the costs of a cat's upkeep. But in fact the station cat at Windermere was not the only one – there were station moggies up and down the country, as lovingly cared for by the railway staff as they had been throughout history. Manchester Oxford Road was at one point rumoured to have as many as thirteen cats, though in recent years, with some of the cats adopted, they were down to four: Jumper, Tom, Jerry and Manx. A white-and-tabby cat, Rabbit, along with her up-and-coming assistant, the black-and-white Quaker, resided at the recently restored Kirkby Stephen East station, Cumbria, in the north-west of England. And even down south, Southend Victoria was home to little Jojo, while Tonbridge in Kent had recently erected sombre memorial plaques in honour of their two felines, Jill and Louis, who had both sadly died in the past few years after many moons of service. It seems having a station cat was not a thing of the past at all – and Huddersfield station was now about to become part of that illustrious tradition.

Angie waved Belinda off through the crowd with a cheery

flick of her hand, though she was careful not to appear too excited that Belinda had given her the nod. As the manager from HQ disappeared from view, however, and Angie turned and headed straight for the announcer's office, her excitement began to build. By the time she had closed the door behind her and turned to face Gareth, who was sitting wriggling on his chair, waiting to hear the verdict, Angie felt ready to burst.

'Oh my God!' she whispered, joyously but cautiously, because there was a rush hour going on outside and she didn't want to alarm the customers with mad screams coming from the office. 'Oh my gosh! Gareth, we're gonna have a cat! We're gonna have a cat!'

Gareth's mouth dropped open in surprise. 'Are you being serious?' he asked.

Angie nodded, not trusting herself to speak.

Gareth leapt up, delighted. 'So we're getting a cat then?!'

'We're getting a cat.'

'We're getting a cat!'

It was like a tidal wave of euphoria sweeping through the station. After a campaign of almost three long years, it was a genuinely emotional moment. All anybody could talk about was the cat, the cat, the cat.

It had been decades – if ever – since Huddersfield had had a station cat. The last known animal residents had been Bess, Dolly and Tommy: the final shire horses employed by the station, who used to act as shunt ponies pulling train wagons into sidings, either to rest them or to enable new trains to be made up from the various carriages they moved about the tracks. But the horses had been made redundant in 1952, and since then there had been no record of any other formally employed animal residents; the greedy pigeons who populated the metal beams of the corrugated iron roof most definitely didn't count. Now, nearly sixty years on, the team at Huddersfield – entirely through their own efforts – had overcome all obstacles to get the 'yes' they needed. A railway cat would be making its home there, so the team hoped, in the very near future.

But who would that cat be?

3. A Star Is Born

'Shh,' said Chris Briscoe, a revenue protection officer with TransPennine Express, 'listen.'

It was the middle of the night on 17 May 2011, and in Chris's semi-detached house in Rotherham nothing should have been stirring. But something had woken him and his wife, Joanne, from their slumber – and he thought he knew what it was.

He and Joanne listened intently into the dark night. Yes – there it was again: a timid squeaking, which sounded as if it was coming from the airing cupboard. Chris threw back the duvet and tiptoed down the landing, rubbing his hands across his bearded face to shake himself awake. Though it should have been shut tight, he could see that the airing cupboard door was standing ajar and, as he edged closer, could hear the multitude of tiny squeaking noises growing louder as he approached.

He gently eased the door open a bit wider and looked down. And there, at the bottom of the cupboard, spread luxuriously across the Briscoes' best Egyptian cotton towels, like a film star in a perfume advert, was his eleven-month-old, black-and-white cat, Lexi. When he'd gone to bed, there'd been one heavily pregnant cat slinking about; now, as he peered down at the wriggling shapes surrounding her, he counted five minuscule kittens and one very happy cat.

Lexi was an affectionate pet, the only cat Chris had ever known who licked him, and she'd become even more so during her pregnancy. While she'd been carrying the kittens she'd barely moved five feet away from Chris: if he sat down for an instant, she'd climb on to his lap; if he got into bed, a moment later he'd feel the warm, solid weight of her as she snuggled down on top of him. He'd known her time was near, so he'd got a special flocked cat bed for her and tucked both that and an old blanket away, somewhere private, so that she could give birth in peace and comfort when she felt ready to do so. Lexi, however, had clearly had other plans – thus the little family currently sprawled out on the softest, most expensive towels known to man.

Chris crouched down and examined his lovely, tired-looking cat and her new children. He reached into the mess of kittens and first checked Lexi over, then did the same with the newborns, making sure that their airways were clear and that their mum had nipped off the umbilical cord properly; all was as it should be. Everything was grand. There was no hissing or biting from Lexi as he did any of these checks; she wasn't that kind of cat. Instead, she happily nuzzled each tiny kitten as it was returned to her, making sure they were all well.

There were five of them: three tabby cats and two black-and-white ones. The latter were so similar that it was almost impossible to tell them apart. They looked the absolute spit of their mum: mostly black, but with almost identical markings to Lexi – a white V-neck bib, and white paws that looked as though the kittens had dipped their paws in paint; or perhaps, given the elegance of their bedding, had slipped on ivory-coloured kid gloves. In fact, all five kittens had those tell-tale white paws: a family trait that had come through strongly in each and every brand-new cat. Having just been born, their eyes were shut tight, and they mewed only for their mother, who attended diligently to each one.

Having made sure all was well, Chris gently closed the

door, leaving it just ajar, as Lexi had wanted, before he and Joanne left them to it.

Lexi's pregnancy had come as something of a surprise to the Briscoes. They owned two cats, Lexi and Gizmo. Both had been found abandoned on a council estate up near Collingwood, and were taken in by Chris and Joanne as they were looking for a pair of cats to help with mousing. Their house had a massive garden and they'd set aside an area at the top of it to keep chickens and a couple of golden pheasants in an ornamental cage. Because of the grain for the birds, mice had soon taken up residence, too, and since the Briscoes hadn't wanted to put down poison to address the issue, a duo of cats was the answer.

Gizmo was an enormous cat, mostly white but with a black head (though white face) and black back. Lexi was half his size. Though he'd been taken in for mousing, he was absolutely idle – so laid back, he was laid down – and daft as a brush. He was a huge, fluffy cat who was patient and kind.

When the cats had first arrived, given they were rescue moggies, the Briscoes hadn't known how old they were. They set about getting them inoculated and had taken them into the vet's to discuss getting them neutered and spayed respectively, as they didn't want any unexpected litters. The vet had looked up from his examination of Lexi and told them somewhat bluntly, 'You're too late.'

Sixty-odd days later, here they were with five gorgeous little kittens.

As the kittens were surprise arrivals, Chris now set about putting the word out that there were five kittens going spare, who needed rehoming once they were old enough to be separated from their mum. Joanne Briscoe also worked for TPE, as a customer host, so both she and Chris tried to spread the message far and wide on the railway network. Their son said he would take one of the tabby cats, and then a train dispatcher from Manchester got in touch to say she'd like the other two tabbies. Only the black-and-white pair were now without a new home to go to.

But they were making themselves rather comfortable in the one they currently had. Over the next ten days, one by one, the kittens slowly opened their eyes. At that age, kittens' eyes are always blue, so first one pair of cerulean peepers, then another, and then another, stretched open and took in the sight of the world for the very first time. But one of the black-and-white kittens – the one who was fluffier than her two-tone twin, which was the only way to tell them apart – took her time. She was the very last of the litter to blink open her bright blue eyes – but once she did there was no stopping her.

Almost overnight, or so it seemed to Chris and Joanne, the basket of kittens was transformed from a blind and help-less mass into five courageous and mischievous individuals, who set out to cause chaos wherever they went. They were so playful! The kittens chased each other all over the house: scarpering up the curtains, hiding in the washing basket, pinching the socks drying on the radiators and treating them like prey. Nothing could be left unattended for a moment or it would be turned into a new game. The kittens had the run of the house and they made good use of it – they darted and tumbled and skidded all over the place, a five-headed ball of kitten mayhem that had suddenly rolled into town like a funfair.

A favourite game of the quintet was to terrorise their dad, Gizmo. He was such a placid cat that the kittens found they could romp all over their father and he'd let them do what-ever they wanted. Eventually, after half an hour or so, he'd have had enough, and would gently ease them all off him and slink out of their way, but he never once chastised them.

Mum, however, was a different matter. All five kittens would jump all over her, just as kittens do, chasing each other and leaping athletically over their mother – a great game – but when Lexi had had enough, she'd give her children a backhander or grab them by the scruff of their necks to tell them: 'Enough. Stop now.' She was a loving cat, but she was also a very 'do-as-you're-told' type of mother, and the kittens learned to stay in line. They learned other things from her, too. When the time came, Lexi – who was an absolutely spotless cat when it came to hygiene – showed them how to use a litter tray so well that all five kittens became impeccably house-trained.

As time passed, the kittens stopped suckling from Lexi and the Briscoes moved them on to the recommended diet of raw mince mixed with egg. They didn't want to use the shop-bought kitten food that some did; nothing but the best for these kittens born on Egyptian cotton towels! Instead, they were weaned on the freshest, highest-quality mince, with raw egg hand-beaten into it. Food of champions.

One of the tabby kittens – the one who became known as Spadge, and who would eventually go to live with the Briscoes' son – certainly agreed with that sentiment. He asserted himself early on and would always be the first at the food; in the Briscoes' own words, 'He was a greedy little oik.' Amid the loud protestations of his mewing siblings, he decided he was getting in first and nobody else could have a look-in until he was finished.

The kittens were a noisy, confident, outgoing bunch. They miaowed when they wanted their dinner and Spadge was in the way, but they also mewed when they were playing, and had been known to let out a chorus of squeals during spirited boxing matches with one another. At night, when they were fast asleep after dinner, wiped out by their mega-exciting day, there were always a lot of soft little purrs coming from the velour brown-and-white cat bed where the siblings all slept.

In addition to Spadge revealing that he was 'the greedy one', the kittens asserted their individual personalities in other ways, too. The black-and-white duo became known as the terrible twins, for a favourite game of theirs was to latch on to Chris's trousers while he was having a quiet sit-down, just like two furry pin badges. The kittens would make themselves quiet and still, so that Chris had no idea they were there. Then, when he stood up to make his way upstairs, he'd suddenly find that he had ten (or twenty) claws stuck into his legs as the cats clung resolutely to his trousers. Those super-sharp claws would scrape his skin when he moved. 'What the hell is that?' he'd cry, feeling them scratch, and one black-and-white kitten or another would cheekily cock its head to one side, enjoying the drama of his roars of pain and the oh-so-sweet sensation of being carried through the air on his trousers. They climbed up his legs *all* the time. So, after only a few weeks, Chris was walking around looking as though he'd made it a new favourite habit to clamber through viciously spiked brambles on a daily basis.

He redoubled his efforts to find permanent homes for the terrible twins. And here, at last, he heard on the railway network that Angie Hunte had been putting out a message of her own: Huddersfield station wanted to employ a station cat. Did anyone know of any kittens who might be up to the job?

It was important to Angie and the team that it was a kitten who joined them. It wouldn't have been fair to an older, former house cat to throw it in at the deep end in a working environment, what with the danger of the trains and the noise and bustle of a busy station. Huddersfield hosted approximately 5 million customer journeys each year, with fifteen trains per hour, which placed it in the top 100 busiest stations in the country. You couldn't teach an old cat the kind of new tricks that a railway cat would need to learn, but if a kitten grew up there it would learn on the job how to be a station cat.

Angie and Chris soon met up to talk all things kitten. At that time Chris was often at Huddersfield for work, so a meeting was easy enough to arrange.

Angie greeted him with one of her classic beaming smiles. 'So, we're looking to decrease our pest control bill,' she said, eyes sparkling with good humour, 'go a bit greener and employ a kitten instead. I hear you might be able to help – how much are you wanting for them?'

'Oh, I'm not wanting anything for them,' Chris replied quickly. Thinking of the scratches on his legs, in the nicest possible way he was going to be rather pleased to be shot of the kittens. To know that he wasn't going to be stuck with at least one of the terrible twins was great news. In addition, given the network nature of the railway, he thought there was also a bit of kudos in the fact that it was going to be *his* cat that would be the Huddersfield station cat; that *he* would be its granddaddy. He would never live that one down.

Above all, though, he and Joanne were simply pleased that the kitten would be going to a permanent, loving home, where the Briscoes could be sure that it was going to be well looked after. In fact, judging by the grin on Angie's face when he agreed that she could have one of the kittens, it was going to be downright *spoilt*.

'We'd like a boy,' Angie added, almost as an afterthought, as they drew the conversation to a close. After all, she and the team didn't want to push it: it felt like a miracle that HQ had agreed to the station cat. Nobody thought that the powers-that-be would appreciate having kittens on top of that, so everyone felt safer if the new recruit was a boy.

As it happened, Chris didn't actually know the gender of the kittens. And when the train dispatcher who planned to take the two tabby cats came to visit her new charges at his home he openly confessed his ignorance.

'I don't know how to sex kittens,' he admitted. 'You'll have to do it yourself.'

Unfazed, the dispatcher picked up the tabby cats and said, 'That one's definitely a boy and that's definitely a girl.' She would go on to call them Percy and Max, respectively. Then she reached over and plucked one of the black-and-white kittens from the basket and turned it upside-down. 'Definitely a boy,' she announced. She picked up his twin, the fluffy one, and did the same. There was so much long-haired fur around its bits that it was a little harder to see, but she made a pronouncement nonetheless. 'Definitely a boy.' She seemed to know what she was talking about.

Chris let Angie know the good news: both the black-and-white kittens were boys, so she could take her pick. There was good news for Chris, too: a lady who worked in the Huddersfield booking office, Pam, had said that her mum would give a home to whichever kitten the station didn't want, so both of them would be off his hands for good.

Joanne and Chris assessed the terrible twins as they scampered boisterously about the house. Apart from the fact that one was a lot fluffier than the other, there was barely any difference between them. They'd noticed only one thing that marked them out. The kittens, as you'd expect, had a heap of toys to play with (some actual toys and some hijacked by the kittens in fun). They had a scratching post with a ball on a string and in their turn all the kittens had climbed up the pole and then dived off, jumping on the ball; there were half a dozen squeaky mice for them to pounce on, too. And it was one of these mice toys that differentiated the twins. It was one of those toys where you'd pull the string at the side and the mouse would vibrate really, really quickly, making it skid along the floor. One of the black-and-white kittens was absolutely terrified of it – but the other was in his element. Over and over, he'd jump on it, pounce on it . . . *boom*: game over. Killer instinct in action.

'So which one do you think should become the railway cat?' Joanne mused aloud. She was a short, smiling woman with blonde highlights and a great sense of humour, though this issue was no laughing matter. It seemed a rather serious question: to be debating the future of these kittens as they gambolled obliviously about the place, investigating every new sight, sound and smell with a kitten's classic inquisitiveness. The five hadn't been outdoors at all yet, as they weren't inoculated, but there were enough new experiences in their home to keep them occupied for weeks. But what new experiences awaited the station cat: the lure of the train tracks, the rhythm of the trains, the hours and hours of walking about on cold platforms in the middle of the night . . .

To Joanne's mind, the fluffier of the two seemed more suited to this occupation. For even at this young age that kitten seemed to be taking after his dad, Gizmo, who was a total fluff-ball and enormous because of it. Surely a nice thick fur coat would stand a station cat in good stead? The other kitten had shorter hair and was nowhere near as large.

Chris described them both to Angie. 'One's really big and fluffy like his dad,' he told her.

'Well, we'll have that one then,' she said decisively. Angie liked the idea of having the fluffiest cat – and this little kitten really was a fluff ball, currently no larger than the size of a man's hand. Chris sent her some snapshots of the kittens – and that's when the team really knew this dream was coming true.

Angie showcased the photographs all around the office, more smile than woman as she did so. 'Meet our little cat,' she said to Gareth as she showed off the photographs as proudly as any new mum would snaps of her newborn.

Gareth grinned right back at her. 'We've done it, haven't we?' he said. 'We've only gone and done it!'

But there was still a lot to sort out before the railway cat could arrive. He couldn't leave his mum until he was at least eight weeks old, so in the meantime the station team began preparing for their little boy's arrival. They got fleecy blankets for him to sleep on, and bought a white plastic double-aperture bowl for his food and drink. There was a lot of excitement around the office at the thought that, soon, the newest member of the team would be joining them. Judging by the enthusiasm on everyone's faces, this little kitten was going to be the most popular colleague at the station by quite some distance.

But not everyone was thrilled by the promise of the new arrival. Some colleagues even started talking up the fact that they were highly allergic to cats, and that therefore the whole plan should be called off – but these 'allergies' were something they had never once mentioned during Gareth's three-year campaign to get a cat, so he didn't really buy it.

But Chris Briscoe, for one, was definitely looking forward to the terrible twins moving out. Each night he and Joanne had to have a roll call for the kittens to find out where they'd got to, as they were forever playing hide-and-seek and trying to get into places where they shouldn't be. 'Right, how many have you got?' Chris would say, his hands full of tiny tabby cat, as Joanne picked her way across the living-room floor and exclaimed, 'There's one at the side of the fireplace!'

Those two would be returned to Lexi's side, placed gently into the snug brown-and-white cat bed, but by the time the other three had been located, the first two would have gone AWOL again. Tiring as it was, Chris's daughter thought she would be very sad to see her new friends move on, as they were due to any day now. Lucy Briscoe was eleven years old and besotted with the kittens. She and the Briscoes' grand-daughter, six-year-old Ellie, had taken the lead in getting the kittens used to humans, so they were forever picking them up and giving them cuddles – as were Joanne and Chris, in all honesty. All five little ones had received an equal amount of human playtime, personal affection and friendship in their formative first eight weeks. The Briscoes would, in some ways, be sorry to see them go.

And that day came all too soon. On Tuesday 12 July 2011, the kittens reached an all-important milestone: they were now exactly eight weeks old. It was time for the members of the litter to say goodbye to each other – and hello to their brand-new homes.

Spadge was the first to leave, moving out to live with the Briscoes' son in Sheffield; a day or so later Max and Percy headed off to their new lives in Manchester. Now only the as-yet-unnamed black-and-white kittens remained. Both would be heading to Huddersfield station on Thursday 14 July. Aged eight weeks and two days, it was time for the terrible twins to take a journey they would never forget.

4. Welcome to Huddersfield

'In you get,' Chris Briscoe urged the terrible twins.

The two little kittens looked blankly at him, not understanding this new game. In the end, he scooped each one up and placed them together in the grey plastic carry case for their journey to the station. They sniffed suspiciously at their new surroundings, and began mewing plaintively at their unfamiliarity. The plastic arched over their heads; at the front of the carrier was a wire mesh door, which Chris now closed firmly.

The kittens cried even louder as it clunked shut, but their mother didn't respond to their melancholy mews. Lexi had wanted to go out, earlier, and was off having her own adventures in the large garden outside. To Chris's mind, she had had enough of her offspring by now and wanted to get on with her own life. Three of the kittens had already left home; when the Briscoes got back to Rotherham that night and let Lexi back in, she would merely sniff at the basket where she'd reared her family, realise the kittens had now all gone, and then carry on with her life, with no visible sign of distress at their departure.

The same could not be said for her kittens at that moment, though. As Chris lifted the carry case and he and Joanne made their way outside, both tiny tots scurried to the back of the carrier as fast as they could, looking for a place to hide. They huddled together, senses alert, as Chris and Joanne made their way to a nearby station: they were catching the train to Huddersfield, taking the Penistone line.

Deep inside the carry case, as close to the back wall as they could get, the kittens clustered together, their ears pricked up as high as they had ever been. The world for them was suddenly full of loud, never-before-heard noises: the slam of car doors, the trilling of birdsong, the electronic beep of the ticket gates. New smells flooded in through the mesh door, too – earth, air, plants, animals, humans – and new sights seemed to burn their very retinas, all spot-lit by the brightness of the July sun. It was totally overwhelming. The terrible twins fell into a terrible silence – and as they boarded the train with the Briscoes and heard the colossal roar of the engine booming into life, they scarcely dared to breathe. What on earth could make a noise like *that*?

Yet, as the journey progressed, and the kittens slowly grew more used to the gentle, rocking motion of the train and the intermittent noises, they found their courage gradually returned. Egging each other on, as they had done when scaling curtains higher and higher in the Briscoes' home, they edged closer to the wire door and bravely peeped out, noses pressed to the gaps in the wire and twitching furiously, as they tried to decipher the cryptogram of smells that accosted their tiny nostrils.

Halfway to Huddersfield, Chris and Joanne decided to check on their precious cargo. But when they discovered the duo at the front of the case, the kittens, spooked by the intrusion, skedaddled to the back once again. They were very, very quiet throughout the whole journey, so Chris and Joanne leaned back in their seats and left them to it. Gone were the noisy, outgoing twins who had caused such mayhem wherever they went. This first trip to the outside world had left the kittens reeling.

After about half an hour the train screeched to a halt at their destination: Huddersfield.

The station cat, though little did he know it, was home.

Yet it wasn't a very happy homecoming. Both kittens had been frightened by the banshee scream of the brakes and the subsequent beep-beep-beep of the opening doors. They started crying again – a mewling noise that seemed to say, 'Mum, where are you? I *need* you' and 'I'm hungry and so cold' and 'Where *am* I?' all at once. But as Chris lifted the carrier and he and Joanne disembarked from the train, the kittens' cries were suddenly curtailed. They felt the swaying movement of the basket around them and realised with a nervous gulp: something's up.

Once off the train, the world seemed even noisier. Though it was a relatively quiet time on the station concourse – about mid-morning, so well after the rush hour – for the kittens, experiencing their very first day in the outside world, it was like landing on a whole new planet. Even the air felt different, colder and fresher than they were used to at home, but it was the loud noises and the alien smells that were really mind-boggling. Station announcements robotically echoed around the chamber of the carrier; running footsteps punctuated every pounding heartbeat in the kittens' tiny little chests; and all the while the terrible twins swayed and scattered inside the roomy carrier as they were buffeted up the platform in rhythm with Chris's purposeful strides.

The party of four was ushered into the communal announcer's office – scene of so many station-cat brainstorming sessions – and the door shut tightly behind them. Peace, of a sort, fell. With the carrying case plonked firmly on an office desk, the team on duty gathered around, all excited whispers and prying eyes, trying to catch a glimpse of the station cat.

Chris and Joanne lifted the lid off the carrier, and each took hold of a squirming black-and-white kitten. Though the cats were used to being handled, having played happily for hours with Chris's daughter and granddaughter at the Briscoes' home, this was now a whole different ball game – and not a fun one.

'Ouch!' Chris exclaimed, as his kitten swiped at him with a well-aimed paw and those tell-tale 'bramble' scratches appeared on his hands. 'Easy now,' he urged. 'It's all right. You're safe.'

Pam, from the booking office, was one of those present at the all-important handover, as her mum was giving a home to the shorter-haired kitten. She phoned her and said, 'Come now, Mum. They're here.'

They were indeed. Bright eyes cautiously flickered as the kittens took in the office environment, peeking out shyly between the fingers of the Briscoes' hands. They had never seen anything like it before: computer screens glimmered and changed before their eyes as new trains came into the station and the programmes updated; microphones crackled and buzzed; and all around were things to climb and roll on: piles of paper, in-trays, filing cabinets and desks.

The team gathered round, cooing at the kittens and fussing over them. Chris had known he'd have no worries about leaving the kittens there, and he didn't; if anything, the team were *over*-prepared for the arrival of their bundle of joy. Joanne and Chris smiled at each other as the kittens fidgeted in their hands. This was it: it was time to let the kittens go, to let them spread their wings and fly.

'So we've nominated this one as the railway cat,' Chris announced to the curious colleagues, nodding at the pie-bald fluff ball in Joanne's hands: the biggest, fluffiest kitten of them all, just as Angie Hunte had wanted. 'And, Pam, I believe you're having this one.'

He handed the shorter-haired kitten over to the red-haired

Pam. In the next few minutes her mum would arrive and whisk him away in her car. The kitten would be named Luther, and he would grow up to become a tall, elegant cat – sleek rather than fluffy – who would live with Pam's mum and dad, together with another cat called Mo, in a house by a river, where there would be plenty of vermin on tap for him to catch. He became a character in his own right, and never again saw his terrible twin, with whom he had once spent so many happy hours playing.

Now, all eyes turned to the station cat. As Joanne gently stroked his fluffy black fur, so soft to the touch, his still-blue kitten eyes darted around, taking in the faces of his new family. They were exclaiming at his tiny size, his snowy paws, at the miniature proportions of his nose compared to his big white whiskers which took over his entire face. Those whiskers twitched as the kitten wrinkled his nostrils, taking in the scents of photocopying, various perfumes and brought-from-home, handmade tuna sandwiches . . . *Hmm,* the kitten almost seemed to think, pausing for a moment. *Food. Now* that *smells good . . .*

His on-alert ears took in all the sounds cascading around him. 'Oh, isn't he handsome!' the team chorused. 'Isn't he just *gorgeous*!' Their voices were like a torrent of noise, washing over the kitten and – at that moment – sounding about as welcome to him as a bucket of iced water.

Joanne bent and placed the little feline gently on the carpeted floor. 'This is home,' she told him.

Whoosh!

The kitten legged it. No messing. He darted straight under the computer table to safety, from where he could work out what the hell was going on.

Everyone in the room chuckled indulgently. There would be time enough for making friends, and for showing the new

31

recruit the ropes. The Briscoes closed up the carrier with a satisfying *click*, ready to head back home.

But, before he left, Chris bent down and locked eyes with the piebald kitten who was now sitting comfortably under the desk. Chris knew what lay ahead for this cat: he was to become the new pest controller at Huddersfield station. He had a job with TPE, and so he was – to all intents and purposes – now a colleague.

A grin lit up Chris's bearded face. 'Bye for now,' he said lightly to the little kitten. 'See you at work on Monday.'

5. First Day on the Job

Gareth Hope quietly eased open the door to the announcer's office and crept inside. Announcers didn't work nights, so he wasn't tag-teaming with anyone else – it was just him, slipping like a pale ghost inside the door, just before 6 a.m. His long hair swung around his ears as he turned at the doorway and surveyed the scene before him.

It was *amazing*. No other word for it. There was this tiny ball of black-and-white fluff on the reddish-pink carpet that he knew so well, the tiniest little thing – and it was moving. It was alive! The kitten was just wandering around the office, having been at the station for less than twenty-four hours, and was clearly still quite confused and trying to take it all in. His white plastic food bowl dwarfed him, he was so small.

Gareth almost couldn't believe his eyes. 'Hello, station cat,' he whispered. For a long time, he just stood in the doorway, staring at the little creature. After all his campaigning, all his eager enthusiasm and blustering banter, *one of his ideas had actually come off*. He had *achieved* something. And now the kitten was before him: living, breathing proof that when Gareth put his mind to something, he really *could* make things happen, no matter how much he might doubt himself at times.

Gareth bent down to say hello, and the kitten, naturally inquisitive, though still somewhat timid, trotted over to sniff out this newcomer with caution. Gareth let the cat's velvety black nose fully investigate his hand, before pressing his fingers firmly into the kitten's fluffy black fur and giving him a friendly stroke.

'Hello, I'm Gareth,' he said cheerily. 'I've been waiting a long, long time to meet you, little cat.'

The announcer's office had a window that looked out onto Platform 1, and Gareth could see, even as he crouched on the carpet next to the cat, that the platforms were already filling up with the morning commuters. Soon, the early trains to Manchester and Leeds and York would be pulling into the station – and Gareth needed to be ready to announce them. But he didn't want to say goodbye to his new friend just yet, so he scooped him up and placed him on the desk where he worked.

The workspace had a keyboard, four large screens showing both the train arrivals and the CCTV images, and a black freestanding microphone for making announcements, as well as the usual office detritus: a computer mouse, a few pens, a clipboard for making notes and a telephone. The kitten padded about on the desktop as Gareth settled himself in his chair, and then curled up, right on top of the keyboard – his bottom on the keys and his head on the desk – and fell fast asleep.

Gareth chuckled to himself. It was just as he had imagined. The kitten was only eight weeks old and had been at the station for less than a day, and he was already taking over. Gareth couldn't bear to disturb him, so he 'worked' (as little as possible, it must be said) around the sleeping form throughout that very first morning rush hour that the station cat was on duty. If anyone came to the window with an enquiry, he would gently lift the kitten – who fitted into the palm of one of his hands – into his cupped hand and carry him over to where he could more easily assist the customer, not wanting to let the little animal out of his sight even for an instant.

Those first customers to catch a glimpse of the kitten were naturally somewhat surprised to see a railwayman bringing a snoozing moggy to the window, but Gareth barely registered their reaction. He had eyes only for the new station cat, and spent most of the shift cuddling him or watching him as the kitten once again adopted what was fast becoming a favourite position: hugging the computer keyboard with a paw stretched out across it. Seeing him shiver, Gareth scurried to get a blanket and draped it around the ball of fur, before returning to his obsessive observation of every slumbering sigh, whisker wriggle and tail twitch as the cat snoozed away the hours.

And that was how Angie Hunte found them when she clocked on for her shift that day. As soon as she locked eyes on the kitten, it was love at first sight. She fell hook, line and sinker for this little creature and, as Angie herself put it, 'There was no work done that day whatsoever. Everything was just second best that day.'

Gareth and Angie couldn't stop staring at him. He was possibly the fluffiest cat they'd ever seen – totally gorgeous. He had ebony black fur, but his bib, paws and belly were the snowiest white. His belly was almost all white, they realised, except for a black splodge just below his heart. White, too, were the inner tufts of his pointy ears, while his tail had just a smidgeon of silver to it at the very, very tip. He was so small that, when curled in a ball atop the keyboard, he still left Gareth plenty of room to type softly around him, for he occupied only the space from the return key to the letter V.

Angie, who had grown up with cats but hadn't had the pleasure of caring for one in over twenty-five years, felt blessed. To be given responsibility for this wondrous little creature felt very, very special indeed. 'I can't believe we've got him,' she breathed softly to Gareth. 'I never thought in a million years we'd ever actually get one.'

As the kitten dozed and Angie and Gareth fussed over him, they also assessed the larger surroundings of the announcer's office. Given the small contingent of anti-cat folk on the team, neither Angie nor Gareth wanted to give a colleague any excuse to complain. So they covered the floor with newspaper – and just as well, for it turned out that the kitten was a rather messy eater and drinker. As he was not yet used to his new bowls at the station, both food and water would get *everywhere* when he dined. Just as his mother Lexi had taught him, however, he was very good about using the litter tray laid out for him, and very few 'accidents' occurred. Whether in the litter tray or elsewhere, the kitten's mess was cleaned up instantly, to make sure it didn't disturb anyone in the office who might have an axe to grind.

The kitten slept for most of Gareth's shift that first day, but he was awake for a little bit, blinking those kitten-blue eyes at his new friend – and Gareth decided, looking at the way the creature's eyes fixed firmly on him, that what the kitten really needed, in this new home of his that was in many ways so transient, with people coming and going on shifts all the time, was a *permanent* friend to call his own. Leaving Angie gazing adoringly at the kitten, he went to knock on the door of the lost-property office.

'Hiya, Gareth,' cried the woman in charge of it, cheerily. She was called Angela Dunn, a friendly lady with short blonde hair and shaded glasses, known for being both practical and kind-hearted.

Gareth subtly scanned the shelves behind her in the office. They were filled with a rather sad-looking collection of abandoned umbrellas and left-behind bags, forgotten coats and jumpers, and much more besides. The loneliest of all the items, though, were the lost-property toys.

They sat morosely on the shelves, their beaded eyes dull

and blank, their once-much-loved woollen bodies misshapen and worn, never to be hugged again by their owners, many of whom were now grown up. There were bunnies and teddies and soft brown bears; dolls and ducks and dinosaurs. Angela kept them as long as she was able to, hoping to facilitate a reunion with a child and its favourite dropped toy, but more often than not the months and then years would pass by and, eventually, as the office grew too full, Angela would gather up the long-lost items with a sad sigh and they'd be redistributed to charity – where, she hoped, they would find another loving home.

'I was wondering,' said Gareth, looking hopefully at Angela, 'is there a cuddly toy we could give to the cat?'

Angela smiled affectionately at him. The lost-property lady was definitely a pro-cat enthusiast and she had already fallen for their little ball of fluff. 'Let me see now,' she mused aloud, 'I'm sure there's something we can do.'

From the rows of toys who had been abandoned longest, she and Gareth picked out a pale-brown cuddly bear. The kitten was so tiny that the bear was about the same size as him on that very first day, but they knew that as he grew older the pair would be well-matched. The bear was made of a fleecy material, a light, malleable creature who could sit upright and be safely chewed – and loved. Gareth thanked Angela for her help, then went to introduce the bear to his new best friend.

The kitten gazed quizzically at it for a second and gave it a good sniff all over and a little taste with his rough pink tongue. Then he curled up right next to it and fell asleep, his head tucked into the bear's neck, looking as happy as Larry, and just as content as if he was snuggled next to Luther or Spadge or Max or Percy, the siblings with whom he had spent his first eight weeks.

'There you go,' said Gareth, tenderly. 'That's better, isn't it?'

It was some hours later, as acting station manager Andy Croughan was clocking on for the night shift, that the manager paused outside the door to the announcer's office, little knowing what he would find inside. Andy had been off on holiday for a few days, so he was utterly confused by the sign the team had pinned on the door:

PLEASE BE CAREFUL WHEN YOU OPEN
THIS DOOR

What's going on here? Andy thought in confusion. *Why do I have to be careful?*

And then, as he eased open the door, he saw *exactly* why. This being night-time, the nocturnal kitten appeared to have woken up – and was ready to party. As Andy eased the door open and looked ahead of him into the room, a tiny dark flash shot past him, chasing a ball of paper that Gareth had thrown. The kitten was darting around like a mad thing, tumbling over his legs and paws and even his own head, just as he had once done at the Briscoes'. He shot across the room, then hid under the table with a squeaky little miaow, observing the newcomer from his place of safety.

Oh my God! thought Andy. *The cat! We've got the cat!*

He peered more closely at the ball of fluff, but all he could see were massive ears and massive eyes amid the downy ebony fur; ears which were way too big for the kitten, but the perfect size for the cat he would become. Andy shook his head in disbelief – and then heard a giggling noise coming from the announcer's chair.

Gareth was sitting there sheepishly, just giggling to himself: an irrepressible burble of joy that burst forth. It was hard to control that kind of happiness. Andy found himself smiling back at his colleague and long-term partner in crime.

'We did it!' Gareth cried, leaping from his chair and offering his palm for Andy to high-five. 'All those crazy ideas – and we actually pulled one off!'

Andy – somewhat self-consciously, as he wasn't keen on high-fives – smacked the proffered palm and gave himself up to the grin. Gareth was right: they *had* done it.

There was only one, tiny niggle dampening the announcer's happiness. The cat had arrived; they had approval from head office: everything should have been grand. But Gareth couldn't help but recall how many times Paul, the former station manager, had said 'no' to him when he'd begged and chivvied for a cat. And although Andy, acting up, had green-lit the idea, Huddersfield was still *Paul*'s station. He was only absent on secondment; he hadn't resigned. And that secondment, as Gareth was horribly aware, was coming to an end in about one week's time. Then Andy would be demoted, and Paul would once more be in charge.

The station cat had landed, it was true. He was here, and Gareth was stroking him and cuddling him and laughing at his funny little antics. But there was a nervousness to those giggles, despite his joy, because a growing terror at the back of Gareth's mind now started gnawing at him.

He pictured Paul coming back onto the concourse. Heading to the office, opening the door, and seeing the cat curled up on the keyboard.

What if his manager took one look at the kitten and said brusquely, 'It's got to go'?

6. What's in a Name?

'Morning, gorgeous!' cried Angie Hunte with even more verve than usual. She had a real spring in her step as she walked into the announcer's office on day two of the station cat's tenure. Somehow, getting up at a quarter to five that morning hadn't been an issue in the slightest – she'd bounded out of bed, knowing that when she got to work, she'd get to see her cat. The early mornings, somehow, just weren't going to bother her anymore: it was now an undiluted pleasure to come to work.

Billy rolled his eyes as he prepared to hand over to Angie for her shift. 'Good morning, Mrs H,' he said dryly.

She batted at him playfully, knowing he was pulling her leg. 'I wasn't talking to you, Mr Grumpy. I was talking to my kitten.'

Said kitten was watching this exchange with eager eyes, all from the viewpoint of his new favourite haunt: the top tier of the team leaders' in-tray. Stuffed with paperwork, and with its metal edges curved up like a hammock, he'd found it an immensely comfy spot, perfect for catching a few zzzs and for watching the world go by.

The kitten's world, for the foreseeable future, was solely the domain of the announcer's office. Kittens cannot start their inoculations until they're nine weeks old, and these usually take the form of a double jab, one at nine weeks and one at twelve weeks, so until that point, to be on the safe side, it is best to keep them indoors. Given the location of this particular kitten's home, too, it was a nicer and safer way to ease him into his life on the railway. Though occasionally the muted thrum of a train's engine or the squeal of its brakes could be heard from a distance through the window, on the whole the office was a much more peaceful and domestic place than the concourse – though, of course, the attraction of the cat itself made the office, at times, busier than Clapham Junction.

'Has he been any trouble?' Angie asked Billy, as the old-timer prepared to head off home.

Billy turned at the door with his hands in his pockets and scowled. 'Trouble?' he echoed tetchily. 'Trouble? Too *right* he's been trouble. Look at where he's sitting! On my paper-work! All night long!'

He kept muttering grumpily to himself under his breath as he cautiously opened the door to let himself out. Despite his hearty moans, Angie couldn't help but notice that he was being awfully careful to ensure that he didn't give the kitten a chance to escape – though he couldn't resist a huffy slam of the door as he exited.

'Have you been winding Mr Grumpy up?' she quizzed the kitten. He cocked his little black head to one side and stuck his pink tongue out cheekily, as if to say, 'Yes, I have!'

Angie got her bits and pieces together, picking up the cat partly to give him a cuddle, but also because she needed the very bit of paper the kitten was lying on. *That Billy*, she mused wryly to herself. He could moan for England, it was true – but it hadn't escaped Angie that, for all his cantankerous words, he hadn't actually *moved* the kitten from his comfy place of rest. Billy, despite the toughened exterior and his prickly ways, was a big old softy at heart – though he wouldn't like her saying so.

Though Billy didn't have the heart to move the kitten, as the shift continued and Martin, Huddersfield's other announcer, arrived for work, Angie discovered there were some colleagues who were not so susceptible to the kitten's many charms. When Martin pulled his chair up at his desk and readjusted his thick glasses on his nose, he looked down to discover the kitten draped across the keyboard, as was now his wont. Martin shook his head: all was not right with his world. He cleared his throat and spoke awkwardly to the cat.

'You can't stay there,' he told him. 'Come on, get down.'

When the kitten didn't move so much as an inch, Martin reached out and closed his hesitant hands around the little body, before lifting him up. He placed him down on the carpet, from where the kitten looked up at him quizzically, his bright eyes drinking him in.

'Go on with you, now,' Martin said. 'I've got to do some work.'

But the kitten kept watching him, as though Martin was the most fascinating creature on the planet. Only when Martin shooed him away did he scamper off, thinking it was a new game, before darting round the office at full speed. For the kitten, everything was a new game.

And there were certainly plenty of opportunities for fun. As the cat grew more comfortable with his surroundings, he grew more daring. The office furniture became an obstacle course for jumping and leaping upon: in three easy bounds, he could dart from the floor to the squishy seat of an office chair, up onto the narrow beam of the chair's arm, and then, the big finish, from his tippy-toes on the beam to the crash mat of the desk, which had a perfect surface for skidding and sliding on, just as a rock-and-roll star might do. The larger pieces of equipment, meanwhile, provided handy nooks and crannies for countless games of hide-and-seek, the skyscraper-like sides of the photocopier giving the kitten a safe cityscape to run and play and hide in.

And the cat had no shortage of playmates. It wasn't long before all twenty-six people on the TPE team at Huddersfield had met him – not to mention the staff from other train companies who also ran services out of the station. Everybody wanted to play with the railway cat.

It was understandably a little overwhelming for the kitten at times: with each new colleague to whom he was introduced, he would at first be timid and shy. Soon, however, he began acquiring favourites. Jean Randall, who worked in the booking office, was one. Her philosophy with animals was that, as you've chosen the animal to come and live with you (and they didn't choose you), you have a duty to make their life as lovely as possible. A cuddle with Jean, whose curly black hair was almost a mirror image of the kitten's fluffy dark fur, soon became a highlight of his day.

But Jean worked in the booking office, where the team were locked in for security reasons, and the cat-burglar kitten wasn't allowed in either, so those cuddles had to happen before or after Jean's shifts, or for a snatched five minutes on her coffee break. The kitten spent far more time with Gareth – sleeping on his lap for the announcer's entire shift – or with the team leaders than with anyone else, and so these people became his closest family and friends. The brown bear, too, was a constant companion: though it was a bit of a struggle for the kitten on account of its size, he'd tenderly clamp his jaws around its arm or leg so that he could drag it around everywhere he went.

With the kitten settling in brilliantly, the next pressing issue was his name. Gareth turned again to his trusty computer and rustled up a new station-cat poster – one he never thought he'd be in a position to create.

Huddersfield Station Cat

Here's your chance to name Huddersfield station's
latest recruit!

Only 50p a go!

Write down your name and your suggestion for the
cat's name and it will be drawn from a hat on
Tuesday the 19th of July.

'Well,' commented Angie, 'we couldn't call him "kitten" for forever and a day.'

There was a great excitement at the station about the competition. It wasn't open to customers, but as is tradition on the railway network, they put the word out far and wide, wanting as many people as possible to get involved. All proceeds from the naming competition were going to Save the Children, so the more people who entered, the more funds the kitten would raise for this very worthy cause. Almost everyone entered, and Belinda Graham even took some entry slips down to the TPE headquarters at Bridgewater House in Manchester, where the team there made their own contribution to the station cat's history.

It was, of course, boy names they were looking for. By now, not only the dispatcher from Manchester (who had given homes to Max and Percy) had sexed the kitten – the little cat had suffered the indignity of having several colleagues examining his nether regions, patting at his mass of fur down below and nodding sagely as they said, 'Definitely a boy.'

Gareth, continuing his tradition of silly ideas, suggested 'David Hasselhoff' or 'Mr T' as suitable names. Others were more traditional ('Socks') or celebrity-inspired ('Keith', after Keith Lemon). Dave Rooney, one of the team leaders with whom the cat was growing particularly close, suggested the very creative 'Aloysius'.

'Aloysius?' said Angie, indignantly. 'What kind of a name is that?' She glared at Dave. 'Please don't let them pick that!'

But Angie would have no control over it – none of the TPE team would. The draw would be made at random and, to ensure it was fair and neutral, they had asked John, a driver-manager from another company, to make the selection. Whatever name he pulled out would be the one. It was a non-negotiable outcome.

The stakes were high indeed. As Tuesday 19 July drew closer, the cardboard box storing all the entries grew fuller. Each name was written on a scrap of paper and, once the entrant had paid their 50p, the scrap of paper got thrown in the box. A close eye was kept on it to ensure there was no cheating – much as Angie might have wished she could throw away some of those names, like another suggestion, proposed by someone with a black sense of humour: Splat. Splat, for a railway cat who'd be out on the tracks! It was hardly appropriate.

Jean suggested Frafty, which had been the name of her children's cat when they were growing up; the station kitten was the spitting image of that much-loved family pet. It was perhaps Terry on the barriers who nailed it, though, when he scribbled four letters on his scrap of paper. His suggestion read: Boss.

Rachel Stockton, a conductor who'd once worked for the RSPCA, had a real liking for a certain cartoon cat. When she first laid eyes on the station kitten, she said to herself, 'He's a right little Felix.' And that's the name she popped into the all-important cardboard box.

The draw was made at about 10 a.m. on Tuesday 19 July 2011. Angie was there, but to make sure it was absolutely neutral she was nowhere near the box as John picked it up and another assistant stood nearby. It was like the lottery draw, with independent adjudicators. The kitten, utterly oblivious, prowled around the office, little knowing that the tall man with wispy grey hair standing above him was about to pluck his name from a forest of potentials.

John was a gruff, fair-minded, no-nonsense kind of man. He was used to dealing firmly with hard-nosed drivers on a day-to-day basis and everything about him said: 'Don't mess with me.' Nobody would be debating the outcome of the draw: that was for sure.

He pushed his hand into the box and swirled it through the scraps of paper. Angie watched him, her heart in her mouth. What would her little kitten be called?

John's hand settled on one and plucked it out.

'Felix,' he announced commandingly.

Felix. It fitted everything about him, Angie thought. It was short, it was nice . . . it wasn't Alowicious!

Gareth Hope was a bit disappointed, however.

'There's probably a million cats in the UK called Felix,' he grumbled. 'I wanted something unique.'

As for Rachel, when she heard the news she pumped her fist into the air and cried, 'Yes!' Felix was a top name for a cat, and it did suit that little piebald kitten to a tee.

Angie bent down to the kitten and scooped him up.

'Morning, Felix,' she said.

He looked at her, nonplussed.

'Morning, gorgeous,' she added. Some habits die hard.

7. Felix Works His Magic

The kitten had been at the station for almost a week now and the transformation in morale was astonishing. Huddersfield had always had a family feel but – just as with actual relatives – along with the closeness of that familial atmosphere could come the odd row or niggle as people rubbed along with each other. But getting a cat had seemed to bring everyone together. Morale was at an all-time high. When the Head of Steam, the pub at the northern end of Platform 1, had its jazz night on a Wednesday, the team were seen literally dancing along the platforms as the bluesy music filled the summer air. The kitten had sucked everyone in and bowled them over.

No one seemed untouched by his magic. Angie Hunte, to her great surprise, had even walked in on Billy playing with the kitten one day, when he thought nobody was watching. The desks in the office had purpose-built holes in, through which, if needed, you could feed computer wires to reach a plug. There was one such unused hole in Billy's desk, and she'd found him dabbling his fingers through it as Felix followed their movement from the floor, completely transfixed by the wiggling digits.

'All right, Billy,' she'd greeted him, in her honeyed Yorkshire burr.

He'd coughed; that gruff smoker's cough caused by his frequent cigarillos. 'All right, Mrs H,' he'd replied. He'd surveyed the cat sitting on the floor who was, by now, washing himself with his rough pink tongue, making his black fur even more fluffy. 'My,' Billy commented aloud, nodding his head. 'He's a grand-looking lad.'

Angie had smiled to herself. 'Yes, he is, Billy,' was all she'd said.

Angie herself thought the reality of having a cat was just heavenly. She and Felix grew closer by the day. If Angie was sitting at her desk working, Felix would come up to her and climb up on her lap. Then, after a while, he'd reach up his paws towards her shoulders. She'd look down at his little face gazing into hers and say, 'Come on, then.' And Felix would climb up and sit on her shoulder, draping himself across her like a warm fluffy scarf, and there he would remain while she tapped away at the keyboard.

Felix, as it turned out, was a big fan of cuddles. When Andy Croughan was on nights, which were always a quieter time with just two team members on shift, he found Felix would latch on to him and follow him around. When he sat to do the accounting, the kitten would sit on his lap or find a crease in his arm and go to sleep. Andy's own cat, Missy, a tabby/tortoiseshell mix, was friendly enough, but she would never, ever sit on his knee. The first time Felix snuggled up to him, he found himself feeling quite touched. But then, of course, every time he sat down the kitten wanted a cuddle, and it became rather like having a demanding three-year-old on his hands!

Somehow, though, he found he didn't seem to mind *too* much.

Felix, when awake, was always more than willing to lend a hand with the cashing up. He was a member of the team, after all. But the lively kitten did not differentiate between work and play – they were one and the same to him. Andy would be cashing up and Felix would keep putting a paw on the cash, almost as if the cat was claiming a high-stakes gambling prize. Or Felix might park his bottom on the cash, or lounge across the balance sheet, or chase a dropped note halfway across the office. Sometimes, just at the moment when Andy had very nearly totted everything up and the neat stacks of money were in ordered, counted piles, Felix would get spooked by a noise from outside, and off the kitten would dart, right through all those piles of money . . . There would be cash *everywhere*!

Gareth, too, found Felix rather a hindrance when it came to doing his job. As the kitten did with Angie, Felix liked to use Gareth as a climbing frame: first to his lap, and then a scramble up his chest to his shoulder. Sometimes he'd lie lengthways across Gareth's back, so that the announcer could move neither forwards nor backwards but would have to stay frozen in that position until the kitten decided to wake up. At other times, Felix would make the daring final step on his ascent: from Gareth's shoulder to his head.

It became a new favoured location for a snooze. He'd clamber all the way up there, then curl up, tail to nose – somehow perfectly balanced on Gareth's skull – and fall fast asleep. If a customer came to the window when the cat was in that position, however, Gareth regrettably felt the kitten was in far too precarious a pose for him to move.

'I can't come to you, I'm afraid!' he would call out to the customer, in as helpful a tone as he could muster. 'You'll have to shout!'

The customers never seemed to mind though. In fact, most were totally charmed by this adorable new arrival and wanted to know the full story about how and why he was there. None-theless, Felix was rarely seen by anyone other than the team in those early weeks as he spent most of his time very much behind-the-scenes, and much of that asleep – cats are reck-oned to slumber for an average of fourteen hours a day and

Felix was, in this regard at least, a typical moggy. However, he never seemed to fancy dozing in the cosy bed the team had prepared for him. Instead – as well as on Gareth's head or in the crook of Andy's arm – Felix would bed down in all sorts of places: across keyboards, in in-trays, in the staff shower room, or on the seat of an office chair. Once, he foolishly chose a wall-mounted letter rack to nod off in: as he awoke and adjusted his weight, the letter rack wobbled unsteadily on the wall. Never had a cat dismounted a letter rack quite so fast!

For all the hours he spent asleep, though, there was still plenty of time for fun. Felix was full of life and every part of the office held possibilities. If Gareth did take him to the window, which was a traditional serving hatch, Felix loved to dabble his paws in the dip in the desk, through which customers might pass money and the team return tickets. Even as a tiny kitten, he wasn't quite small enough to get all the way to the other side, but he would have a good old go. He could get his head in the bucket bit and one white-capped paw out the other side, but could go no further than that. He used to run riot in the office (always watched hawkishly by a member of the team, of course). Gareth tried to get him involved in the station announcements, but Felix merely sniffed at the microphone in confusion and not a single amplified 'miaow' was bestowed upon the waiting customers. Balls of paper were a delight to him, while the pens-on-a-string that were attached to the signing-in clipboards were almost as good as the mice-on-a-string he'd been used to playing with at the Briscoes' house.

Fun as all this was, however, and excepting his cuddly brown bear which was a different kind of toy, as Felix approached the end of his first week, his playthings tended to be brilliantly improvised office accoutrements – not cat-specific objects. But all that was about to change.

Angie happened to be in the office when it happened. She was checking something, so she didn't take in what was going on at first. Martin was on duty, and she remembered him saying, when Felix had first arrived, 'You can't sit there,' and moving the cat from his workspace. Martin clearly didn't do cats, and that was fine: each to their own.

'Come on then,' the announcer was saying now. 'Come on then.'

Out of the corner of her eye, Angie glimpsed Felix leaping up onto the desk. He pottered around, then sat down on the keyboard. Less than a week ago, Martin would have told him, 'You can't sit there,' but it seemed Felix had made a new friend.

As Angie watched, Martin slid open his desk drawer and pulled out a little gift for Felix. It was a small brown mouse on a red pull string. It was the first toy the station cat was ever given by a colleague. And it was Martin – a quiet man who kept himself to himself – who had given it to him.

Angie was amazed to see the transformation in her colleague. Felix had *connected* with Martin; as the cat was doing with so many of the team.

'He's brought so many people down to human, where nobody else could get through to them,' Angie revealed. 'Someone who's just out on their own and they've got their blinkers on . . . that cat can turn somebody like that. He's changed a lot of characters.'

But the question remained: would he be able to change the most important character of all – the one who held the power over whether he could stay? For Paul's secondment was over. The boss was back.

Gareth had never felt so nervous in his life. The first morning back at work with Paul in place again as the station manager, he felt as if he was walking on eggshells. He crept into the office . . . and there was the little ball of fluff to greet him.

'Morning, Felix,' he said, wondering how many more mornings were left to him and his cat. At least the kitten hadn't been banished outright on Paul's return.

As was now their routine, Felix leapt onto his lap, curled up and went to sleep. And that was how Paul found them when he walked into the announcer's office later that same shift. Gareth hadn't told him they were getting the cat – he was far too terrified to take on that particular shoot-the-messenger role – so someone else must have dropped the bombshell.

Paul let the door close softly behind him. He took in the sight of the young announcer with the black-and-white cat on his knee. Up went the eyebrows . . . Then Paul gave a slight, almost amused shake of his head, smiled wryly, and didn't say a thing.

Felix was here to stay.

8. New Discoveries

It took perhaps a day for Paul to warm to the cat. By the second day – like Billy and Martin before him – he was playing with the kitten as happily as the rest of his team. And it was Paul, together with Angie Hunte, who took the lead on Felix's next big move: the feline's first trip to the vet's.

Felix was clearly a very clever cat. Yet he had his moments of foolishness. With his position at the station only just secured – and caring not a jot for the company hierarchy – when Paul tried to place him gently into the cat carrier, Felix fought back. *Swipe!* Three bramble scratches appeared on the station manager's nose. Way to go to endear yourself to the boss, Felix!

Yet Felix clearly remembered all too well the scary journey on his way to Huddersfield station. Even though his own, personal carrier was a different model from the one he'd been transported in by the Briscoes – this time with a sky-blue bottom and an oatmeal-coloured top – when he saw the ominous-looking carry case sitting on the desk, so obviously waiting for him with its yawning plastic mouth, he twigged what was going on and became a wild cat. His mood didn't improve when, after Paul and Angie had wrestled him in and driven him off in the car, they arrived at the vet's.

Animals, perhaps understandably, never like going to a vet. Even though it was Felix's first time, he was already antsy from being put in the carrier, and to wait in the lobby with all the other animals was very disconcerting. The

kitten was here to get a general check-up and his first inoculation jab.

The vet's careful hands held the tiny little cat, who looked
up at him through narrowed eyes, grumpily. Then Felix, to
his intense annoyance, was once more turned upside-down
in the most undignified manner and his nether regions
probed.

'Ah!' announced the vet, knowingly. 'You've got a little
girl!'

Paul and Angie looked at each other in astonishment.
They were stunned. But as Felix was turned upright and
placed back down on the metal table, she washed herself
indignantly without a hint of shock. 'Yes,' she seemed to be
saying, 'get with the programme, humans. I'm a *lady.*'

The reaction to the news at the station was massive; it
caused both a few chuckles and a few dropped jaws. *How*
could this have happened?

Then the next big question arose: should they change
Felix's name?

The outcome of the charity draw was *supposed* to be non-
negotiable, but was it fair to give a female cat a name that had
been intended for a boy? Would *Felicity* not be more apt? All
sorts of suggestions were bandied around.

But, in the end, Felix stuck. It suited her. A girl cat with a
name like Felix seemed a bit different, a bit spirited, and that
was certainly the character of the Huddersfield station cat.
In time, she grew to recognise her name and would even
come when called (if she was in the right frame of mind). She
seemed pretty happy with it. In fact, she seemed pretty happy
with her lot generally – and why wouldn't she be, when she
was getting spoilt rotten?

Every day was play day. As the next few weeks passed, she
had an absolute riot in the offices of Huddersfield station.

Martin's toy had only been the start of it: team leader Dave Rooney got her her first laser toy, and she loved that, especially on a night shift when it was dark and the laser light so bright.

'Felix, what's that?' the team would say as they switched it on. 'What's that?' And she'd look, and they'd turn it off. 'Where's it gone? Where's it gone?' *On.* 'There it is! Go, Felix, go!' And she'd sprint after the maddening light.

She continued her usual games of sleeping or lying on anything that stayed still for longer than thirty seconds, too. Often, she'd spread-eagle herself across official objects so authoritatively that to all intents and purposes she looked as though she was *helping* the team with their duties – but nothing could be further from the truth, whatever Felix's intentions. For example, one of these reclining hotspots was where the conductors kept their cash bags, which might be piled one on top of another. The conductors would be lining up, rushing to get off on a service, but before they went they had to take hold of the very item the cat was stretched out upon so comfortably. In the end, they became adept at performing that old magician's tablecloth trick: pulling them out from under her as she watched proceedings like a hawk, as though looking for the secret of how they did it.

As Felix settled in, Angie and the rest of the team got to grips with how paying for Felix worked. Essentially, the company covered all costs – but they had to be attributed to *something* on the disbursement paperwork: an explanation given as to why the money was being spent. Angie chewed the end of her pen as she sat facing her first form to cover Felix's food costs. *What to put?*

A smile crossed her face as she scribbled it down: *Pest controller needs nourishment.*

After that, they often referred to Felix as 'the pest controller'.

But perhaps another nickname would have been more apt: The Destroyer. For although Felix had a scratching post, she preferred to rake her claws along the office chairs, or the fabric noticeboards, or her colleague's clothes (and hands). She was growing larger and bolder by the day, and had now learned to combine two of her favourite games: the climbing-frame athletics extravaganza she'd perfected with Gareth, and the old-school trouser tango with which she'd used to terrorise her grandfather, Chris Briscoe.

A colleague would be walking along, minding their own business, when Felix would suddenly launch herself at them and run up their back. They'd feel the tell-tale twinge of cat claw, and then the full weight of the kitten as she anchored herself to their work trousers. Then she'd be up, up and away – dragging her claws through the fabric as she ascended their legs, moving on to the slippery smooth surface of a work shirt, giving a trampoline-like push up onto the shoulder, and then the pièce de resistance as she reached the summit: claiming the head. Her claws were such that it rather felt like being skewered with a flag reading 'Felix' when she reached the top.

She tried this trick with lots of people but, unsurprisingly, not many of the team enjoyed the sensation of a cat using them for mountaineering practice, so it was only a hardy few, like Gareth, whom she used consistently for her energetic climbs.

The team's trousers were in a right state: full of tiny holes and pulls in them, from where she'd at least *tried* to run up their legs before being lifted off. It was clear to everyone that Felix was going a little stir crazy.

It was now the middle of August 2011. She'd just had her

twelve-week birthday and her second – and final – inoculation jab. Her age was clear for all to see, for as the weeks had passed Felix's eyes had taken on their adult pigment, changing from their kitten blue to a beautiful, shimmering green; just like her mother's.

It's always a tough thing for any parent to recognise, but Gareth Hope, on a late turn, realised that Felix was now ready to meet the outside world. Up until this point, excepting her trips to the vet, she had resided only in the office with the door always shut tight, preventing any escape. Felix knew that was the way the world worked: people came in and out, but the door was always closed to her.

That evening, as the summer twilight faded to dusk and the night set in, Gareth took a deep breath and lodged open the door.

'Here you go,' he said to his little friend. 'You can have a look outside.'

Felix almost gave a double take – *are you sure?* – before she ran out, tripping over her toes on this great adventure. She ran bravely straight to the public doors, which were just beyond the office door and always open. Then she stopped dead, on the threshold to Platform 1, as though surprised to find that there wasn't simply another office beyond, but instead a very big, and very wide, world. She almost skidded to a halt, as though her senses had been hit by a sledgehammer, and she could go no further until she'd digested all this *newness*.

It was quite late, so the station was quiet. But that was quiet in comparison to rush hour – and in the dark, especially to Felix's little ears, the night sounds of the station seemed amplified a hundredfold.

There were no trains on the platforms. Instead, the melodies she could hear, and which mesmerised her, came from the swish of the public rubbish bags moving in the wind on their frames; from the syncopated rhythm of a woman's high heels as she clicked her way along the concourse; from the constant buzz of electricity coming from the station lights or its signals, which were always switched on. Felix was very alert and seemed very on edge – but she wasn't alone. Gareth loitered, just a few steps behind her, keeping an eye on his charge. She had grown so much, but she was still a kitten, and somehow looked suddenly smaller, standing on the threshold of this brave new world.

Reassured by his presence, Felix turned back to face Platform 1. She sat down in the doorway, perhaps a little abruptly. She took a few moments to take it all in, her head moving from left to right as she assessed everything that lay before her. The concrete of Platform 1 rolled gently to its edge. It was bordered by a shocking yellow line, and Felix felt no desire to see what was beyond its cliff-like edge, where the platform dropped away into nothingness. Beyond, across the blank emptiness, there was another platform, Platform 4; and if she looked to her left, she could just see the outer reaches of Platform 2, located at the very foot of her home on Platform 1. Platform 2 eventually tapered in a slope to the ground, but Felix couldn't see that from the doorway; it might as well have been in Siberia, it seemed so far away to the little kitten. To her immediate right were the bike racks; and they struck her, even on that first scout outside, as a rather safe-looking haven. Perhaps she made a mental note for the future.

As the station cat quietly surveyed the scene, the evening breeze stirred her fur for the very first time, ruffling all that ebony fluff so that each cat hair quivered and moved in the August air. She blinked those big green eyes of hers. She twitched her long white whiskers, sniffing all those brand-new smells. She looked rather as though she was thinking: *Wow.*

Felix, meet the world.

World, meet Felix.

Though the kitten didn't know it yet, all this would be her kingdom.

9. Brave New World

'Coming, Felix?'

Gareth Hope paused at the doorway of the office, a day or so later. The kitten didn't need asking twice. She dived across the office, scampered up his long thin legs, and nestled herself on his shoulder, like a pirate's parrot.

'Today, Felix,' he told her, 'we're going to be doing security checks.'

These were a regular part of every shift, important to make sure that the station was running smoothly and safely. They involved a circuit of the entire station, including investigation of various nooks and crannies, so it was a good way to introduce Felix to the wider parameters of her new home. She was still so small, she wouldn't be walking: instead, Gareth would become her long-legged chariot, transporting her all the way.

Since her first taste of the station's exterior on that summer's night a few days ago, Gareth and some of the other team members had accompanied her outside again. She hadn't gone much further than the doorway, and had only ever gone out late at night. Between the hours of 00.30 and 05.00, Huddersfield station locked its large, panelled, blue front doors and bolted them with a sturdy bronze pole. During the night, they were only opened again sporadically, fifteen minutes before the departure time of the services that ran in the wee small hours, then closed immediately afterwards. When the doors were locked, only Felix and the two team members on duty were around, so it was the perfect time to introduce the kitten to a trainless, customer-less Platform 1. She was too timid to explore very far, but she did like to go behind the bike racks. The metal docking stations towered above her like an iron forest, and she seemed to feel secure behind those thick steel 'branches', with the yellow-brick wall of the office just a pace or two to her back.

That evening, Gareth was taking her out a little earlier than she was used to, before the sun had set. It had been a glorious summer's day, and the heat was still shimmering around the station as Felix and Gareth set off along Platform 1. Felix's enormous green eyes darted this way and that: there was so much for the little kitten to see. More customers were about for a start, and her ears pricked up at the rumble of a wheelie case along the concourse, or the sound of a man's deep laugh. She was very used to people by now, so these noises didn't trouble her; nor did the humans who kept doing double takes at the duo as Felix and Gareth passed them.

Felix bobbed along happily on Gareth's shoulder, noting the coffee bar on Platform 1, and the doors to their right that led through to the main entrance of the station (and, beyond that, to St George's Square and Huddersfield's town centre). She started a little as a strange, moving glass box rose into view like a whale from the deep: it was the lift, which connected the platforms to the subway below. Felix looked back over her shoulder at it, perplexed, but she and Gareth weren't going that way.

Instead, the young announcer trotted down the stairs to the subway. He kept a light hand on Felix as they journeyed underneath the tracks. Huddersfield was a very old, Grade I-listed station – the foundation stone had been laid on 9 October 1846, when there was a public holiday and the church bells rang all day in celebration – and it was a little-known fact that, when it was first built, a vast labyrinth of rooms and passageways was also constructed on the subway level, which today is shut off to the public. In the nineteenth century, they were used as offices, coal rooms, lamp rooms and even the first-class lounge. But they had long since fallen into disuse and now they lay in darkness, their old-fashioned fireplaces no longer flickering with flames; everything abandoned, covered in dirt and dust. Though TPE used a few of the rooms for storage or technical operations, the rest of the crypt was a spooky, subterranean lair, more fitting for ghost stories than travellers' tales. Gareth definitely didn't want Felix to go exploring down there. It was a place that gave the shivers to several team members, and he didn't want Felix to get lost. They stuck to the well-lit, public-access subway instead: a clean and bright tunnel, modern and manageable.

Up they popped on Platform 4. Felix whizzed her head about as they came up the stairs, taking in all the new sights and sounds. Between Platforms 4 and 8 was a buffet room, but it was closed at that early-evening hour; it did a roaring trade in the mornings, when the smell of frying bacon and the clatter of plates tempted in bleary-eyed commuters. Peering towards the south end of the station as they came up from the subway, Felix glimpsed Platforms 5 and 6, which were tucked between Platforms 4 and 8 using a different bit of track. It was just as well she wasn't numerically minded, as the station's layout would have foxed a mathematical genius; but for those keeping tabs, Huddersfield has no Platform 3 or 7.

But Felix wasn't interested in the platforms or the people. Instead, her eyes narrowed sharply as she looked up at the station's roof.

Huddersfield station is only partly covered by its corrugated iron roof. There is a gap in it, running parallel to where the train tracks divide Platforms 1 and 4. But the open sky wasn't what had caught the little kitten's eye – it was the crows.

They lived on the station: a number of big black beasts who claimed the place as their own. The roof was supported by a cross-hatch of several steel girders, providing the birds with plenty of prime perches. They were cocky, confident creatures with slick, oil-like feathers, and at that time were larger than Felix herself. As she watched them swoop down to the platforms to pick over the crumbs the customers had left behind, she gave a worried frown, as though to say she wasn't sure she liked those birds.

As Gareth continued his security circuit by walking along Platform 4, however, something else happened which drove all thoughts of the crows from Felix's mind. There was a silent, still train sitting at the platform as they walked along it: a local stopping service which had been slumbering there quietly before its journey began. The pair were just passing the train when its engine suddenly came to life and revved up with the most enormous *roooaaarrrr!*

Felix was still on Gareth's shoulder. When she heard that booming, jarring sound, her claws came out in fright and she dug in as hard as she could, trying to get as close to her friend as possible, in order to feel secure.

Gareth yelled in pain, and he got the sense that if Felix could have done so she would have yelled out loud, too. As it was, she dug in even harder, until Gareth reached round and gingerly lifted her off. He cradled her in his hands and, seeing that she was scared, rushed her back to the safety of the announcer's office. He ended up with claw marks all over his shoulder, but Felix was OK.

Although it was clear that Felix was none too sure about the thunderous engines, the team at Huddersfield knew – from the success stories of those happy railway cats living up and down the country – that they simply needed to persevere in getting her used to the trains and Felix would be fine. She was simply like a child who puts her hands over her ears at the roar of a jet engine on an aeroplane; in time, that sound would become nothing to fear, just a part of everyday life. Felix was a station cat; she would get used to the noisy engines.

Her colleagues had read about how important it was to expose kittens at a very early stage to the things they expected them to consider normal and safe when they were adults. Anything they don't experience at that young age might be viewed with fear and caution later on in life, to the detriment of the cat. It was why the team had wanted to give a kitten a home in the first place, so that she could learn the ropes as she was learning life itself.

The team took Felix's initiation into station life slowly, though, and were always understanding. The kitten was never rushed into anything, and if she didn't want to go outside, she was not forced to. Yet she rarely ever wanted to stay in – the call of the wild and adventures awaiting her were sirens to the station cat.

As the team helped her to adjust, they made sure that someone was always with Felix when she stepped outside, and she never left the office if the concourse was busy. Her colleagues used to carry her around in a ball in their hands until she got used to the trains and became more confident. Gareth and the others would regularly take her round the station on their security checks and, over the next few weeks, she slowly became inured to the engine noises of the stationary trains rumbling quietly in the station. She was nonchalant, too, about the chimes of the opening and closing doors; the sounds of the station announcements over the crackling tan-noy; and the hiss of the little puffs of air that the trains let off as they prepared to depart. She often wanted to stay close to Gareth when they did the rounds, but she didn't freak out anymore and to Gareth's (and his shoulder's) relief, her claws were not as prominent.

Felix usually sat on his shoulder as they made their way around the station, and for Gareth it became second nature to have a cat perched there. It must have been quite a sight – and this fluffy new member of the station crew certainly seemed to cause a stir among the commuters, who would do a double take as they walked past. Not everyone seemed to approve, however. One afternoon, Gareth noticed a couple of the regular trainspotters huddled in their usual spot at the end of the platform, shaking their heads disapprovingly, as though saying in despair, 'What's *happening* to this railway?'

With Felix now going out and about, the team made sure she had the perfect accoutrement: her very first collar. It was Angie Hunte who had the pleasure of buying it for her – and it *was* a complete pleasure. She had an absolute field day! She got it from a nearby pet shop and spent a long time looking for *exactly* the right one. Angie loved sparkly things, so it was perhaps no surprise that the one she chose was dotted all over with glitzy, diamanté studs. It was cornflower blue – the colour of the tops of the dip-dyed TPE trains – and Felix looked an absolute stunner in it: *so* glamorous!

But while Angie was delighted with her selection, it didn't meet with universal acclaim.

'What is *that*?' said Billy in abhorrence the first time he laid eyes on it. He thought it was an abomination. He looked Felix up and down and then turned to Angie. '*Why*? But *why* would you choose something like that?'

'Because she needs something so that you can see her!'

Angie retorted. You could certainly do that: the diamanté studs dazzled like glitter balls at her throat, catching the September sunlight.

Of course, a collar isn't much good without a tag. It was Christine in the booking office who gave Felix her first one. By this time, everybody at the station was giving the kitten bits and pieces – toys, treats, new bowls and all sorts – and the collar tag was Christine's own special gift for the cat who had transformed the entire station. She went to Pets at Home and got Felix's name and address (Platform 1) engraved on the front of the tag and the team leaders' work mobile number engraved on the back, so that if the kitten ever got lost people would know that she was loved and wanted and missed, and she'd be able to find her way home again.

It wasn't any old tag that Christine bought. Oh no: *this* was a tag for Felix, the Huddersfield station cat! It needed to be something special. Christine had seen the jazzy collar Angie had given her, and as she shopped she was also musing on the poor kitten's gender-confused start in life – so Christine picked out a beautiful, hot-pink, heart-shaped tag for the station's little girl. One can imagine Billy's reaction . . .

Angie had been one of those trying to help her little kitten adjust to the station's noisy exterior. While they all loved carrying Felix about the place, that wasn't a long-term solution: the kitten needed to stand on her own four paws. But there were so many things that could go wrong if she was let loose immediately – she could run off; someone could take her (the volume of strangers coming through the station each day was frightening when Angie really thought about it); not to mention the danger of the train tracks if Felix was released before she understood the threat they posed. She was coming up to four months old, so it was still a lot for her to comprehend.

But Angie thought she had a solution: a cat harness.

'We can get her a little lead!' she exclaimed, pleased with the idea. 'Then we can walk her round and she'll get to know the platforms on her own four paws, but she'll be safe as houses.'

Felix was soon the proud owner of a bright-pink fabric cat harness. It slipped over her fluffy back and fastened around her belly and her neck, and was attached to a long lead so that the team leaders could walk her around.

Billy took one look at it and threw his hands up in despair. 'I'm not walking round with a cat on a lead!' he exclaimed. 'Walking round t'station with a *cat* on a flipping *lead*? There's no way!'

10. Doctor's Orders

Despite Billy's reluctance, the rest of the team at Huddersfield were happy to accompany Felix on a few laps of the station. Before long, she was able to be taken off the lead altogether and could be let loose.

Part of the reason the staff were so confident about doing that, however, was because they themselves were like mother hens – or bodyguards, which was perhaps a more befitting description given the glamourpuss look Felix was rocking these days. Gareth would often accompany her outside, and if she went anywhere near the edge of Platform 1, he would cautiously shepherd her away from the yellow line, making sure she stayed safe. Felix, in truth, showed no signs of wanting to peer over the edge of the abyss. She kept well back, just as her colleagues showed her, and never really ventured of her own accord away from the area adjacent to the office. She never even went down the steps to the subway. In fact, she spent most of her time outside by the bike racks.

They were perfectly located, as far as Felix was concerned, for if she was spooked by anything she could run straight back to the office quick-sharp. If she heard a train coming, she would run for home at once – for its deafening roar (and soon-to-be squealing brakes) still seemed to inspire her with a fear that the sounds from stationary trains had long since ceased to do. Often, she would flee to the lost-property office, which was located right beside the office door, and kindly Angela Dunn would pick her up and give her a cuddle until the train had gone and Felix felt brave enough to explore those bike racks once more. She was very happy sitting there and watching life go by, and it seemed to Felix she had the best of both worlds: fun times playing and snoozing in the office, and the odd promenade with an oh-so-attentive escort.

But for all the mothering the station team gave her, the time was approaching when Felix herself was going to be relieved of such responsibilities. In the middle of September, she passed the milestone of her four-month birthday, and an appointment was made to have her spayed and microchipped. Felix had to go back to the vet.

'How are you doing, Felix?' Gareth Hope asked his little friend.

Felix raised her green eyes grumpily to meet his, and almost scowled. Then she moved her head just a little and he suddenly vanished from her viewpoint, which was very narrow these days, as she had the most annoying post-surgery cone around her neck.

Felix *hated* it. She lifted a white-capped paw to her black shoulder and once more knocked at it, trying to get it off. More often than not, she succeeded. The white cone was supposed to be attached to her diamanté collar, but Felix was clever enough to have worked out how to slide her collar over her head with one paw, so she soon made easy work of giving the cone the slip. She was still tiny, too, so even though the cone was kitten-sized, it still looked too big. It was an absolute nightmare trying to keep it on her and make sure she didn't pick at her stitches.

'Leave her be, lad,' said Billy, who was also in the office. 'She just needs a bit of peace and quiet, don't you, lass?'

The 'grand-looking' cat Billy had once so admired looked

very sorry for herself indeed. The stitches from the operation were still fresh, and she had a big shaven patch on her side where the vet had clipped off lots of her lovely fur. As she was so long-haired, even when it started re-growing it took an awfully long time – two or three months – before her coat was back to normal. Felix looked most put out that her glamourpuss days seemed behind her.

'How are you doing anyway, young Gareth?' Billy asked his colleague meaningfully.

Gareth – the university dropout, who was only working at the station as a stopgap job while he figured out what he really wanted to do – was by now twenty-four and had been there for almost five years. But it was so easy to stay . . . It was family, wasn't it, and how could Gareth turn his back on that, especially now Felix had joined them? The station felt like home.

Gareth didn't reply, but he felt Billy's wise eyes fixed on him as he fiddled self-consciously with some paperwork on his desk. Billy had become almost a father figure to Gareth as they'd worked together over the years. Billy had seen it all on the railway: he knew how people started . . . and then stayed. Blink, and suddenly thirty years had passed and you were still in the same job, making the same jokes with the same people, but you were now wizened and grey.

He cleared his throat and repeated something he'd said to Gareth a few times already, when it was just the two of them in the office and they had some time alone. 'Be aware, young Gareth,' he warned him in his gruff voice, 'you're getting stuck here, son.'

He slipped outside with a cigarillo between his fingers and let the door slam shut behind him.

Gareth sighed, Billy's words of warning rattling around in his head. The old-timer had told him, 'You've got to move on. If you don't move every three or four years, people will think you've given up, and they'll never entertain giving you another job.'

Was he right? Gareth didn't know. Like Billy, during his five years at the station he had seen plenty of colleagues become set in their ways but – funnily enough – for all his years of service, Billy wasn't one of them. Though some long-service employees could become very black and white in their view of things, Billy could not only see shades of grey but also in technicolour – sometimes literally. He liked to open things up and try out new ideas, and one of his recent innovations was to transform part of the station concourse into an art gallery; a vision that would come to fruition the following spring. He was a pioneer when it came to the environment, too, and had already won an award for his novel ways of making the station run more greenly. Billy's philosophy was that the station didn't just have to be a terminus, it could be a hub of the community and the team could make it really nice.

Nor was he the only one at Huddersfield with those ideas – Andy Croughan had started a library where people could leave and take books for free; later, the concourse would display local poetry and get involved in creative writing projects. It was part of what made Huddersfield so special and why Gareth loved working there so much – it wasn't a big, impersonal station as some of the major hubs could be, but neither was it a quiet little place off the beaten track where people had given up. No, Huddersfield was a place where people made things happen.

And he was among those people, Gareth realised suddenly. He glanced down at Felix, who glowered at him from within her big white cone. He had made the station cat happen. It had given him a little bit of faith in himself. *Maybe*

Billy is right, he thought. *Maybe I should keep an eye out, see if anything comes up.*

In the meantime, he had a poorly kitten to care for – and he wasn't the only one on duty. Everyone passing through the office had a kind word – and more – for Felix on her sick bed. Poor thing, she really was very distressed. She took to wandering the office with her favourite brown bear clutched in her mouth, just walking up and down, mewing.

'What's up with you? Do you want to go out?' Angie Hunte would ask her, as Felix cried plaintively. But the cat would just pick up the bear and go back to her slow, sad meandering. Both Angie and Angela thought she treated it like her baby; perhaps, they mused, it was Felix's way of mothering now that she herself would never have her own kittens.

In the light of Felix's fretfulness, lots of the team – independently of one another – took to giving her comfort as often as they could. As Felix turned her big green eyes on first one colleague and then another, the colleague favoured with her gaze would crouch down and slip a hand into their pocket, or their handbag or their desk drawer, from where they would retrieve a bag of treats that they had brought for her. They'd shake one out into their palm and Felix would stick out her little pink tongue and snatch it up, gratefully, as if she hadn't been fed for a week.

'Miaow!' she'd say, plaintively, blinking those big green eyes.

'OK, one more,' the colleague would say, and another treat, or two, or three, would go the same way as the first, as Felix perfected the art of the pitiful stare.

Knowing no better, some colleagues even gave the recuperating kitten saucers of milk, thinking it would cheer her. Of course, she absolutely loved it, lapping it up eagerly and flicking tasty white droplets onto her velvety black nose.

As Felix's post-op health gradually improved and she started going outside again, Angie discovered she was stumbling over her in the most unlikely places.

'Why are you sitting there, Felix?' she would ask in confusion.

But Felix was a clever little kitty. She had sussed out which colleagues – and it was most of them – kept treats for her hidden in their desk drawers or their pockets, and by now she had located all the hotspots. The only one who knew where they all were was Felix, and she'd hover in the relevant area until the magical treats arrived. Every member of the team had a little something on their person to comfort or tempt the cat – but they little realised that every single colleague on each separate shift was dishing out the same. Kittens at that age are recommended to have three meals a day, but as her multitude of carers nursed her back to health, Felix was getting fed a *lot* more than that . . .

But who could resist that lovely kitten face? Felix started to find her voice, too – and if she wanted food she would mew. Loudly. Until you'd fed her. Cats can change their miaows to manipulate humans, often imitating the cry of a newborn human baby when they want food. Felix had clearly mastered this art and was playing them all like a master puppeteer.

But even though her adoring fans readily gave in to her every whim, the kitten wasn't averse to making her own luck too. One Sunday shift, when it was quiet, Gareth decided to nip to Tesco and pick up a bit of shopping for home, including some Go-Kat kitten biscuits for his little Cosmo, who was only a few months older than Felix. He dropped the bag in the corner of the office and went back to his announcing, thinking nothing more of it. It was only at the end of his shift, as he picked up the carrier bag in readiness to catch his train home, that he realised a cat burglar had been at work. Someone had torn through the bottom of the bag with what looked suspiciously like sharp claws, then chewed a hole in the bottom of the cardboard box and helped themselves to biscuits.

Gareth surveyed the damage and glared accusingly at Felix. She was busy washing herself, looking as innocent as anything, and simply batted her eyelashes at him when he said sternly, 'Felix!'

She never did admit to doing it. Gareth supposed it *could* have been Andy . . .

As if coping with the aftermath of the operation wasn't enough for poor old Felix, around this same time she also had to contend with another big change. While she had been settling into Huddersfield station and getting glamorised with her sparkly collar and fuchsia name tag and harness, the station itself had been undergoing something of a makeover too. The back offices were being entirely rebuilt and the new layout was now ready for action. The team would be moving into the swish new set-up, while the old offices would be knocked down.

The new offices were still in the same location – Platform 1 – and they were still by lost property and still had a customer-service window, but they were very different inside. Gone was the large, communal, carpeted announcer's office; that became a tiny, tiled room just big enough for a desk and a microphone. The space behind the scenes was dedicated instead to smart staff facilities: male and female locker rooms, a shower, a mess room/kitchen, and a brand-new office for the team leaders, with enough room for two desks and a couple of filing cabinets. The shower now became a favourite Felix spot and was where her bedding (a black blanket with white paw-prints, among others) was placed permanently for her, at the foot of the towel rack. Some wag made a proprietorial 'this is my room' wooden sign saying 'Felix', which hung above her bed for a while – until she knocked it down, thinking it was a toy. All the new rooms opened off one long corridor which now became the setting for one of Felix's favourite pastimes.

Her brown bear was still her constant companion, but Felix gradually stopped pining over her baby and allowed the bear to be turned into a playmate. One of her very favourite games in the world was to stand between Andy and Gareth as each stood at either end of the corridor. One of them would have hold of the brown bear. Slowly, deliberately, he would seat it on the floor of the corridor, as Felix watched with a keen, excited, beady green eye. The bear would be sitting upright, leaning slightly forward. Then Andy or Gareth would take a step back, a run-up, and kick the bear so hard that it soared high into the air. Down the corridor the bear would fly, and Felix would watch it coming with growing pleasure, then chase it and dive as it got closer, taking total joy in their reunion. She would spend hours darting between Andy and Gareth as they booted the bear up and down the corridor: running, leaping, prowling, chasing, diving . . . never seeming to tire.

With the kitten clearly on the mend, Angie took her back to the vet's for her follow-up appointment after her operation. She was expecting him to say that everything was fine, as Felix was clearly full of beans.

But as the vet checked her vital statistics – and weighed her – he realised she was rather full of cat treats, too.

'She's a little . . . tubby,' he began.

Angie told him about the saucers of milk the team had been giving her.

'Oh, you mustn't allow her to have any milk,' he said at

once. 'It's not good for cats' systems. It's also very fattening: one saucer of milk equates to about four burgers as far as cats are concerned.'

Felix had essentially been stuffing her face; no wonder she was now overweight!

Angie took her back to the station and realised that something serious would have to be done. Felix's colleagues were in danger of killing her with kindness: they had to put an end to the gravy train of treats. It was so important that she knew it was not something she and the other managers could simply mention lightly to their colleagues; unless they emphasised the gravity of the vet's warning, it would be all too easy for everyone to ignore them, and keep on dishing out the treats at a blink of those seductive green eyes. But where would that leave Felix?

So Felix the cat was added to the official, formal station briefing for that week. This was a document containing all the key safety issues staff had to be aware of – and each employee had to sign to say they'd read and understood the topics discussed. It was proper serious stuff.

'We know you want to spoil her,' the managers told the team. 'We know that everybody wants to have a little moment with her, but we also have to look after her health. Please can you refrain from giving her treats, and especially milk, or anything that's not good for her. Please do not feed Felix; please leave it to the team leaders.'

It was the only way to ensure she would lose the extra pounds and then maintain a healthy weight.

Felix tried to get round them, of course. But all the miaows, and fluttering eyelashes, and paw prods came to nothing. Angela thought that Felix's innate laziness was possibly part of the weight problem, too. The cat still loved to lounge anywhere and everywhere, and so enjoyed being stroked and attended to by her many minions that she rarely left the office. Angela used to say to her, 'It's time you went out and did something, you know.'

So far, Felix's trips outside had only ever been with an escort. But now she was spayed and inoculated and five months old, there was really nothing to stop the railway cat from asserting her independence. Felix was about to go it alone.

11. Learning the Ropes

Felix watched the world go by from her favourite position by the bike racks. It really was the perfect spot: close to home if a train came roaring into the station, but it also enabled her to keep tabs on everything happening on Platform 1. She pricked her ears up as she heard the flap of big black wings: a crow above her, landing on its perch. She shook herself huffily – it wasn't a shiver of terror, quite (though perhaps that was only because the scary black crow was so far away) – and then stood up.

Felix had become practised at choosing her moments to explore. From her observation point by the bikes, she was growing used to the rhythm of the station. It was like an industrial ocean in a way: the trains the tide, regularly coming in and going out, washing up people and suitcases on the surf, and then taking away more travelling 'driftwood' as the waves receded and the trains pulled out. She used to wait for the trains to leave and for the last of the dawdling customers to disappear from the concourse, and then she'd go and explore.

The older she got, the more confident she became. On this particular late October afternoon, she made her way all the way along to the very top of Platform 1, passing the Head of Steam pub, then kept on trotting, tail in the air, as the concrete walkway magically transformed into Platform 2. Felix dropped her nose to the ground and had a sniff about. Any crumbs? Any scents that shouldn't be there?

No: all was well. She raised her head again and criss-crossed the platform, veering from the yellow line at the edge to one of her new favourite objects in the station: the abandoned railway carriage.

This was parked permanently on the western side of Platform 2: a navy-blue, ancient, out-of-use carriage with opaque windows. It had been bolted to the ground and had fencing round it, but there were a few gaps in this fence at the bottom, through which a cat like Felix could squeeze. She could then dip down, via the buffer, to the shadowy underbelly of the carriage itself. It all made for a fantastic hidey-hole.

But Felix was staying above ground today. As she slunk and trotted and – yes – rather paraded around Platform 2, she had a little shadow: Gareth, as was his wont, followed her, as vigilant as any mother hen.

Platform 2 was not in use much that particular afternoon, so Felix wasn't spooked at all as she poked her nose about and generally had a really satisfying investigation. Gareth kept glancing back at the station clock: they'd been out five minutes, ten minutes, fifteen . . . There was an automated announcing system in place at Huddersfield, which meant most announcements were triggered by a train coming into the station; the human announcer didn't have to do a thing. This freed up Gareth to enable him to follow the cat about for a fair amount of time. But there were still *some* announcements he had to make . . .

Yet on this day, Felix showed no sign of wanting to return to base. They'd been out twenty minutes; now twenty-five . . . Gareth kept heading towards the kitten, hoping he could scoop her up and carry her back inside with him, but every time he went near her, she moved somewhere else.

After all, there was so much to see! Felix prowled to the very end of Platform 2, where it started tapering down towards the floor, like a bespoke ramp for an inquisitive cat. Beyond this, the yawning mouth of the train tunnels loomed, black and empty-looking. Felix blinked at them with interest, cocking her head to one side – what went on in *there*? Then her head flicked sharply to the right, to look down on the grassy area over which the tracks ran, just before the entrance to the tunnels. Her ears went up, her eyes brightened, and her legs instinctively crouched down.

On the grassy area before the tunnel, she saw a flash of a little white cottontail – and then another. *Boing! Boing!* A family of brown-and-white bunny rabbits frolicked before her very eyes. Felix watched them, captivated, as they darted about and then – perhaps sensing the feline's interested observation – bounded suddenly away to safety.

Felix shook herself and gave a big stretch, all the way along each leg to the tips of her snowy-white toes. The world was so interesting! *What more can I discover?* she seemed to wonder, as she set off once more on her exploration.

Gareth Hope watched her – in contrast to his name – in total despair. He'd been out of the office for thirty-five minutes and he really needed to get back.

'Felix! Come on!' he urged her, but he knew she wouldn't respond. Cats were famed for their acute sense of hearing, but Felix's was uncannily selective when she wanted it to be.

I really need to go, he thought. *But I can't possibly get her back.*

He watched the cat as she sniffed and prowled about, so confident and carefree in this environment that she now knew relatively well. Gareth and his colleagues had been watching her closely outside for almost two months now. They knew she was a sensible cat: that she wouldn't cross the yellow line and go down on the tracks; that she knew where home was and could run for it if scared. Gareth glanced back up at the station clock. Forty minutes!

I'm going to have to leave her, he thought. It was a heart-wrenching moment.

'Felix, I'm going now,' he told her. The cat ignored him. 'I'm walking . . .' he said, as he turned and took the first step. 'I'm going . . .' He hovered, but Felix wasn't even looking at him. His shoulders slumped dejectedly. 'I'll be back in the office if you need me.'

He plodded up the platform, throwing worried looks over his shoulder, but Felix was absolutely fine. With every step, he fretted. *If something happens to her now . . .*

Then he remembered the CCTV and almost ran back into the office. On his computer screen were the various images relayed from the cameras across the station. He scanned through them, looking, looking . . . And there, frolicking in front of the camera trained on Platform 2, was Felix: a flickering black-and-white figure happily sniffing her way along the ground and absolutely *safe.*

Gareth pulled the microphone towards him and made his next announcement, the relief audible in his tone, although the customers listening would have had no idea why.

His little kitten was just fine – and the mother hen could be sure of it.

After that, Gareth would occasionally watch Felix on the cameras when she was out and about and he was stuck in the office, but eventually he knew he didn't even need to do that. His little kitten was growing up fast; she was now too heavy for her climbing trick and was way too big to balance on his head. Where once she could curl up comfortably and settle there, like a cherry on top of a Gareth-shaped cake, she now realised that it was a little *too* wobbly at the summit, and settled for staying on his shoulder instead.

Felix had the run of the station, but there were two

places from which she was banned: the staff mess room, where her colleagues ate their meals and snacks; and the underground labyrinth of abandoned rooms beneath the station (Felix didn't even know of their existence). She soon had a catalogue of favourite haunts: the bike racks, the abandoned carriage, and the lost-property office. The latter was like a little magnet to Felix, for she absolutely loved it in there. She'd wind her way in, give an affectionate greeting to Angela Dunn, then leap up onto a shelf and fall asleep, snuggled up in someone's lost hoodie or wrapped in a stranger's scarf.

Though there was nothing stopping her from crossing the tracks, Felix never did. Her 'training' from the team had worked well; or perhaps it was just her instincts that told her she shouldn't cross the yellow line. The team had worried about her doing that a lot; and with good reason. The station cat at Barnes, Roger, had lost most of his tail under a 455 one day; and he was one of the lucky ones. However, when Gareth asked some of the train drivers he knew about the possibility of Felix getting hit by a train, they'd scoffed at him good-naturedly. They never hit cats, they said. They hit dogs and other animals, but they never even saw cats on the track; the vibrations of the oncoming trains were evident to most felines so early on that if a moggy *was* wandering about, it had fled long before the train loomed into view.

But it wasn't just the trains on the tracks that worried the team. Cats can jump up to six times their length, but even with that special skill, for a kitten like Felix it was an awfully long way down to the tracks from the edge of Platform 1 – and even if she had survived the leap, she might not have been able to get back up to safety. Luckily, she never tested her ability.

Far more interesting to Felix than the lure of the tracks

were the *customers*. And in fact Felix – despite her reputation for laziness – turned out to be far more diligent about her station-cat duties than anyone might have expected. Given the freedom to go anywhere she wanted, Felix chose – day after day – to take up her post at the customer-information window, where she'd sit for hour after hour, her tail flicking back and forth rhythmically, as though it was a pendulum on a clock. Felix became quite a talking point for customers – she started many a conversation between a commuter and a customer-service officer, and everyone went away happier for the exchange.

As the weeks unfolded, and the bite of autumn started to nip the air, Felix settled into her new role as meeter-and-greeter extraordinaire. And it wasn't long before she showed that she was great in a crisis, too.

As it had been in the former office layout, the customer-information window was linked to the now-much-smaller announcer's office, so it was usually the announcers who dealt with any enquiries; along with Felix, of course. Some of those enquiries were pleasant and polite exchanges – which platform do I need? Can you tell me the next train to Leeds? What time will the 16.46 arrive in York? On other occasions, however, when trains had been delayed or cancelled, or there were emergencies on the line, the customers coming to the desk could be rather irate at finding their travel plans thwarted. As Gareth knew all too well from his time on the gateline, hell hath no fury like a traveller stopped in his tracks.

He was sitting at his desk on a late turn one evening when a gentleman came to the window. Unfortunately, a train to Manchester airport had been cancelled and the man was in a pickle, desperately worried that he and his family were going to miss their flight. During the day, there were trains roughly every fifteen minutes or so to the airport, but it was now approximately 7 p.m. and another wasn't due for quite a while – and the family hadn't left themselves much time for their journey.

'I want a word with you,' the man said crossly at the window. Felix was asleep in the in-tray on the desk at the time, and she stirred slightly at his raised voice and blinked open her big green eyes.

'Certainly, sir,' Gareth said politely, coming over to the window. It was a tricky situation for the railway team to be in, as all they could do was apologise for the cancelled service and say, 'You'll have to get the next train.' But when a customer was worried and wound up, as this gentleman was, it was almost impossible to appease them.

As Gareth had feared, his words fell on deaf ears. The man – who was in his fifties and stockily built – launched into a tirade of complaints; he was really rather furious. His family stood beside him as he fumed, his wife nodding her head at his words, and the little boy and girl clearly dismayed that their holiday might be ruined.

Then the man started to shout.

Ordinarily in that situation, Gareth would have stayed behind the glass window and tried to calm the customer from there. As he nodded sympathetically, however, his eye fell on Felix, who was now alert and standing to attention on the desk. *I wonder* . . . Gareth thought. In his campaign with Paul, he had so often said how brilliant having a station cat would be for customer satisfaction – how a cat would calm people down and cheer them up, and make everybody happier.

He glanced back towards the family; the father was puce with rage and his throat hoarse from shouting. There was nothing to lose.

'Excuse me one moment,' Gareth said politely. 'I'll come out and see you.'

Gareth turned from the window and scooped up Felix with one hand. 'Time to prove yourself, young cat,' he told her. He opened the door to the platform and together he and Felix went to reason with the angry man.

'Oh, a cat!' cried the little girl at once, as soon as she saw the kitten in Gareth's arms. She was about six years old and rushed forwards to say hello. 'Isn't she lovely, Daddy?'

She clearly wanted to play with Felix, so Gareth bent down so that the little girl could pet her. Felix blinked up at her with her beautiful emerald eyes and calmly let the child stroke her fluffy black fur. The boy, who was younger, about four years old, was a bit shyer than his sister, but he, too, edged forward and extended a hesitant hand towards the adorable-looking cat.

'As I was saying, sir,' Gareth continued, from his position crouched on the ground with the cat and the kids, 'I'm so terribly sorry about the cancellation. The next train to the airport is in twenty minutes. If you get that, you will still make your flight.'

The man looked rather as though the wind had been taken out of his sails. He glanced at his wife, and both of them stared down at their children, who were purring over Felix as though they themselves were kittens.

'She's so soft, Daddy!' the girl exclaimed.

'In twenty minutes, did you say?' the man asked, more calmly.

'Twenty minutes, yes, sir,' confirmed Gareth. 'It will be on Platform 1.'

Felix had completely taken the edge off the confrontation. As the family thanked him for his help and the children reluctantly waved goodbye to Felix, Gareth stood up and carried his trusty colleague back into the office. As the door closed behind them, he looked down at her and gave her the most enormous grin.

'Good work, station cat,' he told her proudly. 'Very good work indeed.'

12. A Very Special Cat

Felix continued to work her magic again and again as a key member of the customer-facing team of Huddersfield station. She was absolutely superb at calming the angriest customer. As Angie Hunte observed, as soon as they saw Felix, the rage just totally disappeared. In all her years at the station, she had never seen anything like it. And it seemed to work on everyone, from elderly customers to middle-aged mums. Gareth had a teenage customer once, a young woman with short, bleached-blonde hair, who was ranting and raving that her life was *over* because of the cancelled service that had *wrecked everything*! Felix had been asleep under the window at the time, and as the woman screamed at him in a total teenage tantrum, Gareth had fumbled discreetly under the desk for his cat, picked Felix up and put her on display in the window, as though producing a rabbit from a hat.

It changed the conversation completely – and abruptly. 'What on earth . . . ?' the young woman had said.

Gareth had then slipped out of the door with Felix and the girl had held her and stroked her and she just forgot that the train had been cancelled and her life had been ruined five minutes before . . .

Felix wasn't only skilled at diverting angry customers, however – she could also cheer up the unhappiest folk. Because the office window opened onto Platform 1, the announcers could hear everything that went on out there. One day, Gareth's eardrums were split by the most wretched sound of a screaming child. A little girl with Goldilocks curls was crying her heart out and she was standing right outside the office, howling. He could hear that her mum was trying to comfort her, and had been trying to comfort her for the past five minutes, with no luck whatsoever. The child was distraught.

Gareth went out onto the platform with Felix in his hands. He didn't really know much about children, so he had no idea if this would work, but the mum was really struggling. The girl, who was maybe two or three years old, was red in the face; her tears had made watery tracks all down her cheeks. As she took a deep breath in preparation for yet another ear-splitting wail, Gareth interjected hurriedly.

'Look!' he said to her brightly. 'I've got a cat! Would you like to see her?'

The little girl blinked up at him in surprise, and the scream stored in her lungs never came.

'Come and see our little cat,' he said encouragingly, exchanging a look with her relieved mum. The two walked over to Gareth, who bent down so that the child could see Felix properly.

'Here she is,' he said. 'This is Felix.'

He put the station cat down on the platform, and Felix trotted cautiously over to the little girl and sat down at her feet, looking up at her. The child stared back in wonder, whatever terrors had been plaguing her forgotten.

'Say, "Hello Felix",' urged her mum.

''Ello, E-lix,' echoed the little girl, her voice transformed from hiccoughing howl to burbling brook.

Felix stood up again and wound her way through the legs of the girl and those of her very happy mother, pressing her furry body against them both. It was another job well done.

Felix was doing such brilliant work at the station that it was around this time that she made her first appearance in the media, in November 2011. At only six months old, an article was written about her arrival at the station in the *Huddersfield Examiner*, celebrating the employment of this very special member of the team. Angie was interviewed for it, and made an appeal to customers not to feed Felix, for while the moggy had now successfully lost the weight she'd gained after her operation, they didn't want her getting fat again. Angie explained that Felix was going to be a working moggy – the pest controller.

'She's about to start work on keeping pests to a minimum,' promised the *Examiner*.

Despite the media coverage in the local paper, many customers travelling through Huddersfield – who came from far and wide – were still astonished to meet the railway cat, whether they encountered her at the customer-information point, patrolling the platforms or doing a security check with one of her colleagues. If they met Felix when she was on her own, they would often rush up to the nearest member of staff shortly afterwards.

'Do you know there's a cat on the station?' they'd exclaim. Or they'd pick her up and proffer her: 'We found a cat!'

'Yeah, we know,' the team would say casually, maybe even a little wearily after it had happened several times. 'She's ours.'

'But where does she live?' they would ask in consternation. 'She lives here.'

'Oh, is she a stray?'

Felix, at this juncture, would look up at them haughtily, and give almost a toss of her ebony head, so that the diamanté studs on her collar would glimmer and her pink heart tag would tinkle indignantly.

The station team's response would be just as proud: 'She is *not* a stray! She's legal, she's above board and she's very much loved.'

Felix would then start washing herself, licking that oh-so-fluffy black fur to keep it nice and clean. A stray . . . Honestly! Did she *look* like a stray, with her well-kept coat and her glittering accessories? She seemed almost offended by the slur.

But despite the eye-catching glamour of those glitzy accoutrements, not everyone seemed to notice them. There were a few occasions in those early days where a well-meaning customer had picked up the cat and tried to take her home; perhaps because they thought she was a stray, or perhaps because she was so *very* beautiful. Luckily, the team on the concourse always spotted the situation arising before any damage was done. The collar was pointed out and the address read, and Felix – rather than being 'catnapped' – would be safely returned to Platform 1.

But the team couldn't always keep tabs on her. It was a busy station, and a big one, and they all had jobs to do. Felix was an independent woman; at any time of day or night she might be off exploring round the bushes at the southern end of Platform 1 near the King's Head pub, or up at the other end, watching those tasty little wild rabbits. She was becoming more and more fearless – though her hatred of the black crows still saw her running for cover. Sometimes she'd try to style it out on the platform, looking at one of them and striking an 'I own this joint' pose, but the moment the crow started walking or flying towards her, she would leg it – back home if possible, or up to safety on a windowsill.

But then she'd be stuck there, marooned, and the crow would know it. It would caw at her, a cackling kind of call that sounded like a mocking laugh. Angela Dunn, working in the lost-property office, came to recognise that sound. Soon she knew that if the crows started making that noise, Felix would be stuck on a windowsill outside somewhere, too terrified to move. Angela would have to come out onto the platform and shoo the crows off, so that Felix could get down from her little island and run home to safety.

So although the kitten was making great leaps forwards, she was still a vulnerable creature at heart: new to the world and still finding her way, working out what was a terror and what was a toy; who was a friend and who an enemy. As with all parents watching their children grow, the station team were both delighted and chilled by her growing independence. But Felix was a loyal little thing. Almost as if she knew they might be fretting, her explorations never lasted for any length of time, and she never wandered far from Platform 1. Every few hours, several times a shift, the team would spot her hanging out by the bike racks or leaping up onto the customer-service desk to put in her time on the frontline. She gave them no cause for concern.

But then came a day Angie would never forget. The day when she signed on for her shift and Billy had to take her to one side.

'Now, I don't want you to panic, Ang . . . ' the gruff team leader began.

These words, of course, were destined to set her heart hammering hard and fast within her chest.

'I don't want you to panic,' he went on, 'but we can't find Felix.'

Angie looked at him blankly. So Billy said it again, more plainly, more worryingly, and in words that left no room for doubt.

'Felix has gone.'

13. Missing

'What do you mean, you can't find Felix?' Angie asked.

Billy ushered her into the team leaders' office and sat her down in a chair.

'She's disappeared,' he said gently. 'She's been gone all day. Nobody's seen her.'

'What do you mean?' Angie said again, the panic rising in her voice. 'She can't have just *gone*. She must be somewhere!'

But as Billy told her the whole story, Angie realised, with a sinking feeling, that the kitten was well and truly lost.

It had been Dave Rooney who'd first raised the alarm. He'd been the team leader on duty on the early-morning shift, and he'd suddenly realised mid-morning that he hadn't seen Felix since he'd clocked on. That was highly unusual.

'Have you seen Felix?' he casually asked the team, strolling through the station.

But they all said 'no'.

Dave wasn't too worried. He sauntered down to the bike racks, checked in the shower room in case she was sleeping on her fleecy black blanket, and ducked his head into the lost-property office, asking Angela Dunn if Felix had popped by that morning. But the little kitten was nowhere to be found.

Dave walked back up Platform 1, wracking his brains. Felix sometimes liked to hang around the King's Head at the southern end of the station, the boozy little thing, attracted by the thick brambled bushes at the very edge of the station's plot. Could she have gone into the bushes and got stuck, unable to fight her way out? He hurried down there, but he could neither see nor hear the kitten amid the dense, knotted briars.

It was time to call in reinforcements. He radioed Dave Chin, the TPE maintenance man, and asked him to pop by as soon as he could.

Dave Chin wasn't based permanently at Huddersfield, but worked all over the railway network, doing whatever odds and sods needed doing, turning up whenever he was summoned, like a sort of railway fairy godfather. He worked at Dewsbury, Stalybridge, Leeds and Manchester as well, but was often at Huddersfield. The first time he'd met Felix, she was sitting in a watering can on Platform 1 with her head poking out of the top – and it had been a mutual case of love at first sight. From that moment on, whenever Dave Chin came to Huddersfield, he made it his first duty to visit Felix, and it turned out that he was the ultimate Felix charmer. Though she was an affectionate cat with many people, her relationship with Dave was something else. He would pick her up and she would roll over instantly on to her back and loll there in his arms, her head hanging off one side and her legs dangling down the other, so that he could rub her belly or tickle her front paws. He'd walk all around the station with her like that: Felix splayed out in his arms, so loved up and easy and she didn't care who saw it.

'Felix,' Angie Hunte used to tut when she saw her, shaking her head in mock-shame, 'you're an absolute disgrace.'

So when Dave Rooney told Dave Chin that Felix was missing, the maintenance man wanted to do everything in his power to find her. The team leader relayed his concern that the kitten might have got trapped in the overgrown bushes, and Dave Chin clapped his hands together decisively and sprang into action.

'Right,' he said firmly, 'let's get that cleared.'

Dave was a down-to-earth, well-muscled man with a weathered face and copious blond hair. He put every one of those muscles to use that day as he cautiously chopped down all the overgrown bushes on the station, looking under every briar for a little black-and-white cat. But when he had finished there was still no sign of her.

The clock ticked on, and Dave Rooney completed his shift. As he handed over to Billy in the afternoon, he gave him an update – and top of the agenda was that Felix was missing. The old-timer had shaken his head incredulously at all this fuss over the kitten; he was sure that the cat would turn up.

Yet as the hours passed by and Billy did his own searches of the station, and completed his own security checks, he realised he had been wrong. For there was not a hint of a whisker to be seen.

The sun set, and cold night settled like a blanket on the station. Billy, despite himself, began to worry. He often moaned about the cat, as he did everything else, calling her a 'fleabag' or a 'waste of space' or simply 'urgh, that cat!', but despite his mean-sounding words there was always a warmth to his tone. He really hoped she was all right.

The station clock kept time as accurately as always, and all too soon the digits turned to 8 p.m. and Angie arrived for her night shift. Billy knew she would be worried sick at the news he had to share which is why he had tried to break it to her gently by saying, 'Now, I don't want you to panic, Ang...'

Sitting in the team leaders' office, having now heard the full account of the drama from Billy, Angie *was* panicking.

'Have you *searched*?' she grilled Billy, leaping to her feet and pacing the office. 'I mean, *properly*?'

'I've searched, Ang,' he told her.

'But have you checked underneath that disused carriage, on Platform 2? Because she likes it under there, she sometimes goes and hides there . . .'

'I know, Ang,' Billy said. Everybody on the station knew the kitten's favourite places better than the backs of their own hands. 'I've searched.'

'And the bicycle racks?'

'I've searched.'

'And the shower?'

'Angie, I've looked everywhere. She's not here. She's gone.'

A big lump suddenly appeared from nowhere in Angie's throat and hot tears pricked her eyes.

'Ang, she'll turn up. She'll get hungry, she'll come back. It's what cats do.'

'But she's never been gone this long,' Angie said in a wobbly voice, sinking into a chair for support. *Her poor little kitten.*

She was glad, at least, that it was Billy who had told her. They went back a long way, and if anybody was going to see her upset, she wanted it to be him. As a team leader, you couldn't show your emotions out on the station floor – her job was to lead, to sort out problems, to get things done, and crying didn't come into that. But Billy had always understood her. Angie's pet niggle about herself was that she couldn't always find the right words to say what she meant, but if she and Billy were in the same meeting together and she was floundering about, trying to express herself and failing, Billy used to clear his throat and say, 'I think what Angie means is . . . ' and he would get it absolutely right. 'Yes, that's it, that's it,' Angie would say, and he'd nod at her in his gruff way, not wanting her thanks, but knowing she was grateful anyway.

Billy stood up, ready to head home. He placed a rough, weathered hand firmly on her shoulder as he went. 'I'm sure she'll turn up,' he said.

After he left, Angie sat in the office alone. She felt absolutely devastated. She didn't want to do any work; she *couldn't* do any work. She couldn't think of anything but Felix, out there, somewhere, in the dark winter's night.

Who knew what had happened? Had someone taken her? Had she decided she'd had enough of her working life on the station and called it quits? Had – God forbid – she roamed onto the tracks and been hit by an express? Billy had told her that Dave Chin – who was PTS (Personal Track Safety)-certified and wore the all-over orange hi-vis uniform of those who could walk on the tracks – had looked all over the railway lines for her, and there'd been no sign, but even so . . . What if she'd wandered into one of the tunnels?

Angie felt sick. Felix wasn't even a year old. She was absolutely frantic about her.

Every minute felt like an hour. So, when the team leaders' mobile phone rang ten 'hours' into her shift at 8.10 p.m., Angie's nerves were already shot to pieces.

'H-H-Huddersfield station?' she answered tearfully.

'Oh, Huddersfield *station*,' said a male voice on the other end of the phone, as though something now made perfect sense. 'I work for Domino's Pizza.'

Domino's Pizza? thought Angie. *We haven't ordered any pizza.*

But then he said, 'I think we've got something that belongs to you.'

Suddenly, the broken pieces of her world fell neatly back into place. Angie gasped. 'Is she black and white?' she asked joyously.

'Yes!' the man replied with a laugh.

Well, that was it. Angie dropped everything – the station

was secondary and her colleagues could take up the slack. She literally ran to the car park and threw herself into her car. *Domino's Pizza*, she was thinking, *well, I never.* And also: *how the hell did you get there, little kitten?*

For Domino's Pizza was quite some distance away, located right by the busy ring road that encircled Huddersfield's town centre. It was totally out of the area that Felix was known to have frequented on her own, which essentially comprised the length of Platforms 1 and 2. If she hadn't crossed the train tracks – which seemed unlikely since she never had before, and still ran for home if an incoming train was near – then to reach the pizza place she would have had to contend with the traffic in town and cross several busy roads. Unless, of course, someone had taken her . . .

At that moment, Angie didn't care *how* she'd got there; she was just pleased that she knew exactly where she was. She squealed to a stop outside Domino's Pizza and ran in as fast as she could. And there, sat on the floor in the corner, munching away on something the pizza man had given her and relishing the delicious scent of the cooking pizzas, was Felix. She blinked up at Angie as she ran in, then got rapidly to her feet, as though she'd been waiting for her ride.

Angie felt her heart flip right up into her mouth and back again. 'Oh, you've got her,' she breathed in relief to the man behind the counter. 'You've got her.'

She couldn't get to Felix quick enough. She scooped her up from the ground and hugged her. Felix looked happily at her, her fluffy tail swishing, seemingly delighted to be re-united with her mum. Angie stared right into her beautiful green eyes. She was so, so happy to see her.

'How did she get here?' she asked the man behind the counter.

'No idea!' he laughed. 'She just wandered in.'

Angie turned her attention back to her beloved cat. 'You're not going anywhere ever again!' she told her sternly. 'What do you think you're up to? And *where* have you been?' Her worry made her voice quite sharp. She knew Felix couldn't answer, but the questions spilled out regardless.

Angie held the kitten up in the stark fluorescent lighting of the pizza joint and checked her over carefully, as if looking for clues. There was, at least, no sign of any injury, but neither was there any evidence as to where Felix might have spent her whole day away from home.

Angie brought her back down into her arms. 'It is *good* to have you back, madam,' she told her affectionately.

'She's a grand cat,' the pizza man commented from the counter, adding with a grin, 'Can we keep her?'

Angie scowled at him jokingly. 'You've absolutely no chance!' she declared emphatically. 'No chance! Do you know how many people have been out looking for this cat today?'

'She's lovely,' he observed, with a smile.

'We *know*!' Angie cried, holding her kitten even closer to her chest. 'We know she is!'

She thanked the man for phoning her – *thank God for Christine and that heart-shaped tag*, she thought – and carried Felix out to the car.

'Right, you,' Angie told the cat. 'Adventure's over. We're going home.'

Back at the office, Angie put some food in her bowl and Felix wolfed it down at once. While the kitten ate, Angie picked up her phone again and dialled Billy. It was the least she could do after his kindness earlier; she knew that, despite himself, he would be worried too.

He answered after only a few rings.

'I've got her!' Angie said breathlessly, as soon as he picked up.

He didn't need to ask her who. 'Where's she been?' he asked curiously.

'Domino's Pizza,' deadpanned Angie. 'Only Felix could go AWOL and end up at a food place!'

14. Angel Felix?

In the first weekend of December 2011, Dave Chin sauntered along Huddersfield station with his arms full of Christmas tree. TPE always got its Christmas trees delivered from a special farm, and that year Huddersfield had chosen a massive, ten-to-twelve-foot one that would stretch right up to the ceiling of the lobby.

As was his habit, on arrival at the station Dave had already popped in to see Felix, and he wasn't expecting to see her again that shift. Nine times out of ten she was sleeping when he saw her, so he'd just give her a cuddle and leave her be. But on that particular day, as soon as Felix saw what he was carrying, she bounded right up to him and looked on with interest as he and Angie heaved the tree into the entrance lobby and then pushed it into the corner, where it would stand in front of the ticketing office for everyone to see.

'What is *that*?' the station cat seemed to be saying, as she trotted round their ankles and circled the tree, moving back for a better view, then craning her neck upwards, to where the very top of the tree just touched the ceiling.

It was a big, bushy evergreen, with a solid wooden trunk and attractive branches splaying out every which way. Felix thought it might just be the most amazing thing she had ever seen. It smelled heavenly, of outdoors and forest and pine, and it was making the most intriguing sounds as Dave and Angie Hunte pushed and pulled it until it was safely and sturdily in place.

As soon as they stepped back, Felix launched herself at it.

She ran right under the lowest branches until she reached the trunk, then dug in her claws and ran for the stars. It was just like the time when she used to run up her friend Gareth's back, but this was much, much better! It was taller, and it didn't wriggle or wince, and Felix could run fast, fast, fast until she reached the sky!

Suddenly, she was there, right at the very top of the tree. She poked her head out of the branches, and heard the peals of laughter from Dave and Angie below, who were pointing up at her and giggling. This was wonderful! She sat right there, queen of all she surveyed, with her head sticking out of the branches like a feline angel heralding the birth of Christ.

She sat there for ages, just watching. Why come down when one had such a marvellous view? She could see the team in the ticket office processing the tickets; watch as the customers came in and out of the station, many carrying shopping bags filled with festive goods, their breath fogging as they stepped out into the wintry vista of St George's Square beyond the main front doors. And she could see Angie and Dave, who had disappeared for a short while, as they returned with a big cardboard box and started pulling out fairy lights and brightly coloured baubles from inside it.

TPE, by now, had stockpiled a range of festive decorations. They had white lights and coloured lights, blue baubles and silver ones, reds and golds and greens. The team mixed them up for a bit of variety and had different colour schemes each year. Chrissie from the booking office, who had given Felix her pink name tag, took charge of the display, and as Felix watched keenly she now came out of the ticket office and bent to help Dave and Angie.

Chrissie picked up a bauble and hung it on a branch. 'Now, what's this?' Felix seemed to say, as she unpoked her head from the top of the tree and scrambled down the trunk to where the bauble hung below.

It glimmered there in the bright station lights, tempting and teasing Felix just as her laser toy did. The bauble spun first one way and then the other, as though it was taunting her. Felix narrowed her eyes, thinking hard and plotting. Then, in one fluid movement, she reached out a paw and swiped it hard.

Wipe-out! The bauble tumbled to the ground, and Felix jerked her head up, watching, as she heard Chrissie tutting and coming over to rehang it. Felix waited until she'd turned her back and then – *swipe!* Once more, the bauble fell off: 2-0 to Felix. It was game on.

And what a game it was. As soon as Dave or Angie or Chrissie hung a bauble, Felix would knock it off. There were baubles flying everywhere! Felix darted up and down the tree, having the greatest time of her life. Hidden among the branches as she was, all anyone could see was the tree moving a little bit, shaking as though it was chuckling at a fantastic joke, and all these baubles going everywhere.

'Felix, *no!*' they chorused.

But Felix was having far too much fun to stop, as she ducked and dived and swiped and wriggled and made the tree shake even more.

Finally, she tired a little of the merrymaking, and allowed Chrissie to complete the bauble-hanging. She watched proceedings as they continued, once again from the top of the tree, as Dave got out one of his big ladders and started climbing up it. She followed him with her green eyes with a great deal of interest. He had something clutched in his hand. *What new toy-friend is this?* she wondered.

But it wasn't a toy-friend at all: it was an enemy. Though TPE changed the colour scheme of its decorations every year, one thing never altered: at the top of the tree would sit the same little angel, a gold cardboard cherub with a cone for a bottom who could be easily popped onto the highest branch and from there reign graciously over the station's festivities.

Felix watched her coming closer with ever-narrowing eyes. As Dave reached out over the highest branch, Felix bobbed instinctively, and momentarily, below the barrier of uppermost branches, as though concerned he was going to grab her, but Dave merely placed the angel on the top of the tree and then descended the ladder.

Felix scurried back up and poked her head out of the top of the tree again. The angel smiled her painted smile. Felix looked her rival up and down – and the derisive glare she gave her said clearly that she was not *at all* impressed by what she saw.

'*This* is what you want to put on top of the tree?' she seemed to be saying with that disdainful glower. '*This*? When you could have beautiful *me*?'

Felix and the angel stared each other out at their elevated altitude, as though they were cowboys sizing each other up before a high-noon shoot-out. Felix made the first move.

Swipe! A little white-capped paw darted through the green branches towards the golden angel girl. But the station cat missed. She edged a little closer. *Swipe!* The tree wobbled and shook, and the multitude of baubles trembled on their strings. Felix poked and pawed at the angel through the branches: a left hook, a right hook, a swift uppercut. With every blow, she seemed to say, 'Get off! It's *my* tree! Get off! How *dare* you!'

Down below, the team chuckled. This feisty Felix was a rather recent development – but it wasn't always a laughing matter.

Though Felix had not suffered any ill effects from her

adventure to Domino's Pizza, the team had noticed lately that she was no longer quite as pliant and friendly as she had once been. Frankly, you could understand it: from the moment she'd arrived at the station, she'd had scores of colleagues wanting a cuddle, and now she was out and about in the concourse she also had to contend with scores of strange customers, who stroked and poked and picked her up too. It was all a bit much for any cat to deal with. Everybody and their Uncle Fred wanted to play with her and touch her, and by now she was getting a bit bowled off by it.

With those she loved best, though, like Gareth and Angie, she was an absolute sweetheart. She had taken to following the team leaders around on their shifts, like a little puppy. If Angie was on duty and had to leave Felix behind somewhere, the cat would wait for her to finish what she was doing before trotting along beside her heels again; or Felix might turn it into a game of chase, where she would run cheekily ahead of Angie, occasionally looking back over her shoulder to check she was keeping up, then pause, waiting for her friend to catch her. But as soon as Angie's feet drew parallel with Felix's paws, off she'd go again, like a relay runner handed the baton. That was a *great* game. If the pair got separated while Angie was on shift, Felix would wait patiently by the bike racks, and the moment she heard Angie's cheery voice calling out along the platforms – 'Hello, driver!' or 'Good morning, there!' to the customers – she would dart out happily to seek the owner of that voice, her joy plain to see as she scampered along.

Given Felix's new diva-like disposition, however, Angie was understandably apprehensive as she took the kitten for her first grooming session. The vet had told Angie how important it was with a long-haired cat to make sure it was kept well-groomed, and Angie had bought a brush from him for that very job, but it had soon become clear that fluffy Felix was going to need – if not demand – professional expertise when it came to her beauty maintenance. So Angie made an appointment for her at a local grooming parlour.

The first challenge, as with any off-site outing, was getting Felix into her carrier. No matter how grown up she got, this was one terror she would never overcome. It made no difference how many treats Angie used to try to tempt her inside, Felix *knew* what was happening and was far too clever to fall for that little ruse. The moment she saw the box, she'd be off, and neither Angie nor her colleagues could get her inside.

But there was one man who could: Dave Chin, the Felix charmer. Angie used to radio him for that very job. 'Dave! Where are you? Are you anywhere near Huddersfield? We need you – Felix won't go in her box!' Then Dave would come, pick up the kitten in one easy movement, turn her upside-down to give her paws a little tickle, and then he'd slide her inside with a casual, 'In you go.'

Once inside, however, Felix would relax. By the time Angie had carried her to her car and turned on both the engine and the stereo, Felix was as good as gold. Angie and the cat used to listen to reggae music as the team leader chauffeured the station moggy to whichever appointment Felix was attending that day. 'This is our music, in't it, sweetheart?' Angie would say. 'This is our music!' And she'd look across at her and chat to her – 'It's all right, we'll get you there' – and Felix would settle down quite happily, soothed by the reggae beats.

Angie was concerned that even Bob Marley wouldn't cut it as she and Felix travelled to the grooming parlour for Felix's first haircut, however. She felt most apprehensive as she carried the cat into the sweet-smelling parlour, like a mother dropping off her daughter on the first day of school.

The cat groomer leaned across the table to take her.

'She's never really done anything like this before,' Angie said, hesitantly. 'Are you *sure* she's going to be all right?'

'Oh, she'll be fine,' the groomer replied airily. 'We deal with them all the time!'

Pfft! Angie thought. *You haven't dealt with ours* . . . She had visions of Felix throwing a diva strop in the middle of the parlour and quickly hurried out before she could change her mind.

An hour or so later, she returned to collect her girl. 'Has she been all right?' she asked nervously.

'Oh, she's been absolutely brilliant,' they said.

Angie thought they meant the groomer who'd been attending to Felix. 'No, no, I'm talking about *Felix*. Has *Felix* been all right?'

'Oh yes!' they said, laughing. 'She's been great. She sat and let us wet-wash her; she's had the blower; she's had the whole job lot. Here – see for yourself.'

And there was Felix, sitting on the table with her head up high, her fur going everywhere as though in a wind machine, looking for all the world like a movie star on a magazine shoot. She looked *amazing*. Her coat was clean and bushy and out to here, like a glorious Afro. Angie had never seen her look so glamorous and gorgeous. When she picked her up, a heavenly scent wafted towards her. Little Felix smelled *divine*. Angie couldn't wait to get her back to the station to show her off.

There were a lot of oohs and ahhs as Felix trotted out onto Platform 1 with her new look. But the instant she hit the mucky concrete, she flopped to the ground and started rolling, rolling, rolling, wriggling her back and her oh-so-fluffy fur into the dirt, trying to get the nice clean smell off her!

'Felix!' Angie hollered. 'Come back here! We've just had you cleaned!'

But Felix wouldn't be told.

Felix wouldn't be told, full stop, these days. As Christmas drew closer, the station team and customers had to contend with a classic Yorkshire winter: rain, rain, snow and more rain. Through the open roof of Huddersfield station, raindrops fell and landed on Felix's fur as she huddled on Platform 1, that thick furry coat of hers – just as Joanne Briscoe had anticipated – keeping her snug as a bug in a rug. But wet as Felix's fur got, her feet got wetter still. When the weather became too gruelling and the cat retreated to the cosy comfort of the lost-property office, she used to leap up onto Angela Dunn's desk and walk all over it, leaving filthy pawprints on her paperwork. Angela had never seen such a mess!

'Now, now, Felix,' Angela would scold, '*please* wipe your feet before you come in.'

The station cat didn't make herself popular with the team working on the concourse, either. They might just have finished mopping the floor for the hundredth time that day when in would walk Felix with her elegant strut, diamanté collar flashing at her throat, and she'd leave muddy brown pawprints all over the clean white tiles.

'Felix, *really*?' they'd cry after her in disbelief. 'We've just cleaned that floor!'

But while Felix was merrily having a whale of a time misbehaving, her carefree antics were about to get her into some serious trouble on the railway.

One afternoon that December, Felix decided it was the perfect time for a spot of rabbit hunting. Off she trotted to the end of Platform 2, where she paused, sniffing the air. She stood quite still, waiting.

There they were. Out came the little brown-and-white bunnies, hopping about on the grass by the tracks, right by the yawning mouth of the train tunnel. Felix dropped close to the ground, every sinew in her body pulled taut as elastic, every sense on high alert. Slowly, slowly, she crept forward, and started edging down the ramp that led her straight to the rabbits' playground.

The team, watching her from further up the platform, shook their heads. *You haven't got a cat in hell's chance of catching those rabbits, Felix,* they thought to themselves – but Felix wasn't going to let that dissuade her. She was having fun! Down the slope she went, nose to the ground, bum wiggling in the air, stalking those wild rabbits as though her life depended on it. Closer and closer she got to them, down and down . . . until Felix the railway cat was stalking the rabbits right by the tracks. She was very, very close to going beyond the safety of the platform and clearly hadn't a clue as to the danger she might put herself in.

Luckily, someone had been keeping as close an eye on Felix as she was on those bunnies: the driver of the train that was dawdling at Platform 1. Concerned, he called over the Huddersfield station train dispatcher and spoke to him from the door of his cab.

'Look at that cat!' He gestured at Felix, who was busy striking hunting poses on the very edge of the platform. 'She'll be in proper danger if she doesn't watch out.' He made a decision. 'I'm not going to risk it. I refuse to move this train until that cat is safe!'

Chris Briscoe, Felix's 'grandfather', happened to be working at the station that day and was witness to the ensuing chaos his kitten caused. What a palaver! Felix caused quite the scene. There she was, gaily gambolling about with the rabbits, while further up the station there was a train stuck in its tracks, customers wondering what was causing the delay, and a railway team up in arms trying to sort it all out. Felix had brought the whole station to a standstill. In all likelihood, the moment she heard the train's engine start, she would have run for home, but the driver was so frightened of running over the popular station cat that he wouldn't move his train one inch.

Eventually, Felix finished with her fun and lolloped back up the ramp to safety, completely oblivious to the chaos she had caused. The train's engines roared, the driver was waved on, and the station started running at full speed again.

'Who are we going to put this down to?' the team asked crossly as they filled in their forms; they had to account formally for any hold-ups.

All eyes turned as one to the little black-and-white cat.

'*Felix*,' they said in unison.

15. The First Farewell

That was the one and only time Felix ever brought the station to a halt. Like any kitten, she tested boundaries and had her fair share of cheeky and mischievous antics – but this kitten was undeniably growing up. By now, her blue kitten collar had grown too small for her, even with its adjustable strap, so just before Christmas Angie Hunte gave her a new one, this time a glittery pink number, in which Felix looked dolled up to the nines. It coordinated with the pink heart tag perfectly. Felix would certainly look smart on Christmas Day.

Where Felix would spend her first Christmas was a topic of some concern to the team. Huddersfield station is staffed twenty-four hours a day and *almost* 365 days a year, but is always closed on Christmas and Boxing Day. Felix couldn't possibly spend the festivities on her own in a deserted station, so Angie started asking the team which of them might be prepared to host Felix over Christmas.

She would have loved to take her herself – though she joked that if she did, the cat would probably never come back to the station, being held hostage at home! But Angie's daughter was asthmatic, so she wasn't able to do it. With so many of the team having their own cats at home, it proved quite tricky to find someone who had a feline-free household and was willing to take her. In the end, Andy Dyson, one of the team leaders, offered his home and Felix spent her first Christmas in a domestic, family environment.

Gareth clocked off on Christmas Eve pleased to know

that Felix would be in safe hands. He *really* wanted to have her at his own home, but he knew that Cosmo would not be keen on the idea. But there was a special reason Gareth had wanted to spend as much time with Felix as he possibly could, for Gareth Hope, after all these years at Huddersfield, had got himself a new job. His last day at the station would be Friday 6 January 2012.

Throughout the autumn, Billy's words of warning had rattled round and round in Gareth's head. In the end it was Paul, the station manager, who had given the young announcer a bit of a leg-up. Knowing that Gareth had a background in computer programming, he'd asked him if he could use his experience to help improve the announcing system. Gareth had therefore been involved in developing a new announcing programme that the network had installed, which had required him to spend some time at Control and to go down to Leicester to test the new system. In November, a new job had come up at Control and – perhaps partly thanks to Gareth's recent experience there and his developing the programme – he'd got the post. He would be a customer information controller, based just outside Manchester Piccadilly. It was a fantastic promotion, one that would really challenge him and test his skills.

'Well done, lad,' Billy had said when he'd heard the news. He didn't smile, or anything so extravagant as that, but Billy just didn't smile; it wasn't his way. He gave Gareth a proud look, though, locking eyes with him as he nodded his grizzled head. 'That's grand,' he said simply.

Gareth knew in his heart that he was ready to move on, but that final week at work he suddenly wasn't quite so sure. He was really clingy with Felix all week, insisting that she spend his shifts with him in the tiny announcer's office, which she was quite happy to do. She'd adored Gareth ever since she had arrived at the station, and the two of them were best buddies.

Everything they did that week seemed to be for the last time. The last time Gareth would kick her brown bear down the corridor for her. The last time she would join him on a security check. The last time he would offer her the microphone and she would turn her head away contemptuously, as though to say, 'You're the one who does that job, sonny. Don't expect me to lower myself to your level: *I'm* the railway cat.' He couldn't believe he wasn't going to be seeing her, day in, day out, for eight hours a day. He knew he could – and would – come back to visit, but they would never again have the same close connection.

In the six months Felix had been at the station, she had transformed his working life. With Felix there – no matter what else was happening that day, whether the trains were cancelled or he was in trouble with Paul or simply not enjoying the company of his colleagues for whatever reason – he could enjoy Felix's company; he could sit in his office with his cat and everything was fine. The other members of the team felt the same: 'She's my favourite colleague as she never complains,' one had confessed to Gareth. 'She's just another member of the team, but easier to work with than most.'

'She's brought a lot of good feeling to the station,' Angie agreed.

At the end of every shift that final week, Gareth would try to get a cuddle from the cat. He knew how special she was, and as he faced up to life after Huddersfield, he felt a certain amount of pride that he had been so closely involved in bringing her to the station. All those posters and pitches had been worth it. There might not yet be bouncy tarmac on the platforms, or slides where the stairs should be, but there *was* a station cat, and that was an incredible legacy to be leaving behind. It felt *meaningful.*

Friday, 6 January 2012 arrived far too soon. As his last-ever shift at Huddersfield drew to a close, Gareth completed his rounds of the station, bidding farewell to his colleagues in the booking office and the concourse. He and Andy parted with a long, warm handshake.

'Don't forget the little guys,' Andy told him – in joining the team at Control, Gareth would be making decisions that would affect the station staff.

'I won't!' Gareth promised. The two friends grinned at each other, their sadness at parting tempered by the fact that their roles would require them to remain in regular contact. Nevertheless, their flights of fancy would never quite reach the same heights as they had at Huddersfield.

With an increasingly heavy heart, Gareth walked back into the announcer's office, ready to pick up his bag and catch his train home, which would be leaving in the next few minutes from Platform 1. Martin was there, to take over the next shift, as well as Angie and Angela – and of course Felix too – ready to see him off.

'Right, then,' Gareth said brusquely.

He bent down and picked up his constant friend, Felix. Used to these nightly cuddles goodbye, she didn't realise: *this is the last time.* But Gareth knew. He felt suddenly tearful.

Felix, sat in his arms, raised herself up on her back legs and put her two front paws on his chest. They stared at each other, green eyes into blue, then Gareth took her paw and shook it, formally, as he took his leave of this most special of colleagues.

'Goodbye, little cat,' he said, and was surprised to find that his voice cracked as he said the words. Behind him in the office, Angela Dunn started crying. Gareth didn't know what else to say to Felix – there weren't the words to tell her what she meant to him, how much she had helped him, how she had given him the courage to believe in himself again. 'Thank you,' was all he said, and he found that those big green eyes of hers swam slightly, as his own flooded suddenly with unshed tears.

There was a soft clunk as the office door closed: Angie Hunte, saying nothing, having no words either, just ran out of the office and left them to it. But the door being opened let in another sound: the arrival of Gareth's train. As its doors chimed, he knew he had to run.

He squeezed the cat in his arms one final time, kissed her on the head, and put her down gently on the floor of the office. There was just one last opportunity to give her a rub behind her ears – she leaned into his hand, as if squeezing him back – and then he ran and got on the train. There came the beep of the closing doors, the lurch of the engine and then, as he sat in his seat, staring blindly out of the window at the station he knew so well, the train pulled unstoppably away, taking him from Felix; from his friend.

There was no shame in it, Gareth thought, as he gave himself up to the tears. This was simply what happened when you found you had to leave a cat like Felix.

16. On the Night Shift

'What are we going to do tonight, Felix?' Angie Hunte asked the not-so-little-anymore black-and-white cat.

Felix looked up at her, as though she completely understood Angie's words.

'Are you coming with me?'

Felix got to her feet: yes, she was. And off the pair trotted to complete their security checks.

With Gareth Hope gone, Felix now strengthened her relationships with the team leaders even more. Most of that bonding took place on the night shift – a shift the team fulfilled on rotation – when a hush would fall over the station and the big front doors were shut tight. Especially in those cold winter months of early 2012, Felix wouldn't always be outside on the deserted platforms during the wee small hours. Often, she and Angie would be in the warm team leaders' office instead, where Angie would be working on the computer. The team leaders' jobs were complex, including accounting, finance, revenue and retail duties amongst many others, and Angie often had to focus hard as she went through her night-shift responsibilities.

But Felix was not the sort of cat to let you focus hard.

She'd sit up on the desk.

'What do you want, lovely?' Angie would ask her distractedly, her attention fixed on whatever spreadsheet was onscreen.

Felix would raise one snowy-white paw and place it carefully on Angie's arm, as though she wanted to tell her something very, very important.

'What is it, sweetheart? Are you after something?' Angie would turn and face the cat, and Felix would repeat the movement, a little more firmly.

'Do you want a cuddle?'

Felix would nestle close into Angie and then reach up even higher to touch her nose: claws safely tucked away, using the velvety pad of her paw.

'Give over,' Angie would say, rubbing her nose. 'I don't know where you've been.'

She would turn back to the screen, but – *prod, prod, prod* – those little paws would soon be back at work. Then, all of a sudden, Felix would roll over on to her back, stretching out across the desk.

'Oh ho!' Angie would say. 'You want your tummy rubbing, is that what it is?'

She'd reach out a hand and stroke Felix on the soft underside of her fluffy white belly, and Felix's tail would hang off the desk, flicking from side to side happily.

'Felix,' Angie would say after a few moments, 'you do know that I've got work to do, don't you? I *have* got work to do.'

But, for the next few minutes at least, Felix the railway cat would demand that the only team member Angie would be leading that evening would be *her*. Back and forth that tail would go, just like a wagging dog's.

It was the opinion of Jean Randall, in the booking office, that Felix was having a bit of an identity crisis. There were never any other cats on the station concourse, but by this time in her life Felix had observed a fair few dogs being taken on day trips on the train. They wagged their tails when they were happy . . . Felix did the same. They followed their owners around obediently, trotting at their heels . . . Felix did the same. They sat on command, especially if a reward was on offer . . . and Felix did the same. It was as if she thought she was a puppy.

And, just like a little dog, one of Felix's favourite games on the night shift was a flat-out race.

It was usually team-leader Andy Croughan who would challenge her to the contest. It would be bang in the middle of the night, with the station absolutely deserted. Platform 1 would be empty and wide and just too tempting to resist. If Felix was hanging around at the top of the stairs on the platform, and Andy happened to find her there on his way back to the office, he would assume a position beside her, as though they were each in lanes at the starting blocks.

'I'll race you to the office, Felix,' he'd tell her, seriously. The office was located at the other end of the platform, so it was a fair distance – enough time to get up a bit of speed. 'Reckon you can beat me?' he challenged.

Felix would look over at him with a withering stare. 'What do you think, mister?' she seemed to say. She'd be up on her feet, and Andy would crouch down a little, the two of them locking eyes.

'On your marks, get set, go!' Andy would cry. Then he and Felix would sprint along the deserted platform to the office door. Felix just loved it: she'd bound along as fast as her little legs would carry her – and she was *fast*. All that time sleeping meant that when she was awake she had heaps of energy, and the team found they had to find ways of helping her burn it off – or they'd get no peace. They would still throw her favourite brown bear for her to catch, and they'd also throw the odd treat down the long corridor too, so that she would run, run, run for it, like a Marine released for war, before taking down her prey with one military manoeuvre: a satisfying swallow and a lick of her lips. Then her tongue would be out again, almost as though she was panting, 'Come on,

I'm ready for the next one!' and they'd fling a second treat and all you could hear was a clattering as Felix went tearing down the corridor again.

Felix was good company on the night shift. There were only two human team members on duty, and each had their own responsibilities, so it could be a lonely and even, at times, intimidating shift to work. But with Felix there, it was as if she were an extra person. She kept them going. 'Come on, lovey, let's go down here,' Angie would say, as they wandered into one isolated corner or another. Felix would follow, and her presence would take their minds off what *could* be waiting in the dark . . .

Before the doors were shut at half past midnight, one of the major jobs of the team leaders was to organise the shunt movements of the carriages. At Huddersfield, there are some sidings – essentially, a train 'car park' – alongside the main tracks. Innumerable trains came in at night, which would then lie dormant until the early-morning services the following day, and the team leaders had to find them all somewhere to sleep. Yet it was a complicated process. The trains would arrive in a higgledy-piggledy order, but the team leaders had to make sure that they 'slept' in a pattern that would enable the early-morning services to run on time. The team leaders were told the night before which train would be leaving at 5 a.m. and which at 5.25, for example, so they had to ensure that the 5 a.m. train wasn't stuck behind the 5.25, even if the earlier train had come in first. The shunt movements were the movements of all these carriages late at night, and executing the movements successfully was rather like completing a Rubik's cube, as one 'twisted' and transported the trains first one way and then another.

An additional complication was that customer services were still running while the shunt movements were going on, and these of course took priority. Platforms 1, 4 and 8 had to be kept clear at all times for express services, and God forbid there was any hold-up.

In order to keep track of it all, one of the team leaders' jobs was to sort out what was called a 'unit diagram'. A 'unit' meant the train or carriage; it was a diagram of all the station platforms and the sidings, showing which unit had to sleep where, so that they could be shunted into the relevant positions before the station shut down for the night.

Frankly, Felix felt exhausted just *watching* them do it. She, of course, remained safely on Platform 1, observing the activity from a distance, as the team leader directed proceedings and the shunt drivers, in their orange hi-vis outfits, moved the trains to the sidings, then crunched back along the gravelled tracks to return to the platforms. It was a collegiate sort of atmosphere, late at night, and Felix's ears would twitch as she heard the cheery human voices carrying easily in the still air, and then again as the drivers started to leave and their car engines would fire up, then fade away to nothing.

After that, it was just Felix, the two team members and the cleaners on duty, who steadily made their way around all the sleeping trains, dragging Henry the Hoover behind them. As for Henry, Felix would follow him closely with her eyes as he rattled along the platforms, as though he was some sort of scarlet smiley animal that she had to keep tabs on – but he never did anything but noisily trundle along before disappearing inside the dark, slumbering trains.

Felix perhaps liked the station best at night. There were no roaring trains; the crows were fast asleep. It was a time when it truly became her domain – and she asserted herself as soon as the heavy front doors were locked. Every night, as soon as the huge pole had been bolted across the towering doors, Felix would prowl around, running her own security checks, as though to find out: 'What have those humans been doing with my kingdom today?' She investigated every corner of the concourse, casing the joint with her emerald eyes, leaving no stone unturned. She padded silently on her four white paws. Though often, in the daytime, if she shook her head or leapt from floor to desk her pink metal heart tag would jangle against her collar, at night she seemed to have perfected the art of the silent assassin, and not a footfall could be heard as she tiptoed through the station. She moved thoughtfully, not rushing as she sometimes did: the station cat was very much in charge.

Silence reigned everywhere. The ticket office windows had been closed since 8 p.m.; the room behind their drawn shades was dark and still. At either end of Platform 1, both pubs had long since shut for business, and the clink of the beer bottles joining their fellows in the recycling bins and the raucous laughter of the revellers had long since faded away. Above Felix's head, as she continued to stalk along Platform 1, the train display boards no longer showed a continuous list of services, the orange digits updating every few minutes. Only three services ran at night, and in between their arrival and departure Felix ruled the roost.

She faded into the shadows along Platform 1, her inky black fur camouflaging her in the dark. Only every now and again would an observer see a flash of white at her tail, neck or paws. If she was looking in a certain direction, her white patches concealed from view, you wouldn't spot her at all. Only when she moved would you realise: *cat*, not shadow.

But there were still plenty of jobs for the station cat to do. The team in the office would print out the reservation stubs at night, and Felix took it upon herself to oversee proceedings. She liked to watch as the details were printed out on the thick white card, as though checking that no customer was going to be without their booked seat – not on her watch. The *Metro* man would drop off his delivery of newspapers and Felix would sometimes observe as he threw them into the pink metal display holder that stored them in the concourse, ready for the commuters to collect in a few hours' time. Felix was always fed at night, too, so she made it her number-one priority to hassle whichever team leader was on duty as soon as she felt a bit peckish. She would miaow demandingly for food, her tail wagging constantly in anticipation, licking her lips, until her meaty meal – made by the cat-food company 'Felix' – had been squeezed from its shiny pouch into her bowl and she could devour it hungrily.

At 05.00 every morning, the team leader would once again walk to the main entrance and slide back the bolt to throw open the doors. The night shift was almost over. The station lights were on a timer, so as soon as the first streaks of sunrise started to show themselves in the sky, a sensor would be alerted. As daylight began to spill across the station, the electric lights would automatically switch off.

In the April of 2012, however, the night shift being over didn't mean that night-time was. Sunrise was around half past six when the month began, so it was still dark as Felix and her colleagues at the station went about opening up their world again: pulling up the shades in the ticket office, which opened at 5.45 a.m.; firing up the coffee machines in the catering concessions, so that the scent of freshly ground beans began to fill the air; wiping down the paintwork and the walls with a clean damp cloth to make sure that everything was shipshape before the working day really began. The sleeping trains on the platforms stirred, engines starting to rumble and whir. Many headed off immediately, due to begin their services at other stations, while others waited expectantly for the customers who would be boarding at Huddersfield.

Felix was often on duty for the morning rush hour, too, though she tended to avoid the evening crush. As she waited by the bike racks, seeing the sun come up, the little station cat seemed very much at home. She listened as Martin made his announcements; watched as her colleagues strode about, assisting and guiding customers on the platforms. Everybody was hard at work.

Felix was too, of course. She had a routine by now, which usually involved a stint or two at the customer-information desk. She had proved that she was great with customers, and she had saved the day in several stressful situations. All in all, she was a fantastic colleague – everyone agreed.

There was just one problem.

With Felix approaching her first birthday, the so-called 'pest controller' had still not caught a single mouse.

17. The Pest Controller

It wasn't as though she hadn't tried. Felix was well-practised at her prowling technique. She knew how to drop to her belly and creep along; knew (in her head, at least) that she had to stay still until the last possible moment and then pounce. But none of her oh-so-serious stalking sessions was ever successful.

She'd given it her best shot with the rabbits, but they had bounded away infuriatingly fast. Next, she'd turned her attention to the pigeons (much less scary than the crows). It was easier said than done to catch a bird, however, not least because the savvy pigeons tended to save their scavenging trips for when the railway cat was AWOL. You'd sometimes get one doing a reconnaissance trip, soaring the length of the platform with its cat-seeking radar on high alert, a drum-roll sound echoing under the iron roof as its flapping wings beat out a rhythm. If she was there, the bird would keep on flying, doing a graceful curve at the end of Platform 1 before ascending into the girders in the roof, where he would join his fellows to coo the warning: 'Not yet.'

But, every now and again, one brave (or foolish) pigeon would totter along the platform within Felix's sights, its head bobbing like a woodpecker's as it greedily tried to pick up crumbs from the platform, moving its beak so fast it was a blur.

Felix would be hiding in the bike racks: they acted as a kind of camouflage to conceal her from pigeons as well as noisy trains and people. She would crouch on all fours, the tension in her limbs palpable, as slowly, slowly, slowly she sneaked forwards like the predator she knew in her bones she was. There was a certain pride in her movements, a commanding authority, as though with every calculated step she was broadcasting the message: 'Look at me, I'm a predator. Watch out, world!'

But, somehow, even though Felix's brain was saying, 'Easy . . . easy . . . ' the closer the cat grew to the pigeon, the more excited she became. Maybe *this* time she would do it! Her impatience and pure exhilaration at being in the hunt would bubble up and get the better of her and, way too soon, she would spring up and rush headlong at the bird. It was always long gone before she got anywhere near it. So, to cover her humiliation at once more losing her prey, Felix would be forced to sit down incongruently and start washing herself, trying to give the impression that she had just fancied a change of scene for her ablutions. 'Pigeon? What pigeon? I don't know *what* you're talking about,' said her too-focused licks of her fur. She had nailed the nonchalant, nothing-to-see-here look at least.

She'd even tried to have a go at dogs. Well, they were another animal, weren't they, and they were on *her* patch. She'd try all her usual stalking techniques, but they would always end in failure. Felix would be concentrating hard on the canines in her cross-sights, but had she looked up at their human escorts, she would have seen the shock writ plain across their faces at seeing the station cat trying to hunt their darling dogs. Depending on the size of the canine in question, the object of Felix's attention would sometimes find itself swooped up into its owner's protective arms.

But the dogs were hardly in danger. Despite Felix's best attempts – and she spent hours practising pinning down her soft mice toys, a skill she had mastered since kittenhood – she seemed unable to catch a thing. It was all a bit of a poor show for a pest controller.

Felix's failure to hit her 'targets' hadn't gone unnoticed by the team.

'Waste of space, you are,' Billy would say to her, though there'd be a smile in his voice. He'd shake his head in mock disgust. 'Call yourself a pest controller? Useless. Absolutely useless.'

But Billy was forced to eat his words one day. He and Angela Dunn had been out on Platform 1 and were making their way back into the office when they suddenly noticed that Felix was acting most peculiarly in her lair by the bike racks. She was absolutely transfixed by something on the ground, and looked almost as if she was smiling.

'What's she got there?' Angela asked Billy, as the two of them paused, then crept closer to the cat.

There, laid out before Felix like a sacrificial offering on a silver platter, was a mouse. It was still alive, and it looked uninjured so far, but it had clearly wandered right into Felix's field of operations and was very, *very* much regretting that decision.

Felix, on the other hand, was delighted. She gazed down at the mouse, not letting it out of her sight – but had she made eye contact with Billy, she might well have been tempted to tell him with a flash of her green eyes that she very much hoped he savoured his enormous slice of humble pie.

The only problem was that now Felix had caught the mouse, she wasn't quite sure what to do with it.

She lifted one of her white-capped front paws. The mouse, eyes alert, trembled where it lay on the platform, fearing the blow that must surely come. But Felix merely patted it with her paw, as she did with Angie's arm when she wanted a cuddle. The mouse shivered and quivered, but Felix didn't scratch or skewer it; she simply patted it gently with her paw. She moved it along the platform, she pushed and poked at it. She looked rather like an engineer pondering a complex piece of machinery, thinking, *But what does it* do? *How does it* work?

Slowly, the mouse started to recover its equilibrium. As Angela and Billy watched, and Felix kept on with her somewhat simple-minded patting, the mouse assessed its options. Like an SAS expert, it quickly recalled to mind its own mental 'blueprints' of the immediate station vicinity, and the nearby location of all the mouse-sized subways, tunnels and holes.

Tap, tap . . . went Felix's paw. She looked down quizzically at her prey.

And then the mouse legged it. Operation 'Escape the Cat' was underway.

Stunned at the sudden movement, Felix narrowed her eyes and tried to follow the darting mouse – but it was far too quick for her. In the wall at Felix's back, just behind the bike rack, was a small metal grate, with holes just big enough for a tiny rodent to squeeze through. Felix dashed to the wall, but it was too late. As she pressed her frustrated face to the bricks and the metal grate, the mouse was home and dry.

Angela and Billy burst into laughter.

'Oh, Felix!' cried Angela affectionately. 'Bloomin' heck, love. You're not supposed to let them go!'

Poor old Felix. But the pest controller of Huddersfield station was a clever cat and, now she had some hands-on experience, like the most eager intern she was as keen as mustard to land a real job with the skills she had learned.

She stayed by the bike racks. It had worked for her with mouse number one, and she trusted its sturdy metal docking gates like firm friends. Felix shrewdly started using the bike racks to help her in her quest to catch her first mouse. She used to trap the rodents by the silver limbs of the bike rack, and pin them there with her paw. She was starting to feel she'd got the hang of this mouse-catching business now. For a game, she would let them go a certain distance, then she'd pin them again. Let them go . . . Bring them back. Let them go . . . Bring them back. Felix started to enjoy herself. Then, one day by the bike racks, when Felix was about a year old, she jumped all over the mouse she'd caught – she just went for it, fearlessly, claws and teeth and all – and it was game over for the mouse. It was an instinctive assassination.

Felix felt so, so, *so* proud of herself. She picked up the dead mouse in her jaws and trotted up to the door of the office, where she knew Angie Hunte was working. She wanted to show her what she had done. Her tail stood tall and straight as she walked: a flagpole that perhaps she wished she could run a banner up to read: 'FELIX CAUGHT A MOUSE!' Her hips and her shoulders almost shimmied as she walked the few short paces to the door, the pride rippling down her back. Just *wait* till her mum saw *this*.

Angie opened the door and saw the dead mouse hanging limply in her baby's mouth. She nearly had a fit.

'Felix,' Angie said, trying to control her queasy dismay, as the cat looked perkily up at her, waiting for the shower of praise she knew must come, 'I love you to *bits*.' Felix's tail wagged proudly. *Yes, here it comes* . . . 'But I really, *really* don't want your presents, my darling.'

Angie was more than a bit squeamish about the dead mice and rats that Felix now brought to her, again and again and again, as the station cat got into her stride. But Angie couldn't bear to deal with dead vermin. The lads she worked with helped out instead.

'I'll get rid of it, Angie,' they would say. And when they

came out to collect up the bodies, Felix would finally get the praise she was after. 'Well done, Felix!' her colleagues would chorus. 'Who's a clever pest controller?'

With Felix's career going from strength to strength, someone at the station clearly thought her achievements needed formal recognition. On the wall in the team leaders' office hung a hierarchy chart of the company: a diagram with everyone's names and job titles listed, showing who reported to whom. The chart was shaped like a pyramid, the general members of staff at its wide bottom, the team leaders in the narrowing middle and above them, at the apex, Paul, the station manager.

Someone – and no one, to this day, has ever confessed who – now took a pen and drew a little box *above* the manager's name. In it, they wrote: FELIX.

'Well,' said Angie, 'as far as we're concerned, she *is* the Boss!'

18. Stranger Danger

Felix the railway cat, pest controller extraordinaire, leapt lightly to the ground from the metal benches arrayed on Platform 1. As well as spending hours sitting there, it was now part of Felix's exercise regime to use the benches as a piece of athletics equipment, for they had three thin armrests on them and when Felix ducked her head beneath these armrests, they formed a tunnel for her: she would squeeze through them, as low as she could get, before jumping down to the floor.

Sometimes, a customer would join her on the bench – or vice versa – and the two would sit in companionable silence. Felix, on the whole, got on well with the customers. By now, the regular commuters knew her of old; some would even bring the occasional treat for her, which endeared them to Felix even more, for the way to the station cat's heart was most definitely through her stomach. Though she hadn't lost that grumpy assertiveness she'd started to showcase towards the end of 2011, as the summer of 2012 progressed Felix's personality, on the whole, was sunny enough to match the weather. She was quite comfortable winding through people's legs, and even enduring the patting hands of young children.

She could be cheeky at times, and had perfected the art of being loving when she wanted something; indifferent when she didn't. She was a favourite of older people and little kids especially, and she seemed to take their interest with reasonably good humour. Having grown up on the station, she was a very confident cat in that environment. She needed to be, really, for although she was well-known to the regular customers, most of the people travelling through were strangers, who didn't know who Felix was or that she lived there. Others, perhaps, took *too* much interest.

As the late summer slid into early autumn and the nights closed in, it turned out to be fortunate indeed that Felix was so popular with the everyday users of the station – for they knew that she belonged there.

One night shift that autumn of 2012, Angie Hunte was on duty. She was working alongside a colleague called Pamela. It was perhaps shortly after 8 p.m., and it was already pitch-black outside.

Nights at the station could be quiet affairs. There tended to be very few people about: the odd concerned parent or partner waiting at the entrance to greet their loved one off the train, or a cluster of youths sharing a stolen cigarette on a bench. The customers came in dribs and drabs: a young woman clicking in her high heels, anxiously clutching her handbag to her shoulder; a teenager eating takeaway chips; a small group of bald and round-bellied Yorkshiremen who had sunk a few pints in the pub. It was too early for the drunks and a bit too late for those commuters working overtime in the office, so things were pretty peaceful on the concourse.

Suddenly, the two women heard running footsteps coming towards them. They looked up to see one of their regular customers pelting in their direction, looking absolutely distraught.

The woman was panting. As she drew close to them, she cried, 'Somebody's just taken your cat!'

'What?' exclaimed Angie in horror.

'Somebody's just picked up your cat and walked out!'

'No!' Angie stood up angrily, a mother instantly on the warpath. 'They can't touch my Felix!'

She and Pamela flew to the front of the station, running after the thief as fast as they could. The woman had said it had only just happened, that the person had come into the concourse, snatched the station cat and run off, so they were hopeful that they would locate Felix immediately.

But as they burst out of the station into St George's Square, Felix was nowhere to be seen. Angie stood panting at the top of the station steps, peering into the dark night. To the left was the station car park and the King's Head pub – no one on foot would have gone that way. To the right was the taxi rank and the Head of Steam. It was brightly lit by the cars' waiting headlights, and it was clear that no running person with a cat clutched in their arms was spot-lit in that direction. Immediately in front of them were the fountains of St George's Square and the bronze Harold Wilson statue, and beyond that was the road. It was a large square, and they could see all the way across it – no little black-and-white cat was in sight.

'FELIX!' Angie hollered. 'FELIX!'

No sign. Then, through the darkness puddled at the edges of the square, where it was pitch-black beyond the reach of the streetlights, Angie saw a tiny flash of white. All of a sudden, little snowy paws were running towards her and there was Felix, bounding down the road and sprinting as though her life depended on it.

'Felix!' Angie cried, as the cat mounted the steps and she could pick her up at last. 'Well done, little cat, well done,' she said in relief. 'You got away!'

Angie carried her back into the station. Frustratingly, at that time Huddersfield didn't have full CCTV coverage, so when Angie checked the tapes there was no record of the stranger who had wandered onto the concourse and stolen the station cat. Dave Chin's money was on a character like Cruella de Vil in *101 Dalmations*: someone who had coveted Felix's fluffy fur coat and then stolen her.

They never did find out who took her, but they were very grateful to the customer who'd brought the crime to their attention. It didn't bear thinking about what might have happened if she hadn't raised the alarm.

Felix settled back into station life. Angie and the others tried to keep a closer eye on her, but as they were all working shifts and no one other than Felix was always on duty, it was inevitable she had some experiences that none of the team saw. As the autumn progressed, it became apparent that some of those experiences were not very nice at all.

'Are you coming, Felix?' Angie asked her chirpily one day, as she was heading out to do security checks on a morning shift. Normally, Felix would accompany her enthusiastically: Angie's magical assistant. But on this day, as Angie pulled open the door that led out to the platform and held it open for the cat to pass through, Felix backed off, as though she didn't want to go outside.

'All right, lovey,' Angie said, not too concerned about this behaviour; Felix did sometimes choose to stay at home. 'Day off, is it? You have a nice nap then. I'll see you later.'

Angie's next few shifts were at night, when Felix happily came out and trotted around after her, so it wasn't until a couple of weeks later that it became evident that something was seriously wrong.

In the daytime, when it was busy, Angie noticed that the confident cat she had always known and loved so well had vanished. Instead, if Felix was outside at that time of day, she would cower against the platform floor as the customers passed her by. Jean Randall noticed that she flinched if she heard children playing and would not go near them anymore. But it wasn't just children: she suddenly seemed terrified of everyone who was not a station employee, and the sunny, sociable cat became a thing of the past.

'Somebody's hurt her,' Angie fretted to Dave Chin. 'Somebody on the platform.'

They didn't know who, of course. It could have been an unwitting, overly enthusiastic child who had unintentionally pulled her fur too roughly. Or it could have been something more malevolent – perhaps an adult with a chip on their shoulder and an unforgiving black boot. The result was that Felix now withdrew into herself. She would back away if a colleague opened the door for her to go out at rush hour, and spent most of her time at the window in the booking office, looking out, feeling protected by the presence of Jean and Pam and the other women who worked there. She stayed indoors, and would only brave the outside world during the night shift, when the station was deserted and she could once more claim the platforms as her own.

It broke everyone's hearts to see her that way; she wasn't the same cat at all. They gave her a lot of love, a lot of care, and they hoped against hope that she would somehow be able to find her way back to them – and start to trust again.

It took a long, long time. One month passed, then two. Not until the Christmas carollers were singing in the square outside did Felix, gradually, start to become a bit more confident again. She still spent her days in the booking office, but she gained the courage to sit in an area of the windows where the customers could gain access to her. It was terribly brave, but as she was sitting right next to her colleagues working the windows, she wasn't entirely alone. They would look out for her, she knew.

One busy day that December, Felix was with one of the

girls, who had a jaunty Santa hat on her head as she served the customers. The cat was sitting tall and upright and proud – perhaps still a little tense and stiff – taking everything in and courageously facing the world.

A male customer reached the front of the queue and approached the window manned by Felix and the Santa girl. 'Hello, there,' he said warmly to Felix.

While the girl processed his order, he reached out a rough, flat palm and gently stroked the cat. Felix leaned her head into his touch and let her chin rise contentedly into the air. He tickled her underneath that chin, then she dipped her head and asked for another stroke. He was more than happy to give it.

And just like that, Felix was back to her old self. It was the best Christmas present the team could have wished for.

19. The Final Hurdle

Felix gazed up at the iron roof girders with an increasing sense of annoyance. The crows were sitting up there, looking down at her, staring her out. Now aged two, Felix wasn't quite so terrified of them as she had been as a kitten, but that didn't mean that the crows were any closer to showing her the slightest sign of respect. They would cockily fly down to the platform and walk around when she was on duty, as if she was nothing.

Felix wasn't going to stand for that. She would prowl at them, then rush at them, but they would merely rise into the air like supersonic spaceships, fly up to their iron roost and sit there, cawing down at her. They seemed to take a great deal of pleasure in winding her up, knowing there was nothing she could do about it.

They even teamed up to do it. One day a single crow left the safety of his perch and landed on the platform. Felix was out and about and he had started crowing at her. There was a mocking tone to his caws: 'na-na-na-na-na'. Felix had narrowed her green eyes and started to creep towards him. She had not got far before her attention was diverted by a second crow, who swooped down and landed behind the cat, so that Felix was like a piggy-in-the-middle between the two birds.

'Na-na-na-na-na,' the second crow chorused. He and his buddy were now either side of Felix, taking the mickey out of her as her black head flicked in frustration between them, as if she was watching a tennis match. She made a decision and started to edge towards one, but then changed her mind and tried to go for the other. The crows thought it was a great game and continued to tease her, cawing loudly, until Felix lost her temper and rushed at one of them. Then both took off with a colossal flapping of their inky wings, and Felix was left behind. If she could have growled, she would.

What was probably most annoying for Felix was that the crows were the only creatures who didn't show her respect. For Felix, at age two, had blossomed into the most beautiful adult cat you can imagine, and everyone else she encountered seemed to fall at her fluffy white feet.

Her fluffy coat was what attracted people's attention first. She really was the most remarkably downy cat, and her regular trips to the grooming parlour and Felix's own attentive ablutions ensured her coat was kept in tip-top condition. Her fluffiness went all the way down to her tail, which acted as a glorious boa for this glamourpuss; Felix was constantly draping it over the edges of the furniture she was sitting on and flicking it back and forth as she swung her hips and sauntered about the station. It was her eyes, however, that really had her admirers swooning. They were those classic reflective cat's eyes, a gorgeous pale green, like summer grass, but with a hint of silvery moonshine to them. With those, and her enormous white whiskers fanning out from her ebony nose, she had the loveliest little face. She had finally grown into her pointy black ears with white tufts, too. The whole look was enhanced by the pretty pink collar Angie had bought for her, and that shiny hot-pink tag. Whichever way you looked at it, Felix the cat was all grown up.

But there remained one final hurdle Felix had not yet managed to clear. Perhaps mindful of her colleagues' warnings when she was a kitten, Felix had not yet crossed the train tracks.

When Felix arrived at Huddersfield station, she was just eight weeks old.

She was too tiny to venture far – spending most of her time snoozing in the back offices.

Felix soon started to take up a bit more desk space…

But while initially she may have been more of a hindrance than a help to the job at hand, Felix eventually became an integral part of the team.

After several years of hard work, Felix earned a well-deserved promotion to the role of Senior Pest Controller.

Team leader Angie Hunte: 'Felix has always been special. I love her to bits. I can't imagine being without her.'

Dave Chin, the maintenance man, a.k.a. 'The Cat Whisperer'.

Andrew McClements, who formed a close bond with Felix when he joined the Huddersfield team.

The cat flap that was installed for Felix (but which she refuses to use).

Felix guarding the entrance to the station with Terry.

Felix, with her colleague Andy Croughan, draped in the livery of TransPennine Express.

Felix has many fans amongst the customers at the station, including Pauline and Mike Dyble (left) who made a special visit to see Felix as a treat for their 55th wedding anniversary.

The Fairy Bricks charity created this Lego Felix when she raised over £5,200 by 'running' 5k.

She stuck to the side of the station she'd grown up on, and her manor comprised Platforms 1 and 2 only. There was plenty to entertain her there: the bunnies bounding around near the tunnels, the abandoned carriage, the lost-property office and the sanctuary of the bike racks. Though as a kitten she'd been carried to Platform 4 via the subway, riding like a feathered parrot on Gareth Hope's shoulder, Angela Dunn reported that she never used the stairs herself. So with Felix obeying the painted warnings to 'keep behind the yellow line', there was no way for her to cross to whatever magical world might lie beyond the tracks on Platform 4 – or further afield.

Yet as she grew older, Felix found that she wanted to explore that world. The Huddersfield team had almost come to believe that she would never cross to the other side – but never was a very long time.

So, as Felix glared at the crows in that early summer of 2013, perhaps she watched them with a certain amount of envy, too. They had the freedom to fly wherever they wanted, but Felix's world was bordered by the bright yellow line.

Nevertheless, she was an adult cat now. Maybe, just maybe, she was old enough at last to learn how to walk the tracks safely, like Dave Chin and the shunt drivers did in their orange hi-vis uniforms.

Well, there was no time like the present to find out. Felix got up from her favourite position by the bike racks and gave herself a little shake. She yawned, showing her sharp white teeth and her rough pink tongue, and stretched along her tippy-toes. She was ready. She was going to try.

She walked nervously to the yellow line on Platform 1. There were a few customers milling about, but it wasn't especially busy and no one was paying her much attention. She looked left; she looked right. She listened hard. By now, having lived at the station for two whole years, Felix knew the schedule of the services possibly better than anyone else around, and indeed a train was not due. She walked to the very edge of the platform, and bunched her paws together on the ledge. To a human observer, it might have looked reckless, but Felix knew exactly what she was doing, and how to do it safely.

With one powerful leap, she dived off the edge of the platform and down onto the tracks. Once more she paused, listening with every potent sense she had, with her front paws balanced on the first metal rail. There were no vibrations through it. Cats are very sensitive to the slightest tremors; they are said to be able to detect earthquakes ten or fifteen minutes earlier than humans can. But there were no pulsations on the rails at that moment; no train was anywhere nearby.

Grey gravel had been laid out between the two metal rails that formed the train track running beside Platform 1. Felix now picked her way across it carefully. As she crossed the second rail of this first train track, she paused once again, her front paws safely across the rail and her back ones still on the wooden sleeper, as the ridge of the rail touched her fluffy belly. She stood as still as a statue, assessing, adjudging, and then determined it was safe to move on.

She had made it successfully to the midway point between Platforms 1 and 4. Beyond was another set of train tracks, the ones that ran alongside Platform 4 – but Felix suddenly decided that *two* sets of tracks was rather too much to tackle on her first trip out. Halfway across would do for today.

She turned back to face Platform 1, seeing her home turf from an entirely different perspective for the very first time. Felix carefully checked both ways before once more crossing back towards Platform 1. At the foot of the sheer wall she paused, gazing up at the precipice above. The platform was *awfully* high up. Yet she had confidence in her abilities. In one lithe, athletic jump Felix ascended from the tracks to the platform, and once more crossed back over the yellow line. She was home and dry.

She had an even greater desire to explore.

To begin with, however, her track-crossing adventures were always curtailed at the halfway point. She would get so far, then turn tail and retreat. But Felix's courage and confidence were building by the day, and soon she felt secure enough in her knowledge of the railway to cross not one but two sets of tracks and make it all the way to Platform 4.

Angie Hunte, watching her little cat making her way in the world, thought that Felix's new accomplishment in learning how to navigate the tracks safely needed formal recognition. On the railway, employees have to complete what is called a Personal Track Safety (PTS) course before they are allowed to work on the tracks. As walking on the tracks is so dangerous, employees are not allowed to set foot on them until they are in possession of a PTS certificate to show that they have successfully completed their training. They are also issued with a PTS ID card, bearing their photograph; these cards expire every two years.

As it happened, around the same time that Felix completed her own personal track safety 'exam' and became adept at crossing the tracks, maintenance man Dave Chin's latest PTS card expired.

'Could I have that please, Dave?' Angie asked him, a smile playing on her lips and a twinkle in her eye as she cooked up a little plot.

''Course you can,' he told her, intrigued.

So Felix was soon the proud bearer of her own, personalised PTS card, granting her the authority to walk on the tracks. Angie carefully stuck a photograph of Felix in the appropriate space on the cream-and-red card, then scribbled on it in a black marker pen: ACCESS TO ALL AREAS.

It was official: Felix had the run of the place, and she had a PTS card to prove it.

20. Queen Felix

The customer came rushing onto the concourse. 'There's a cat on the track!' he exclaimed in horror. 'She's going to get run over!'

The team in their hi-vis jackets sighed — not another concerned customer.

'She's fine, sir,' they reassured him. 'She knows what she's doing.'

'But what if a train comes?'

'Trust us, it's fine. She'll get up and walk away.'

Outside, at the centre of all this fuss, was Felix, sitting calmly at the midway point of the tracks while commuters gathered in concern, looking as though she was saying, '*What?*' with a disdainful flicker of her big green eyes. In truth, it had become a bit of a favourite game of hers to saunter out to this centre-stage point, a bit of a wind-up that gave everybody on the platform a good old fright; clever as she was, people never, ever saw her on the tracks when a train was actually due.

Felix herself was no longer frightened of those trains. The kitten who used to run for home whenever they roared into the station now blinked at them nonchalantly. If she was in the middle of a really thorough wash, she might not even look up. The lack of fear didn't mean that she was less cautious, simply that she felt completely confident in her skill and in her knowledge of the station.

That knowledge grew wider day by day. With her access-all-areas pass, Felix's horizons expanded. She started coming back to the station with brambles and bushy bits in her fur – clear evidence that her explorations were taking her further afield. Even on the station itself, she would strut about authoritatively, strolling along the front entrance as if she owned the place – and what a place it was.

The façade of Huddersfield station, rather aptly for such an elegant cat as Felix, is a grand classical portico with majestic pillars; its design was based on the palazzi of Renaissance Italy. The poet John Betjeman once said it had the finest façade of any such building in the country – and English Heritage agreed, selecting it as one of its top ten favourite stations in England. An architectural journalist, meanwhile, thought it so magnificent that he described the station as 'a kind of stately home with trains in'. It has to be said: it suited Felix down to the ground. And at 416 feet in length, such a stunning façade provided quite a catwalk for the railway cat.

It was almost as if Felix knew she fitted the part. Drawing on her stately surroundings and her new-found confidence and maturity, Felix's gait now took on an unmistakeably regal air. When she strolled or even simply sat down, her striking head would be held high, as though she were looking down upon her subjects; her imperial procession through the concourse announcing, 'I'm ready for my public . . . I'm making my entrance now.'

Something in the proud way Felix carried herself reminded Angie Hunte of royalty. It is indeed apt that female cats are called 'queens', for Felix was most definitely cut from royal cloth. So emphatic was the imperial impression she gave that Angie now nicknamed her 'Her Majesty'.

And, as befits a monarch, Felix made sure that she chose only the best spots on the station for her latest adventures. Beyond the car park and the King's Head was a somewhat unkempt, overgrown area that lay beyond the white picket fence of the station's boundary. Filled with long grass and wildflowers, this became her 'country retreat', where she could play among the sweet-smelling grass and rub her back along the plants. Inside the station, as the summer of 2013 drew on, she asserted her ownership of the place by taking up residence on the concourse, where the large windows created glorious sunbathing spots on the white tiled floor. The sun would stream through the windows in shafts of light, creating spot-lit patches in which Felix could indulge in a luxurious catnap.

And those catnaps wouldn't be quick. Felix would bask in the warmth of the summer sun for hours on end. She didn't care that she might be spread-eagled in the middle of the queue for the ticket office: this was her kingdom and she wasn't moving for anybody. Her subjects should circle around her, like the planets do the sun – *she* was as immovable as a star. If someone addressed her, perhaps asking her to shift so they could move forward, she would look up at them with a supercilious scowl, but she would not move, and in the end they would simply step over her and carry on.

By far Felix's favourite spot on the station, however, now that she had mastered the art of crossing the tracks, was Billy's garden.

Billy's garden was the station garden: another of his inspirational ideas to create something a little bit different for everyone who used the station and for the local community.

For years, there had been a patch of near-jungle located just back from Platform 4 – it was formerly Platform 7, but it had been taken out of use years before, allowing ugly weeds and gnarled trees to take over. Whenever he passed it Billy had used to mutter what an 'absolute waste of growth' it was.

'It needs chopping down and then you could have a lovely

garden,' he would say, moaning about how dreadful it was that something wasn't being done to improve it.

Well, as was Billy's way, he had moaned and moaned and moaned – and eventually, after years of complaining in the right managers' ears, he had got a green light to do something about it at last. He had even roped those managers – and the British Transport Police – into his vision. 'You lot can come down and help,' he'd told them bluntly, and there had been a weekend when the station was alive with the puffs and pants of Billy's assembled motley crew as they tore apart the thick undergrowth with secateurs and chopped down the tangled trees.

That clearance had taken place when Gareth Hope still worked at the station. But getting rid of the bulk of the jungle had only been the first step – Billy then had to put in hours and hours and hours of work to clear it all, enhance the soil and pull out all the knotted roots, and eventually choose new plants and nurture them. The garden was Billy's passion and he was the only one who worked on it, so it had been years in the making. Billy gave it what time he could, and even did a bit of maintenance and horticultural work while he was on duty, if it was a quiet shift. Yet there were many times when the team at the station would see him over there on his day off, dressed in his overalls and digging away with his own tools, one of his cigarillos clutched in his hand whenever he took a break. In Billy's opinion, if you were going to do something, it was worth doing properly. Within that gruff exterior beat a heart of gold. Billy *cared* – and every green shoot that flourished in that garden was proof of it.

He didn't care at all, however, for the regal cat who now decided that his growing plants and damp soil bed were the perfect setting for her royal commode.

'Felix has been in my garden again!' he would complain to

144

Angie – and with good reason, for he often heard his fellow team leader say to the railway cat: 'Isn't that a lovely garden? Are you going to pay it a visit?'

'Don't you dare encourage her, Mrs H!' Billy would say grumpily. He had a real love/grump relationship with the station cat.

As she did with the other team leaders, Felix would follow him around devotedly on his shift. Billy was still as unimpressed as he had been when Angie had first proposed he used the cat harness; he'd look down at his little shadow and mutter, 'I'm not wandering round with a cat at my heels.' But Felix wanted to be with him because he was *fun* . . . occasionally. Time and again his colleagues would walk in on him dabbling his fingers through the hole in the desk for Felix, as the cat's captivated eyes followed their every move.

There were times, though, when Felix *thought* he was playing, and Billy was most definitely not. During one infamous night shift, Billy was working on his period-end paperwork, stacking up all his papers in tall, organised towers that literally took him hours to erect in the correct order. Felix slipped inside the team leaders' office and surveyed those towers with glee. Then she flew across the room, pouncing and playing, sending the papers flying all over the office in her wake. The Destroyer had struck once more.

Felix may not have been endearing herself to Billy very much at that time but she had clearly impressed the railway powers-that-be. In the June of 2013, Huddersfield station installed electronic ticket barriers at the main entrance for the first time – and Queen Felix found she had her own personal cat flap installed to allow her to come and go as she pleased.

As with any royal event, it was covered by the press: once again Felix made the hallowed pages of the *Huddersfield*

Examiner. This time it was the station manager, Paul, who spoke to the journalists, telling them, 'Customers and staff hold Felix in great affection and she's very much part of daily life here at the station. We strive to offer the best service possible to both customers and their four-legged friends and we know Felix is certainly the cat that got the cream with her very own VIP entrance and exit!'

It was a very smart creation, edged in blue and with a cartoon image of a black-and-white cat on the flap itself – and cartoon trains on the surrounding framework. TransPennine Express had commissioned original artwork, for the cartoon cat, just like her real-life inspiration, wore a hot-pink heart-shaped name tag. The pièce de resistance and final flourish was that, above the flap itself, Felix's own name was picked out in handsome blue lettering, leaving no one in any doubt that this edifice was just for her.

But despite their commendable efforts, Felix was not impressed. In a diva-like response that was typically Felix the station cat utterly refused to use the bespoke cat flap installed for Her Majesty. If she wanted to get from the main entrance to Platform 1, she would run straight at the booking office and leap up at one of the serving windows, little caring if her sudden appearance made the customers standing at the counter jump ten feet in the air. She would bestow on them a gracious nod, then head straight on through, jumping down from the desk inside the office and sauntering confidently to the interior door. There, she would sit and wait, wagging her tail, until a minion had opened the door for her and she could continue on her way.

If the booking office was shut and Felix was forced into a tight corner, she *still* wouldn't use the flap. People had seen her heading towards it but, at the last moment, choosing to squeeze round the edge of the frame that held the cat flap – for there was a slim gap between the frame edge and the wall, which she could just slink through – rather than going through the flap itself.

It was just the sort of behaviour her colleagues were coming to expect from Felix. Angie had noticed that she no longer drank the water regularly laid out for her in her bowl. Instead, she would jump up to the sink, where the tap would sometimes be dripping. Felix would carefully shuffle on her bottom to the very edge of the sink, gracefully thrust her head forward and stick out her tongue to catch the fresh water drops, as if tasting manna from heaven.

She was a bit of a fussy eater, too. Though sometimes she would wolf down her 'Felix' cat food hungrily, at other times she would merely lick the jelly from the chunks of meat, as though selecting the choicest morsels, and leave the rest.

Billy thought she was spoilt, especially with her brand-name cat food.

'Oh, just go into town and get a tin of any old cat food,' he used to tell Angie. 'She'll eat it, mark my words. When she's hungry, she'll eat it.'

There came a day when one of the other team members completed the food shop for Felix and indeed picked up a tin of any old cat food. It was a household brand name, so it was tasty, high-end stuff, but it was not the eponymous 'Felix' that Felix herself had always favoured.

That night, as usual, Felix wound her way through Angie's legs and miaowed for her dinner. She had had a hectic day patrolling the station and was in need of nourishment. Angie scraped the new branded food into her bowl and set it down, to the musical accompaniment of Felix's satisfied purrs that her demands for food were being met.

Then the purrs stopped abruptly. Felix's nostrils and whiskers quivered as she inhaled the unfamiliar aroma of her dinner. She dropped her head and looked at it quizzically. She edged a little closer and gave a deep sniff, as though making absolutely sure. Then she sat back on her haunches haughtily and looked up at Angie with an imperious glare, as if to say, 'What is *this*?'

Angie shrugged her shoulders. 'Eat,' she encouraged her. 'It's good.'

Felix bent down again to her supper dish and gave it one more sniff. Back up to a sitting position she came again, and once more gave a demanding 'Miaow!' But there was no other food available.

As soon as Felix understood that, she took off from her meal and made a disgruntled exit: a most dissatisfied customer. She left that unappetising new food in her dish, and did not go near it again.

Angie fretted to Billy about it, but he gave her short shrift.

'She's ruined, that cat,' he said bluntly. 'She's spoilt. When she gets hungry enough, I promise you, she'll eat anything. Ours do at home. Just leave her be and she'll come round.'

But this was a battle of wills that Billy was not destined to win. He and Felix both dug their heels in, but Felix was adamant she would not break. She was Felix the station cat and she liked 'Felix' cat food – and she would eat nothing else. In the end, Angie ended up going out mid-shift to the shop on the corner and buying some 'Felix' for her to eat. Felix gobbled it up gratefully, glad the stand-off was over and all was right with the world again.

With such grand behaviour becoming infamous in and around Huddersfield station, what happened next was perhaps no surprise.

Felix was summoned to the theatre. Her star potential had been spotted – and she was about to take to the stage.

21. Curtain Up

Felix had already proved herself a consummate performer. When interacting with the team, she had soon learned that mastering some little tricks made it much more likely she would be able to elicit a treat or two from them. (For with the station cat's weight now normal and a formal feeding regime in place under the direction of the team leaders, the rules about giving the occasional cat treat had been relaxed a little.)

So Felix had learned how to sit at a colleague's desk and raise one white-tipped paw, Oliver-style, to ask, 'Please, sir, can I have some more?' She had also perfected the most starving-hungry, Puss-in-Boots look with her great, green eyes, which rendered admirers powerless to resist her pleas for *just one more treat* . . .

With food-laden customers present every day on the platforms, it hadn't been long before Felix had started plying her trade with them, too. She'd developed a sixth sense for knowing when someone was about to eat. Even before the flapjack had been unwrapped or the sandwich taken from its packaging, she would be in position a short distance away but still within the person's eyeline. Closer and closer she would creep. Her tail would wag charmingly. She'd lick her lips in anticipation. Surely, any moment now . . .

And if this opening performance failed to elicit a response, she would up the ante. Sometimes she'd jump right into the customers' laps if they were sitting on the benches with food. Inches from their faces she would stare fixedly at them, imploring them to give her *just one little titbit, it was all she asked* . . . and often they would feel so guilty under her gaze that they gave in. At times Felix would even hold people hostage, leaping onto their suitcases if she suspected they had food; the team thought it very likely that some people had even missed their trains because of her, not wanting to shift her but instead choosing to wait for the next service so they could have a few more minutes playing with the famous station cat. Even though her colleagues always told her off for this shocking behaviour – both the begging and the hostage-taking – Felix was Her Majesty, and she did as she pleased.

Some regular customers began bringing in cat treats for her, and Felix was delighted to see bags of Dreamies emerging from rucksacks and handbags as she waited on the platform and begged with those big green eyes. But Felix was a remarkably clever cat and knew all too well that the bags weren't empty when they went back into their owner's luggage. How could she get even *more* treats?

She started putting on a little show, in order to get as much as she possibly could. She could already sit on command, and now began expanding her repertoire. People used to say to her, 'Come up for it,' holding the treat above her head, so Felix learned to balance on her hind legs and reach for the stars. She would grab the customer's proffered hand with her front paw and then take the treat, as though accepting it from them with a formal handshake. Or she might eat the treat directly from their hand, gobbling it down in one greedy guzzle. Then came the showstopper, the party piece, the big finish: Felix learned to catch treats with her two front paws.

She'd be balanced on her hind legs, watching the treat dangling above her, preparing to catch it with the precision of a heat-seeking missile. The treat-giver would ask her, 'Ready . . . ?' Then they'd drop the treat. And Felix, clever little Felix, would slam her paws together and capture the titbit between them on its way down. *Nom, nom, nom . . .*

Naturally enough, Felix was rewarded for her antics and was more than happy to keep performing them; they became a regular spectacle at Huddersfield station. People would get out their cameras and smartphones and snap away – and the cat proved herself to be quite the poser, a performer who never suffered stage fright and would merrily execute her tricks for the cameras . . . at a price, of course (one cat treat). Across the local area, Felix soon became well-known for her talents.

Which was partly why, in July 2013, she got the call to join the world of entertainment. The station cat – for one day only – was asked to swap her railway duties for a turn in the spotlight, on stage at the Alhambra Theatre in Bradford.

The producers there had spotted the rising star and invited her to make her theatrical debut. They were putting on a production of *Rising Damp* and needed to cast a brilliant cat in the role of Vienna, Rigsby's moggy. Felix bore a real resemblance to the cat who'd played the role in the 1970s TV series, so as soon as the creative team learned of her existence – and saw her adorable face in the local paper – they knew she *had* to join the cast.

At the time the call came in, Felix was already familiar with some of the razzle-dazzle of drama and dance. The Head of Steam wasn't the only pub in the station to have a live-music night; the King's Head regularly played host to several bands, too. So Felix was accustomed to hearing the strains of the musical instruments drifting out over the platforms, and she and Angie would often walk along together in rhythm with the tunes.

'Come on, Felix,' Angie would say, 'let's have a little boogie!'

It was Paul, the station manager, who took the call from the big-shot producers, and he and Dave Chin were the ones who drove Felix to her appointment in the limelight. She wouldn't be performing live – instead, she had been invited onto the set to meet the cast, and with them would be having some staged photographs taken which would be used in publicity and on the theatrical posters displayed outside the theatre. Given her temperamental disposition at the time, however, neither Paul nor Dave was quite sure how she would behave. This would be one of the first times Felix had been taken away from the station and into an uncontrolled environment . . .

The Alhambra is a Grade II-listed building, named after the Alhambra Palace in Granada, Spain. As that heritage suggests, it is a supremely grand edifice, with a domed turret supported by striking Corinthian columns. Inside, Paul, Dave and Felix could see that it was just as magnificent: the theatre was exquisitely adorned with highly decorated gold-and-ivory plasterwork curving below the balconies, elaborate boxes for the well-to-do theatregoers, and traditional scarlet seating in the stalls and circles. Felix was making her stage debut in a proper theatre with 1,456 seats.

The cast were already on stage when they walked in. There were handshakes all round, and then it was time for Felix to meet her new colleagues and compatriots.

Dave bent down and gently opened the door of the cat carrier. Felix – looking a little grumpy, as always, at her enforced imprisonment – emerged somewhat uncertainly, then stood on the stage, taking it all in. Her quizzical expression very evidently said: 'Where on *earth* am I?'

It must have been confusing for her. For not only was the theatre itself a never-before-seen and rather glamorous landscape, but in her immediate vicinity, on the stage itself, was the set for the production. Rigsby's living room had been recreated. Felix's green gaze took in the centrally placed settee, the chairs, the scenery, the false walls . . . She looked back at Dave. 'Where on earth am I?' her confused look seemed to say once more.

There was only one way for her to find out. Let loose, Felix the railway cat started to explore. She wandered all over the stage, twisting between the legs of the chairs and tables, sniffing at all the props and the people and giving everything a thorough investigation. The theatre folk asked if it was OK to let her wander around and Dave reassured them confidently: 'Yeah, let's just leave her, she'll be all right.'

The humans continued to talk; then Dave suddenly said, 'Where's she gone now?'

For Felix was thoroughly enjoying her adventure. Having given the 'living room' a comprehensive examination, she had now turned her attention to what went on *behind* the scenes. Flicking that fluffy black-and-white tail that had so enamoured the producers, she had disappeared off-set, weaving her way behind the scenery and the fake walls and figuring everything out in her super-smart way.

Only once she had completed her study of the entire set did she return centre stage and leap up onto the sofa – and onto the lap of the gentleman who was playing her owner. The cast gathered around, and with Felix positioned at the heart of the group the photographer stepped up and started snapping away. Just as she did at the station when the customers pulled out their camera phones, Felix posed and postured and vogued with all the swagger of a supermodel. Oh, she had a whale of a time! The actors made a great fuss of her. But in Felix's opinion, of course, that was just as it should be. After all, she *was* their leading lady.

The photographer took a number of shots. Felix sat with all the cast behind her as the flashbulbs popped, looking for all the world like a feline West End star launching her latest theatrical triumph. She was as good as gold and every bit the professional.

Paul and Dave felt rather proud of her as they drove her back to Huddersfield later that day. Of course, to the station team she was already a pin-up and a poster girl, for snapshots of Felix from throughout her life decorated the staff notice-boards back at the station – just as much in pride of place as the formal school photographs of beloved offspring in houses up and down the country.

As for any parent, though, with the good comes the bad. A little later, pride in Felix wasn't *quite* the emotion Paul was feeling. Owing to her bad begging habits, Felix, very occasionally, scoffed something that really didn't agree with her system. And one day she'd evidently eaten something that she shouldn't have. Rather than take herself off to any number of places that might have been more suitable, however, Felix chose to call on Paul.

He was sitting doing some paperwork at his desk. In strutted Felix and leapt up onto the wooden surface of the table. Paul had recently discovered that he was allergic to cats, after finding himself sneezing violently anytime Felix sat on his lap, so she rarely came into the station manager's office these days. Paul looked at her enquiringly and wondered what she wanted.

What she wanted . . . was to vomit all over his desk. Then she neatly leapt down, and walked out.

Well, she was a diva. Paul could clear it up.

And he did.

22. It Must Be Love

Felix the railway cat was the queen of Huddersfield station, as regal as Queen Elizabeth II and as single as the Virgin Queen. Yet as 2013 drew on, it turned out that, like that red-haired beauty Elizabeth I, Felix attracted her own fair share of suitors.

'Felix has got a boyfriend.'

Angie and Angela were catching up on the latest news, and this hot gossip was spreading like wildfire around the station. Their little Felix had an admirer.

He was a stray black tomcat. Very few – if any – cats ever appeared on the concourse, but it seems word of Felix's fame had spread in the feline world too, and this new fellow had suddenly started appearing at night. Felix, the fluffy feline goddess, was quite the catch, and the stray began to appear regularly on the night shift as he hung around the station hoping for a glimpse of her. He'd sometimes wait for her at the customer-information desk, looking for all the world like a lovelorn teenager, choosing to settle in this spot that smelt so strongly of his sweetheart.

Angie Hunte, eyeing him up and down from a distance, was none too keen on the look of him. Though he was a bit bigger than Felix, for his shape he was skinny and scrawny, and even from where she stood she could smell his unpleasant, feral scent. Unlike her beautiful fluffy Felix, this cat was short-haired and his coat was unkempt. Oh, he was no good. Angie, like so many a worried mother before her, thought she should intervene.

'Look, Felix,' she said, trying to reason with her charge. 'He's rough. And when you start with them rough it continues, girl!'

As she observed the two cats together, Angie had reason to hope that her words had hit home. One night shift, Felix was sitting on the customer-information desk when her fella wandered into view. At last, his vigil had paid off. The tomcat sat down and stared wonderingly up at her: this vision of fluffiness so dedicated to her role. But Felix paid him no mind whatsoever. Nose in the air, she kept her head held high.

Ooh, she's playing hard to get, thought Angie, watching through the door. *Good on you, lass, good on you!*

But it seems Felix's curiosity soon got the better of her – or perhaps it was the dedication of her suitor that paid off. 'Felix, your bloke's out there for you,' Angie would say with a disapproving tut, as the black cat prowled around the platforms looking for her girl.

But Felix wasn't about to let her 'parents' see her courting. The team never saw the two of them playing together or even interacting closely. But when the tomcat looked steadily at Felix one evening and then tottered off, *she* tottered off as well, and they started to follow each other around in the cooling autumn nights.

It was perhaps partly because of these developments – and on the direction of the vet – that Angie determined it would be wise to give Felix a preventative flea treatment the vet had recommended. The station cat didn't have fleas, but the medicine would ensure that she wouldn't get them, plus keep her free of them in the future. Given the company she was keeping these days, Angie thought they had better get on with it straight away.

The medicine came in the form of tablets. Angie knew

that wasn't going to go down well with Felix – and she was absolutely right. She tried hiding the tablet in Felix's food, but the canny cat just ate around it and when she'd finished her meal the tablet would still be there, utterly untouched. Angie tried everything she could think of to get the medicine down her, but eventually it became clear that they were going to have to try another way. It was for Felix's own good, of course, but Angie knew in her bones the cat wasn't going to like it one bit.

It took three of them in the end: Angie and two other team members called Dale and Louise. They caught up with Felix in the team leaders' office.

Felix looked up at them as they entered and her eyes narrowed. Every sense she had told her something was up. When Louise picked her up she kicked up a hell of a fuss, but eventually she resigned herself to the inevitability of it, and Louise was able to hold her still. But Felix was still not happy – and it was written all over her face.

'Sweetheart,' Angie said, trying to reassure her, 'I would not do this unless I *had* to, I promise you that.'

Then she gently opened the cat's jaw with her fingers and placed the tablet in her mouth before closing her jaw again.

Felix looked as if she wanted to hawk it up like a hairball and glowered indignantly. Then, as they watched, Felix licked her lips in a way that seemed almost involuntary.

Well, that's done it, everyone thought. Just in case, they kept hold of her for a moment longer, to make sure the tablet really had gone down.

'Let's just make certain she's OK,' Angie instructed.

But Felix was. She licked her lips again and Louise set her down on the floor. The trio clapped their hands. *Great, we've done it*, they thought.

'Job's a good 'un, team,' Angie declared. 'No more stress. Let's give her a treat.'

But as she opened the door to fetch the Dreamies, Felix made a beeline out of the room. Unusually, she wasn't hanging around to receive her reward. Angie followed her out into the corridor and watched her go, nodding her head understandingly. She knew Felix hadn't enjoyed that experience, yet she knew, too, that what the cat needed now was simply to be left alone – Felix would come round in her own time.

She bustled back into the office, really pleased that, at last, Felix had taken her medicine.

'Well,' she said complacently to her colleagues. 'That wasn't too bad, really, was it? Not too bad at all.'

'Angie,' said Dale, slowly.

'What?'

'Look down there.'

On the carpeted floor was a little white tablet. Felix had spat it out before she'd made a beeline for the door. And she knew exactly what she'd done so she'd legged it before they could try to make her take it again.

Angie shook her head, nevertheless feeling a grudging admiration for the cat's antics. Obviously Felix's recent experiences onstage at the Alhambra had stood her in good stead – for the performance she had just given was truly worthy of an Oscar.

But it left them with a problem: how could they get Felix to take her medicine?

In the end, it was Billy who provided the solution. It turned out that the medicine didn't come only in tablets: you could get it in the form of drops, too, which you placed at the back of the cat's neck and then the treatment worked just as well. So it was in Billy's arms that Felix finally received the protection she needed. He held her steady in his rough, weathered hands, stroking her fur reassuringly as he picked up the bottle and administered the drugs.

'There you go,' he said gruffly to her. And Felix was very grateful that he had ensured she never had to take those tablets again.

It marked the start of a softening in the relationship between Billy and Felix. The two seemed to reach a kind of understanding. And in Felix's occasional grumpiness towards people – which she displayed more and more often, the older she got – one could perhaps see something of the cantankerous nature of Billy: Mr Grumpy himself. The two were kindred spirits. At any rate, he didn't complain quite so much when she came to his garden anymore.

However, the horticultural experts who lived in Huddersfield might well have argued that perhaps he had never *really* wanted her to stay away. For amid the lavender and the Shasta daisies, the orange montbretia and the blue geraniums that Billy had planted in his garden, there was also another plant: nepeta, commonly called 'catmint'. It has silvery-grey leaves and spikes of purple flowers, and gardeners know that cats *love* to roll in its aromatic leaves.

Perhaps he had planted it there just for Felix.

23. The Battle for Huddersfield Station

'Eh up, here she comes,' said Dave Chin with a hearty chuckle, watching an exuberant Felix bounding along the platform towards him in December 2013. Beside him, Chrissie from the booking office was carrying a cardboard box that Felix recognised oh so well: it was full of the Christmas tree decorations. Every year, as soon as that box of decorations came out, Felix came out too. For it meant only one thing: game on. Party time. Let the merrymaking begin . . .

By now it was a well-established tradition that, every December, Felix 'helped' to decorate the Christmas tree that stood in the station concourse. Just as she had done as a kitten, she would dart up the bare trunk, right to the top, then sit there for ages, queen of all she surveyed. Just because she was now an older cat, it didn't mean she had forgotten how to have fun: when she wanted to be, Felix was still just as playful as she had been when she'd first arrived at the station as a little kitten and had run riot over all and sundry. As the decorating commenced, she would determinedly wage war on the baubles and on the gold cardboard fairy that Dave and Chrissie tried to hang on the tall tree, playing football with the ornaments as she batted them across the ticket hall – to the great amusement of the watching customers. As soon as she saw Dave staggering about the station with the enormous Christmas tree in his arms, she was right there with him, and this year was no different.

Eventually, Felix shook the pine needles from her fur and left the twinkling tree behind. Time for a patrol outside.

She exited through the front doors. Felix perhaps liked the grand wooden doors best of all – though not just because they were the most fitting for Queen Felix's regal appearances. Although Felix had heaps of character, her stage presence – in the opinion of the automatic doors, at least – wasn't quite sufficient to trigger their electronic sensors and make them open. If she found herself shut in the ticket hall with her colleagues on the other side of the glass, she would have to wait for a cleaner or a member of the public to assist her. Far easier for Felix was the grand entrance, the central door, through which she could come and go as she pleased.

She trotted out and stood at the top of the steps, sniffing the cold winter air. The station's façade looked as pretty as a picture: round its stately columns were wound strings of ice-white fairy lights; apt enough for this festive season, though in fact they were there all year round. Above Felix's head, at the tip of the towering columns, was a traditional triangular gable, and at its centre was an old-fashioned black-and-white clock with Roman numerals. Though Felix couldn't read the position of the hands, they always indicated the same thing anyway: time for adventure.

She scampered happily down the steps and headed out. Immediately in front of the station steps in St George's Square, modern fountains burst sporadically from the ground in tall spurts of icy water; at night, they were lit in ever-changing shades of purple, green and blue. Felix, savvy as she was, neatly avoided the fountain holes that could suddenly spring to life with a shock of cold water, and headed off to explore.

Across the square, directly opposite the station, was a building that might just have caught her eye. It was the Grade II-listed Lion Building, and atop its soaring, three-storey silhouette was a life-size statue of the King of the Jungle. Leo stalked the rooftop with his enormous feline paws, looking as predatory and proud as his miniature relative did below, his luscious, moulded mane as regal as Felix's own unique personality.

The Ashlar sandstone Lion Chambers were built in 1853 – but the incarnation of Leo the Lion that gazed down upon the railway cat that evening was a much more recent model. In the 1970s, after over a century's accumulation of fractures, the original Coade stone lion was retired from duty and on 13 November 1977 a new, lighter, fibreglass model was installed. He certainly looked imposing as he surveyed his kingdom: at night, he was lit up like a Roman god in the floodlights trained upon his feline form, and he dominated the skyline – just as Felix dominated proceedings down below.

Felix was having a brilliant time at the station that Christmas. With her and Billy now the best of friends, Felix would contentedly potter around him when he was on shift. If he was sitting in the office, she'd sit with him while he did his work; occasionally, Billy would even pick her up and she'd snuggle into his lap. If he went outside, she would go too and twirl in and out between his legs as he worked, wagging her fluffy black tail. He'd look down at her as they were doing security checks, or she might even be allowed to join him while he laboured in the garden, dressed in his overalls, on his day off. 'Y'alright?' he'd ask her, with a bit of an unfamiliar twinkle in his eye.

Angie Hunte and Dave Chin watched with a sense of pleasant incredulity as Billy enjoyed a bit of a play and a tumble with the black-and-white cat. Felix, in her own special way, had undeniably brought out the soft side of Mr Grumpy. Even as the duo watched, Billy actually *smiled* at the little cat – a proper, Yorkshire beam of a smile – and Angie and

Dave heard him laugh. Billy was *laughing*. They weren't used to that.

And it was Felix who had made it happen.

The team at Huddersfield knew she was a very special cat. But what they hadn't realised was just how many other people were starting to know it too. It had been quite a year for Felix, what with the bespoke cat flap being installed on her behalf and a stint in the limelight on stage in a major theatre of the North, not to mention her high-profile appearances in the local rag. But it was still a shock to Angie when she learned that Felix had been chosen as the cover star of the official TPE Christmas card of 2013.

Knowing nothing about the behind-the-scenes discussions at head office in Manchester which led to Felix being celebrated in this way, it came as a complete surprise to the Huddersfield team when they opened their envelopes with the official cards inside and found Felix, looking as happy as Larry, beaming out and wishing them season's greetings!

The illustration was of a railway station and a group of carol singers. And there, right at the front of the picture, was Felix, sitting listening to the performance, wearing her pink collar and heart-shaped tag. The artist had caught her so well: the intelligent angle of her head, her pricked-up ears, her regal air that seemed to say, 'Well, of *course* I'm on the Christmas card! Who else could it have been?'

Angie was beside herself; she was dancing forever and a day, holding the card aloft and telling everyone she met about her little girl's achievement.

'Have you seen it? Have you seen the card?' she excitedly asked her colleagues, who had not yet opened theirs.

'No,' they said, wondering why their team leader was so enthusiastic about the annual Christmas card from head office.

'Look, look!' she cried, waggling it in their faces. 'Take the card, take the card! It's got our Felix on!'

They looked at it and their jaws dropped.

It was *so* lovely – and the perfect way to round off what had been an amazing year for the railway cat.

But there was someone who was none too pleased about the moggy's masterful ownership of the station. Well before Felix had ever placed a paw on the platforms of Huddersfield station, another animal had once roamed the railway and claimed it for his own. He was most put out that this feline was getting ideas above her station. And one night in the winter of 2013, he decided it was time to do something about it.

Angie was over on Platform 1, midway through a night shift, when she saw him appear. She gasped and froze, for this creature could strike fear not only into the hearts of felines, but into human hearts too.

Weaving his way through the softly swaying plants of Billy's garden on the opposite platform was a thin-nosed urban fox.

There was something about foxes that Angie couldn't bear. She whispered frantically to her colleague, Carl, who was also on duty, 'Carl, Carl. I can't move.' Even though the fox was on the other side of the train tracks, it didn't matter to Angie how far away it was. The simple fact that it stood there, glowering at her, made her heart race and her palms grow sticky with sweat. She wanted to get inside as fast as she could.

The fox fixed her with a lazy look, and continued to prowl about amid the scented plants of Billy's garden, picking his way through the tall grass, his reddish-brown coat brushing the bushes.

'Get me inside, Carl,' Angie whispered urgently to her

colleague as they watched the fox asserting himself, as confident as could be, 'get me inside.'

Carl just laughed at her, good-naturedly. 'He's not going to bother you,' he said reasonably. After all, the fox was on the other side of the train tracks – they weren't close enough for him to do them any harm.

Yet it wasn't them whom the fox had come to see.

As Angie watched, a little black-and-white cat came trip-trapping her way along Platform 4, far out of Angie's reach. Felix had not yet spotted the insurgent fox who had infringed upon her territory, wanting to claim it for himself. She had not a care in the world as she sauntered along, on her way to Billy's garden where she had spent so many happy hours of late. She walked swiftly, eagerly, little knowing the danger ahead.

And it was a very real danger. Several years back, Jumper, the Manchester Oxford Road station cat, had been savaged by what was assumed to be an urban fox; it was a vicious attack, and the poor station cat had lost her back leg in the ensuing violence.

Angie felt the bottom fall out of her world. 'Felix is over there!' she cried to Carl in alarm. But there was nothing she could do for Felix – she was too far away and the fox could strike in seconds. As Angie watched, the fox turned his eyes away from the humans on Platform 1 and looked levelly at the approaching station cat. He took a stealthy step forward on one strong front paw. He was ready for this battle. He hadn't even had to hunt her: Felix was coming to him.

Angie watched his preparations with a sickening, sinking feeling. 'He's gonna kill her, he's gonna kill her, he's gonna kill her,' she whispered fearfully. The fox crouched down, as though preparing to spring, and bared his teeth: those sharp white incisors that Angie now feared were going to tear Felix apart before her very eyes. 'Oh my goodness,' she moaned in horror. 'He's gonna eat her. He's gonna eat her, Carl!'

Then Felix clocked the fox. The two claimants to the station throne made eye contact – and Felix held the fox's gaze. 'What's going on here?' those assertive green eyes of hers seemed to say. This was *her* patch.

Neither creature moved an inch: they just stared, and stared, and stared at each other. And then Felix, perhaps channelling the King of the Jungle on the Lion Building outside in St George's Square, decided she was *not* going to walk away from this battle. She was the Queen of Huddersfield station and, like so many monarchs before her, she was going to defend her crown.

As Angie watched in terror from Platform 1, she saw Felix's fluffy black back begin to rise in the middle. Soon every hair on the cat's body was standing on end. In cats, this *can* be a sign that they're frightened – which, considering the fierce nature of the fox Felix was facing, might have been the case – but it can also indicate that they are *really* annoyed.

The fox had chosen to mess with the wrong cat. Felix was angry, and her body language was shouting, 'This is *my* territory here!'

Felix's ears flattened. Her back was arched as high as Angie had ever seen it. Tension radiated from the cat's body as Felix stood her ground. This was *her* station – and the fox had to know it.

The stand-off continued. Angie felt her heart hammering in her chest. Cats' hearts beat nearly twice as fast as those of humans, yet given her intense fear, Angie felt certain that, at that particular moment, her and Felix's hearts were beating as one.

Still, the station cat and the fox continued to stare each other down. Felix's back went up a touch higher – and the fox turned tail and ran. He vanished into the dark winter's night, back to wherever his lair was located. The battle for Huddersfield station had been won by Felix the cat.

Seeing him go, the moggy relaxed and carried on with her plans for the evening, strutting along the platform on her way to Billy's garden. The enemy had been vanquished, much to her satisfaction.

It wasn't the last time the fox appeared on the station. At about four or five o'clock in the morning, every now and again, the night-shift team would see him pottering around and walking hesitantly along the platform, maybe on his way to hunt the tasty wild rabbits who frolicked at the bottom of Platform 2. But following their encounter, he and Felix had reached an understanding: the fox ignored her and she ignored the fox. They respected each other's boundaries.

Nevertheless, the pest controller would watch him with a keen green eye as he made his way along the platform. She was in charge here, and if the fox put a foot wrong Felix would know of it.

Yet the fox always toed the yellow line. He now knew all too well what the team at the station had known for years: Felix was the Boss.

24. Clever Felix

The big black crow cawed its mocking caw.

Felix raised a weary eye from her lair by the bike racks and stared at the bird impassively. The crow was a real poser and kept flying about as though trying to impress his fellows. He had made it his habit, that spring afternoon, to keep landing on the platform to squawk at the station cat, trying to wind her up. Over and over he did it: flying off to his iron roost, then coming back down, his harsh cry getting more and more frustrated the longer that Felix didn't respond.

But Felix merely sat there and watched him. She refused to get riled by his antics. She was Queen Felix – and even though she couldn't fly, she had learned to rise above it.

Felix's new maturity, and her confidence in her position as a gracious monarch, showed itself in her other interactions, too – in particular, in the way she behaved with her fellow residents of Platform 1. Though she still enjoyed a good stalking session with the posse of pigeons who scavenged at the station, the team were astonished to see that, when one of the pigeons was poorly, Felix could – in opposition to every instinct in her bones – actually be quite caring towards the suffering bird.

One afternoon, as Michael Ryan, who worked in revenue protection, was hard at work on Platform 1, he spotted Felix acting most strangely over on Platform 4. There was an injured pigeon, unable to fly, squatting helplessly on the ground over there, and Michael watched with a sense of grim fascination, safari-style, as Felix skulked over to the bird, expecting the station cat to slay the stricken creature as a lion might take down a gazelle on the slopes of the Serengeti.

But Felix did no such thing. First of all, she sat with the bird, as though she was a night nurse keeping a bedside vigil by her patient. Then she reached out a velvety white paw and patted the pigeon reassuringly, in a manner not unlike that which the same nurse might have used to mop her patient's brow. There was no aggression nor even a mocking playfulness in that pat – she appeared to be comforting a friend.

At her encouraging touch, the pigeon, who had been trying to get to Platform 8 and given up, made a valiant effort and hopped a little further. Felix, her claws still retracted, gently touched its purpley-green feathers once again, and once more the pigeon moved on. Every time it stopped, Felix tapped it one more time, and thus escorted that pigeon all the way to Platform 8.

One could argue, of course, that she was just playing with it, and that the ailing pigeon, fearing for its life, had no choice but to ask, 'How high?' when Felix's tap said: 'Jump!' But that wasn't how it appeared to Michael Ryan, observing this strange scene from over on Platform 1. It was weird, but it really was like seeing Felix interacting with a friend.

The unlikely truce was maintained even when the pigeons weren't poorly. Sam Dyson, who had worked with Felix ever since she'd arrived at the station, doing platforms, announcing and the booking office, watched one day as she and another pigeon kept each other company for roughly two hours of his shift. The pigeon had sat down on the edge of Platform 1, settling in as though he was an elderly gentleman with a rug over his knees at the seaside, wanting to watch the tide turn. He'd been there for quite a while, and Felix had eventually tottered out of the concourse to see what he was up to. She got closer and closer to him – not prowling, but rather moving with an interested, enquiring walk that took her, in the end, all the way up to him, so that she was standing right next to the bird.

The pigeon didn't flinch or fly off, and neither was Felix fazed by him. She got so close that it was almost as if she was going to cuddle him, but eventually she decided to simply and gracefully sit down. And then she and the pigeon sat together on the platform and watched the world go by, like two old friends nestled on a comfy park bench, having a good old natter and setting the world to rights.

For all Felix's maturity, however, in the spring of 2014 she showed Angela Dunn, at least, that she wasn't always the smartest kitten in the litter.

'Hiya, Felix,' Angela said that day, as the cat appeared in the lost-property office, hopped over her open desk drawer and greeted her affectionately. Every now and then, Felix would lick Angela's hand: a sign of real love. Given the cat's sometimes grumpy behaviour with other people, the little rough-tongued kiss always took Angela by surprise. But she and Felix were old friends, and Angela made a point of never picking her up or pestering her, believing that the cat had enough people petting her to last a lifetime; and it seems that the cat genuinely appreciated the peace and quiet she promised. Angela was one of those figures who had been around for all of Felix's station life too, like Angie Hunte and Billy – and Felix's own brown bear (who was still a firm favourite, even after all these years).

Felix miaowed plaintively for a treat and, when Angela obliged, she performed her little trick of catching it with her paws. Ta-da! But although she purred and pestered Angela for an encore, to Felix's immense disappointment her colleague tucked the little orange bag of Dreamies back in her middle desk drawer and shut it tight, telling Felix firmly that she had had enough for today.

Felix sniffed at the desk, from where the tantalising scent of the Dreamies drifted, and fixed her molten eyes on Angela, begging for more – but Angela had already turned back to her work. A moment later, when Angela looked up again, Felix had disappeared. Though she still loved to doze among the soft treasures of the lost-property cave, that activity was clearly not on the cat's agenda for today.

A little while later, Angela shut the big bottom drawer in her desk with a satisfying clatter. Done! That was her paper-work completed: now for a platform patrol. She slipped on her yellow hi-vis vest – the colour all members of the TPE team wore on the platforms at Huddersfield station – and stepped outside to join her colleagues.

They were standing there chatting when they heard a dis-tant: 'Miaow!'

They looked around for Felix, expecting to see her behind the bike racks or further along the platform, but there was no sign of the fluffy black-and-white cat. *That's odd*, thought Angela, *I wonder where she's got to.*

'Miaow!' They heard again. It was a deep, echoey sort of sound, quite unlike Felix's usual voice, but it was unmistake-ably her.

'Where's Felix?' Angela asked her colleagues, but nobody had seen her.

'Miaow!' The cat's cries sounded more urgent now, so Angela started looking around for her properly. She searched in the station manager's office and in the team leaders' room; she checked Felix's bed in the shower closet and called for the cat in both the male and female locker rooms. These were a favourite retreat as they offered peace and quiet . . . and copious comfy bedding options. She caused absolute havoc in the men's room because the team often left their spare uniforms in there, and Felix would bed down in the cosy clothing and get cat hairs all over them. Once, a team member forgot to lock his locker, and when he came back the door was wide open and there was a cat all rolled up in his smart jacket inside the metal cavern: just two emerald eyes peeping out. *Well*, he thought, *I can't be mad with her; it's way too cute!* As well as sleeping in the lockers, Felix was also known to doze on the snug wooden shelves in the ladies' locker room, or even on top of the locker units themselves: she had a perfect view out to the town of Huddersfield from the summit of the lockers in the men's room, and it was one of her favourite spots.

But as Angela searched for her high and low, there was no sign of the cat in the locker rooms today.

'Has anyone seen Felix?' she asked. But no one had. 'Where are you, cat?' Angela wondered aloud.

'MIAOW!' Felix replied, as though trying to tell her. By now, the chorus of mews was impatient and demanding. Felix was quite patently saying, 'Let me out! I'm stuck!' but Angela had tried all the usual places and Felix was not in them.

Angela scratched her head and stood quite still, hovering by the customer-information point, always a popular place for Felix, and where, opposite the desk, the stable door of Angela's lost-property office lay half-open.

'MIAOW!'

Where is she? Angela wondered. She listened more closely as Felix called again.

That's odd, she thought, as she edged towards the noise, *it sounds like it's coming from my office . . .*

She opened the stable door and stood on the threshold of her room. There was her desk: no Felix. There were the shelves packed full of all the abandoned items: no Felix. Angela walked in and marched up and down those shelves, moving things around in case Felix had got stuck behind a suitcase or caught up in a cagoule.

'MIAOW!' ('I'm right here!' Felix seemed to be yelling.)

Angela slowly turned round and stared again at her desk. *I wonder* . . . she thought.

She walked over and pulled open the big bottom drawer, and out leapt Felix, looking ruffled and a little bit dazed to find herself freed from her dark and unexpected prison. Angela had never seen her move so fast. She was off!

As Angela shut the drawer again behind Felix, it was obvious to her what had happened. Greedy Felix, wanting more treats, had tiptoed into the big drawer, wondering if she could somehow help herself to the bag of Dreamies located teasingly in the middle drawer above. The big drawer had been roomy and looked a rather fun place from which to plot her cat burglary. But the cat criminal, having silently stepped inside, had then found herself trapped when Angela had unwittingly shut the drawer on her.

Well, thought Angela, watching Felix dart away up the platform, very glad to be free at last, *that will teach her not to try and get treats on her own!*

As Felix approached her third birthday, however, her plots to get more food grew more complex. Cats are very, very clever creatures. Their brains are more like ours than those of dogs – and Felix certainly had human levels of cunning when it came to the thorny question of how to hoodwink her colleagues into feeding her more.

The answer seemed an obvious one, given Felix's experiences the year before. Diva Felix was required to make another unforgettable appearance in the limelight: acting was clearly the way for this drama queen to go. It was once more time for the railway cat to tread the boards with her white-capped paws.

The first Angie Hunte knew of the scheme was when she came on shift one morning. The team leader on the night shift was *supposed* to feed Felix, but as Angie bustled into the office and wished everyone a cheery good morning, the canny cat was waiting for her with a heart-rending complaint to make.

Felix staggered up onto Angie's desk the moment the team leader sat down in her chair and boldly pushed her way into Angie's eyeline.

'Miaow!' she mewed, terribly feebly, as though she could barely muster the energy to call out, so weak was she from lack of food. She fluttered her eyelashes and blinked her mournful green eyes at Angie. Out came one velvety white paw, which she pressed desperately to Angie's skin, begging her to help her. She had been left alone all night with this other, mean team leader – and it was only Angie who could save her now.

'Now then, what's all this?' Angie said in concern. She knew only too well which of Felix's mews meant, 'I'm hungry,' and recognised that Felix was currently employing it at top volume.

Felix edged closer to Angie, channelling every flick of her tail into the act, placing her paws on Angie's shoulders so she could stare straight into her eyes, pleading for mercy, for food, for this unwarranted starvation to be brought to an end – before it was too late.

'Has he not fed my Felix?' Angie said aloud in horror.

Dave Rooney had been on shift the night before. Unfortunately for Felix, he just happened to be passing through the office at the time she said it, and he stopped in his tracks and looked at Angie with an I-can't-believe-you-fell-for-that face. 'You know I have,' he deadpanned. 'That cat is trying it on.'

And it wasn't the last time she did – not on your nelly. Felix had twigged that the multitude of carers she had as a railway cat, and the nature of their ever-changing shifts, meant that she could try time and again to get more food out of them whenever the changeover of team took place. Angie found that it was often she who was on the receiving end of the cat's amateur-dramatics performances. So convincing were Felix's interpretations of near-death hunger that Angie would find herself staring in genuine concern at the cat, when in would walk the colleague who'd been on duty the previous shift.

'Oh, soft touch is here,' they would say to Angie, teasing her, and only then would she realise that once again Felix had been pulling her leg.

But Felix did manage to grab an extra meal every now and again, and only after her subterfuge had been successful would the team leaders confer and realise that she had been given a double dinner. In the end, to ensure they were not hoodwinked by this master criminal, they decided to write on the noticeboard exactly when Felix had been fed, so that if they genuinely forgot on a busy shift, the team would know that she *did* need feeding if she cried; but if she was just trying it on (as nine-and-a-half times out of ten she was), they could send her packing with her fluffy black tail between her legs.

Of course, she never went far if her plans *were* foiled – only as far as the gateline team. With them, she'd twist in and out of their forest of legs to get their attention before it would start all over again.

'Miaow!' she'd say, making eyes at them, all the world a stage. 'I'm *so* hungry . . . '

Felix's family was even larger now than it had been when she'd first started working at the station. With the introduction of the ticket barriers in June 2013, a new team of staff members had been added, so that the crew at Huddersfield now numbered thirty-six humans and one black-and-white cat. Not everyone was a fan of the moggy when they met her, however – there was a new team leader called Geoff who would yell, 'Get out!' whenever she walked into the office while he was on shift (he may also have been guilty of rudely writing 'Fleabag: fed' on the team leaders' noticeboard). Yet when he bellowed, 'Gerraway!' at her as she sauntered in, Felix merely turned around and strolled nonchalantly out again, the carefree wag of her tail seeming to say, 'OK, Geoff, I'll be back in a bit when you've calmed yourself down.' Like any boss managing a crotchety employee, she just needed to work out how to deal with him. She was confident that she would succeed: after all, look at her and Billy these days.

It was plain to see from the way Felix trotted around after Billy that she simply adored him – and the feeling was mutual. In fact, Felix loved him so much that, in spring 2014, she focused that clever brain of hers on to a problem she *really* wanted to solve: how could she make sure Billy stayed at the station *all* the time and never left her? Angie was there the day she came up with the answer.

Billy had been working nights, and as usual he and Felix had spent much of the time together. It had been a twelve-hour shift, so no wonder he was exhausted as he made his slow and steady way out of the station just after 6 a.m. He and Angie walked together, chatting as they went, finishing off the last of their handover before Billy headed home for a well-deserved sleep and Angie took charge of the station.

'And Felix?' Angie asked.

'Fed,' Billy said as he ticked off the items on his hand. He coughed abruptly, somewhat hoarsely, and then continued, 'Watered. But not present and correct – I haven't seen her since you signed in.'

While the team leaders had been talking in the office, Felix had vanished from view.

'She'll turn up,' Angie said confidently, knowing that the cat would come back soon; she was always on duty for the morning rush hour.

'I dare say,' Billy replied, stifling a yawn.

They stumbled down the station steps and passed the King's Head pub on their way to the car park. Billy could see his silver people carrier looming into view and it had never looked so inviting. He couldn't wait to slip into the seat, click his seatbelt into place and drive straight home to bed.

But a cat-shaped someone had other ideas.

As they rounded the corner and had full view of the car, they also saw that Felix was sitting proudly on the roof, having selected it specifically from all the motors on offer. She looked as pleased as punch at her brainwave to stop him leaving the station. Perhaps she'd taken her inspiration from her hostage-taking triumphs, when she would jump up on the suitcases of those customers with food, trying to keep them on the platform for as long as she possibly could. For Felix looked pretty comfortable on top of Billy's car – it was obvious she was not planning on moving any time soon.

Billy shook his head in disbelief.

'Come on, cat,' he said. 'I want to go home.'

But Felix didn't budge.

'Get off, please, Felix,' he went on. 'I've just done a twelve-hour shift. I want to go home, cat. I want to go home now.'

Felix merely lifted her beautiful head just a touch higher,

and every sinew of her fluffy body said, 'I'm not moving any-where.' She flicked her tail back and forth, wagging it with great pleasure at the success of her scheme. Looking levelly at Billy, her big green eyes unmistakeably said, 'Gotcha.'

'*Please*,' he begged.

Angie, chuckling away and not at all sympathetic to Billy's situation, quickly snapped a photo of the stand-off between the two. There was Billy, absolutely exhausted, pleading with the cat, and facing him was Felix, sat squarely on the roof of Billy's car, refusing to shift an inch. Angie thought it so funny that she showed the image to Billy's wife and the team; she captioned it: 'Preventing the team leader from going home.' It was a ruse that Felix would try over and over again – because her heart was really in it.

As far as Felix was concerned, Billy's home was here – with her. And with her was where he should *always* be.

25. Meet the Boss

Billy's garden was now complete in terms of planting and design – but as any gardener knows, a gardener's work is *never* finished, so he was still doing regular maintenance of the little patch of land on quiet shifts and on his days off, occasionally with a fluffy black-and-white shadow at his feet.

However, Billy had recently had another bright idea about who could help him with the garden maintenance – and it wasn't Felix! Instead, Billy had wondered if he could perhaps get some of the local community involved; he had a vision that maybe a group of young people he knew, who all had learning difficulties, might be able to join him in helping with the garden. They'd then have a patch of the station they could take pride in. They could enjoy seeing the plants grow and come to appreciate how their care of those plants created real beauty. Their involvement was a way off yet – there were lots of hoops to jump through first – but when Billy had a vision for something he kept plugging away at it, and he planned to be no less dog-with-bone with this concept than he had been with so many other projects he'd turned his mind to over the years.

The station – as the team knew well – was much the better for his input. Not only was his 'Art Station' project still running, after a successful two years of exhibiting local artists' work on the concourse, but Billy also won an award in 2014 for his environmental innovation (his second in five years). Over time, he had transformed the station's green credentials, putting in place a traffic-light system for switching off plugs (to cut down on unnecessary electricity use), installing water-saving gadgets in the public toilets and revolutionising the recycling processes. Even in the garden, he'd recently devised a rainwater-capture system to keep the garden green. When new 'young un' Chris Bamford joined the station in 2014 – he would be doing a bit of everything: the gateline, announcing and customer service on the platforms – he found Billy's work impressive; and the man himself very funny, even though he was *incredibly* blunt and direct (some might even have said rude). Mr Grumpy was still in position, but despite his best efforts he seemed to be endearing himself to more and more people by the day.

Yet Billy, the relatively important team leader, wasn't the colleague to whom Chris was introduced first when he joined the team. That honour, naturally enough, went to Felix. In fact, the very first thing his colleagues said to him on his first day – as they did to all new recruits – was, 'Have you met Felix yet?'

'No,' Chris replied, intrigued. 'Who's Felix?'

'Let's get you introduced to her,' they told him, smiling. And they made sure those introductions were complete before they commenced any of the induction formalities. They had their priorities right: 'Meet the Boss, and then we'll deal with the station.'

In truth, in Felix's three years at Huddersfield she had confidently assumed a supervisory role over *every* department, so perhaps it was only fair that Chris should meet the colleague who would be keeping a very close eye on his performance. When Felix wanted to be, she was immensely curious about every aspect of the station team's work – and had the attention span to sit and watch everything she possibly could. As she did so, she seemed to take a step back from the colleague she was observing, as though she was about to scribble thoughtful and perceptive notes on a (very well concealed) clipboard.

It was like having an inspector in. She would sit for a long time watching the booking-office team serving at the windows, appraising their performance. She would balance on top of the monitors or the printers, and keep tabs as the tickets came out. When the cashing up was being done or the Securicor man was dropping off more money, Felix would be there, keeping a close eye on the cash: the multi-talented, multi-disciplined supervisor extraordinaire.

Chris laughed when he realised just who 'Felix' was. A friend of a friend of his had worked at Huddersfield station just before he'd joined, so he had heard on the grapevine that there was a resident cat at his new workplace – but he hadn't known her name. Now, he did.

As it happened, Chris was allergic to cats. But it wasn't as if he could do much about that! And, as he settled into the station, over time Felix seemed to help him build up his tolerance until he was absolutely fine in her presence.

That first week, however, he was perhaps apprehensive about working with her in more ways than one. For as Chris learned the ropes, just as his colleagues had warned him, 'the Boss' was on his tail. On one of his very first shifts, Felix joined him on the gateline. Yet she hardly set a good example: she sat squarely in the stream of customers coming through the gates so that they had to move around her. Worse still, she just glared, Medusa-like, at every single customer coming through.

Her grumpiness had become more pronounced as she grew older, and Chris was seeing it in action today. There were some people she liked – such as the Felix charmer, Dave Chin, into whose arms she would still leap for an upside-down cuddle – but many others whom she didn't. If she didn't know someone, she was likely to regard them with deep suspicion until they had proved themselves trustworthy.

Given this reputation, perhaps Chris gulped as this temperamental terror headed straight towards him, insolently swishing her fluffy black tail. Felix had evidently decided to assume a new gateline position. She suddenly (and rather unexpectedly) sat down firmly on Chris's money bag, which he'd momentarily left out on the side while he got himself sorted.

Chris needed that money bag in order to serve his customers. But now, with an adult cat sitting heavily upon it, he couldn't get to his cash.

'Uh, Felix?' he asked, feeling somewhat self-conscious to be talking to a cat. 'Could you, er, move, please?'

Felix stared at him stonily and yawned her most bored and uninterested yawn. Chris rubbed his hands over his black-bearded face and sighed, thinking hard. It seemed like the worst kind of initiation ritual imaginable for one's first week in a new job: a deliberately difficult boss who seemed set on sabotage. He'd expected there to be lots of skills he'd need to acquire to become adept at his new role – he hadn't expected one of them to be mastering the art of removing a cat from a money bag.

But he did it, in the end, and in time he began to learn other things, too, including how to shift Felix without waking her if she was spread-eagled across the keyboard in the announcer's office when he needed to use it. The desk had always been a favourite location for a catnap, but she took up rather too much room now.

Despite Chris's growing skill in handling her, Felix, mischievously, seemed set on making the new boy's life difficult. She would plonk her bottom on the microphone button, stopping him from making an announcement – and as she did it, she would gaze at him with a twinkle in her big green eyes, as though she knew exactly what she was doing. Or she might paw at his arm to demand his attention *just* at the time he needed to focus on a CCTV image, or even when he was midway through broadcasting an announcement over the tannoy. He would somehow manage to finish what he was saying without making an error, then turn to Felix.

'What do you want, cat?' he would ask.

And she'd flick that fluffy tail of hers, as though to say, 'Wouldn't you like to know.'

There came a day when it was *very* clear what Felix wanted. She was miaowing insistently for her dinner – and, this time, she really *was* hungry, for the team leader on duty had been caught up in an emergency. Seeing this, Chris said to his human colleague, 'I'll take care of t'cat.' So he and Felix had gone into the kitchen together and he'd sorted out her supper.

After that, Felix's assessment of this 'young un' seemed to change. *Oh, this one feeds me, I'll follow him* . . . she seemed to think. Whether he wanted one or not, Chris now had a buddy for life.

Angie Hunte could have told him that Felix was the very best buddy you could wish for. It's lonely at the top, and with the way the shifts worked for the team leaders, nine times out of ten they would be on duty on their own – managing a team, sure, but with ultimate solo responsibility for the station. Only very rarely would Angie get a chance to sit down with Billy or one of the others with a cup of tea to talk through the frustrations and worries of the job. Yet she found that Felix, ever-present, was always willing to listen with an attentive twitch of her white-tufted ears – and the cat made the perfect sounding board for gripes about work. Sometimes, she was the only 'person' around whom Angie could talk to.

'For God's sake, Felix,' she might rage at the cat when one thing or another had come up. 'I'm fed up. I'm absolutely fed up!'

Felix would jump up onto the desk and come padding over to Angie's side. She would sit down, yet she wouldn't beg or paw or purr as she sometimes did. Instead, she seemed to listen, as if she knew that that was what Angie needed of her at that moment. Felix could be a diva, it was true, but she could also be a very good friend.

Which was why Angie always had the same response whenever customers asked her what would happen if Felix jumped on a train – or was escorted onto one by a joker. 'What if I took her on a train?' they might query, provocatively.

Angie would narrow her eyes. 'You'd have me and thirty-five colleagues after you,' she would say tartly. 'It's really *not* worth it.'

But while Felix was going nowhere, one part of her – a part that had become rather famous – now completely vanished.

In the summer of 2014, Felix's long-time glitzy pink collar and her heart-shaped name tag went missing without a trace.

To this day, no one knows what happened to them. One day Felix was wearing them, looking as glamorous as always; the next, her neck was bare. Did she slip the collar off herself, as she used to do with her kitten cuff? Or did it get caught on something during one of her explorations, and was even now hanging from a prickly bush or dangling over a precipice?

Whatever the story, the cat wasn't telling it. She preened and fussed in Angie and Angela's hands as they exclaimed over the pretty collar's absence, but Felix's head-tossing look wasn't quite as effective without her bling.

Much more important than her fast-tumbling glamour credentials, however, was the fact that, without a collar, Felix was wearing nothing that told people she was a railway cat who belonged to the Huddersfield team. Without a tag, she could be stolen – or get lost. If she ended up in Domino's Pizza now, there would be no happy ending to the adventure.

It became a priority to get Felix's identity back as quickly as possible. The team wanted everybody to know that Huddersfield station was where she lived; where she belonged. Angela Dunn went out to buy the new collar, and she raced as quickly as she could to the pet shop.

But there was disappointment as she surveyed the collars on display. Felix had looked so stylish in her pretty pink collar that Angela had been planning to get her the exact same shade again – but there were no pink collars available except for really over-the-top designs with bling literally hanging off them, which were totally impractical for a railway cat who every day went travelling across the tracks. Yet Felix needed a collar *today* – no one wanted her to go one more night without some form of ID. What if tonight was the night someone snatched her, as they'd done two years before? What if tonight was the night that Felix got hurt far from home and no one knew to call the station when she was found? It didn't bear thinking about.

Angela frantically rifled through the offerings: a panic search of the whole stand. Nothing seemed appropriate for Queen Felix. She took every single collar off the hooks, searching, searching, searching . . . And there, at the very, very back, practically the last collar she examined, was a glittery deep-purple number that exactly matched the colour of the TransPennine Express logo.

It was perfect. 'On brand' for the company cat. Elegant and smart. But most important of all, of course: *glamorous.*

With the pink heart-shaped tag now gone for good, Chrissie – who had originally bought that distinctive

ID – kindly commissioned a new identifier for Felix: this time it was a slim gold circular disc. It was engraved with the same details as before: Felix's name and address on the front, and the team leaders' mobile-telephone number on the back, so that Felix's family could be found if she ever went missing again.

With a tiny purple bell added as a final flourish, Felix's new ensemble was complete. What a stunner she would be in it!

The station team cooed over the cat like true fashionistas as she strutted up and down her platform catwalks, displaying the purple accoutrements just as a supermodel would the new Dior couture in Paris. Yet – to Angie's surprise – when Billy saw the cat's new glittery get-up, he didn't say a word. There was neither commendation nor condemnation; a far cry from his outspokenness when Felix had first got dressed up to the nines all those years before.

But Billy had not been feeling well lately. In October he started suffering from a spot of heartburn and a bad sore throat, an affliction which seemed to grow steadily worse as 2014 drew towards its close. Come November he was feeling so poorly that he called the station manager, Paul, and informed him that he'd regrettably have to take a bit of time off sick.

Felix, however, was not under the weather at all. Rather, she went from strength to strength. That December, to Angie's delight and pride, the station cat was once again chosen to be the star of the official TPE Christmas card.

As for where Felix would spend the holidays, it was Jean Randall, in the booking office, who that year volunteered to take the cat home for Christmas. She didn't know it when she signed up, but it would turn out to be a Christmas she would never forget.

26. Santa Claws

'Here we go, then, Felix,' Jean said as she opened up the door of the cat carrier. 'Welcome home.'

Felix stepped gingerly out of the blue-and-oatmeal carry case and looked around with interest. Jean lived in a lovely two-bedroom cottage, built in 1802. On the ground floor it had a long kitchen/diner, as well as a huge living room with wooden floorboards and plain cream walls. The focal point of that living room was the fireplace, which was framed by a beautiful stone mantelpiece set before an open chimney. When the fire was lit and the white voile curtains drawn across the glass French doors, it was a wonderfully cosy place to spend a winter's night.

Felix had a good old nose around, sticking her twitching whiskers into every nook and cranny, familiarising herself with this environment which was so very different from the station. She had stayed with Jean for Christmas 2012, too, but showed no sign of recognition as she padded round the living room on her white-tipped toes.

It had been a great Christmas two years ago with the little black-and-white cat, so Jean had been more than happy to volunteer to look after Felix again. In 2012, when Jean and Felix had first got home from the station on the afternoon of Christmas Eve, after investigating her new pad Felix had simply curled up on Jean's lap and fallen fast asleep, exhausted by the novelty of being in a family home.

On Christmas Day, however, it had been Jean who'd been exhausted, for Felix – bless her – had spent the whole of

Christmas Eve night crying and howling. She'd been lonely without the night-shift team around her and was clearly disconcerted by the stillness and the silence, where normally there were trains coming and going through the night. Jean had got up and sat with her at least three times – but they didn't see Santa. Instead, they'd snuggled up on the sofa together and listened to the radio as Christmas morning had broken across the town.

Christmas Day had been a fine affair with Felix receiving a special festive treat of fresh prawns while Jean and her visiting family and friends ate their dinner; it was a very full house, and Jean was convinced that at least some of the visitors came because they knew the railway cat was the guest of honour that year and wanted to meet her. Felix had been as good as gold as they'd pulled their crackers and told the jokes, so used to the noise of the station that the bang of the crackers didn't even make her start.

But busy and well-populated as the celebrations were, Felix had been far more interested in her hostess than in her new admirers; she'd followed Jean around devotedly, and every time she'd got close to her she'd purred loudly, delighting in the familiarity of her friend when everything else was so strange. Yet it didn't take her long to adjust to her new environment: before she came home, Felix was sleeping through the night without a peep and Jean thought she'd adjusted very quickly to domestic life.

That said, the cat returned to work with far more enthusiasm than most workers do following the Christmas break. Jean and Felix had spent both Christmas Day and Boxing Day 2012 together, then Jean had carried Felix back to the station on 27 December, which was also Jean's first day back in the booking office. When Jean had opened the door of the carry case, the railway cat had come straight out as if she'd never been away and immediately got on with her work. She'd sauntered along the platforms, giving a contented nod to the customers as if she was saying, with some satisfaction, 'I'm *home*.'

Not that she didn't enjoy her holidays. Felix was a curious and adventurous cat with many human friends, and her annual jaunts to stay in the different homes of her colleagues for Christmas had always been fun affairs. This year, naturally, would be no different. As always, her first priority was to suss out the lie of the land.

Jean let the cat get settled before changing out of the uniform she'd been wearing for her shift that morning. She pulled on some tartan pyjamas and shrugged a cosy pink dressing gown on over the top. She liked to get changed after work, and she and Felix wouldn't be going out again that evening; it would be just the two of them on the sofa instead: the cat lady and the cat. Nice company for each other on this Christmas Eve night.

Jean padded back down the stairs to see how Felix was getting on. Perhaps she would be lying on the new fleecy blanket Jean had bought for her bedding. Or maybe she'd be in the kitchen/diner, where her litter tray was laid out. Well-trained by her mother Lexi, Felix was still diligent in using the litter tray, even though she tended to do her business outdoors at the station. It seemed there were some things you never forgot.

Because Felix was a cat so accustomed to being outdoors and to coming and going as she pleased, the only hardship of her holidays was that Jean would be keeping her indoors for the entire visit, as she had done two years before. Felix was far from home and had travelled to Jean's house in a car – Jean didn't want her getting lost or running off. The idea of returning to the station after Christmas *without* the station cat and having to break the news that she'd lost her didn't bear thinking about. Team leader Angie Hunte would probably kill her.

When Jean got downstairs, Felix was pottering happily about in the living room, swishing her fluffy black tail as she wandered this way and that, her whiskers quivering as she sniffed all the exciting new smells. Jean joined her.

'All right, my darling?' Jean asked as the two of them ambled about the big living room, Felix still exploring and Jean doing some tidying up. There was a large coffee table in the middle of the room; Jean was standing on one side of it and Felix on the other. As it was now late afternoon on Christmas Eve, it was dark outside the French doors: a thick blanket of black had already settled upon the town.

Jean chattered away to Felix, conscious of the cat's eyes upon her as she moved about the room. When Felix was staying at her house, the feline often followed her movements obsessively, as though she didn't want to let Jean out of her sight.

Which was why, when the cat's gaze was no longer trained upon her, Jean felt its absence, as surely as if a spotlight had been suddenly switched off.

Jean was a mother of grown-up kids, and she felt an eerily familiar sensation as the cat stopped looking at her. It was just like when her boys had been small: she'd always instinctively known they were up to something when they went quiet.

She glanced over at Felix on the other side of the coffee table. The cat had turned away from Jean and was facing the unlit fireplace, sitting there and looking, as though deep in thought. As she watched, Felix's head inclined to one side and her whiskers twitched. There was a tension in the cat's body, as though she was about to do *something*, but what it was Jean couldn't imagine.

'Felix?' she asked uncertainly.

And then Felix ran up the chimney.

She leapt over the hearth in one jump and dived athletically up into the open chimney above, through which – perhaps – she could smell fresh air and freedom. All Jean could see was her tail and her two back legs as she scrabbled and scraped against the sooty chimney in her bid to climb up, up, up and away.

'FELIX!' yelled Jean at the top of her voice. She scrambled round the coffee table, which suddenly seemed like an obstacle upon which Felix had counted for a few seconds' delay. Nevertheless, somehow Jean managed to grab those wriggling back legs with both hands before they completely disappeared from view.

Her heart was pounding. *I can't let her escape, I can't let her escape* ran the mantra in her head.

Felix writhed and wiggled against her, trying to find some traction. It was a sort of 'dog-leg' chimney, where the channel curved round and then narrowed, and Felix was trying to get round the bend, her front paws scrabbling hard against the chimney as she attempted to find a way through. As she struggled, she dislodged centuries of puffy black soot, which fell in thick ebony drifts around both her and Jean, coating the two of them.

Jean was panting. She genuinely thought she was going to have a heart attack. *Oh my God, it's Christmas Eve*, she thought to herself. *It's Christmas Eve – I can't let her go. What if she gets hurt? What if she escapes? Or what if she gets stuck in the chimney?! I'll have to call the fire brigade!*

She could just imagine *their* reaction.

'You do know it's supposed to be Father Christmas coming down the chimney tonight, madam,' they would chortle behind their hands, 'not Santa Claws . . . '

But never mind the firemen: Jean was far more concerned about what the station team might say. Even though Jean genuinely believed she might keel over at any moment from the stress, she knew it wasn't *her* that her colleagues would be alarmed about.

'Oh, Jean's had a heart attack?' they would say, so blasé. 'Well, never mind that. How's *Felix*? How do we get the cat back? If she's stuck up the chimney, we'll just have to demolish Jean's house!'

Jean tugged harder on Felix's squirming hind legs, trying desperately to drag her back to safety in the living room, and the cat mawed and dug in to something within the narrowing chimney, holding on tight to her escape route. Jean pulled and Felix howled, Jean yanked and Felix squealed, and every second felt like an aeon as Jean's heart hammered in her ears.

And then Felix let go. *Whoosh!* Cat and cat lady fell backwards from the chimney. Felix did a commando roll and shot away into the kitchen. She was safe. Peace was restored. Home sweet home.

Yet that home was no longer *quite* as sweet as it had been before Felix had made her bid for freedom. As Jean sat panting before the fireplace, she surveyed the damage.

She was covered in soot. Felix, she had seen, was *totally* covered in soot. The wooden floorboards, the hearth ... *everything* was covered in soot.

But more pressing than the dirt, to Jean's mind, was the need to block up the chimney. What if Felix did it again?

Jean couldn't believe what had happened. On her visit in 2012, Felix hadn't shown the slightest interest in the fireplace – and now this!

The escape artist was mewing in the kitchen, a kind of 'Well, I say!' mew at all the commotion, but she wasn't grumpy or bothered by what had happened. Her attitude seemed pretty equable: 'I tried that, it didn't work, so let's move on.'

But just because Felix didn't seem concerned about it now, it didn't mean she wouldn't turn her attention to the chimney again in the future, perhaps in the middle of the night when Jean was sleeping and no one would be awake to watch her go . . .

Jean tiptoed to the kitchen door and shut it firmly so that Felix was, at least, safe for the time being in there. *I'm going to have to block the chimney*, she thought. She picked up a cushion, but realised it was way too small. She debated pushing something in front of the fire, so that Felix couldn't get to the chimney, but whatever she placed there would inevitably have cat-sized gaps at the sides, through which the lithe Felix would easily be able to squeeze. In the end, she went upstairs and grabbed an old duvet. Pushing and shoving, she rammed it up the chimney till the hole was completely filled.

'There!' said Jean when she had finished. 'That will have to do.'

That particular mission accomplished, she now turned her attention to what was evidently going to be a big job: the clean-up. Jean walked from the fireplace through to the kitchen. Following in Felix's footsteps was easy as the cat had left a sooty black trail everywhere she went. Jean decoded the evidence like a crime scene investigator. Here was where the cat had landed from her fall and rolled across the floor. Here was where she'd had a good old shake to get some of the soot off. And here was where she had curled up in a big fluffy ball in the corner.

'Felix,' Jean said to her, and the cat looked up. They stared each other out, and Jean shook her head reproachfully. 'Don't you *ever* do that again, do you hear me? I nearly had a heart attack!'

Felix gave a little purr, as though to say, in conciliatory fashion, 'I won't!' She got up and started twisting through Jean's legs.

'Friends?' asked Jean.

And friends it was.

Jean grabbed an old hairbrush and Felix stood still, ready to be groomed. Her trips to the parlour had never been quite like this. First Jean stroked her, and a lot of the soot came off in her hands. Then she pulled the brush through Felix's fluffy fur, and brushed and brushed and brushed her till she was clean. Felix stood there, letting Jean minister to her, until there was a solid black circle of soot all around where she stood. Only once she was totally clean did Jean let her go. She then wiped up the living room and the kitchen and all of Felix's sooty pawprints, then let the cat back into the lounge.

Felix tiptoed in and went straight over to the fireplace as though drawn to it by a magnet. She cast a look over her shoulder at Jean, who was watching her like a hawk.

'Don't even think about it, Felix,' she said dryly.

Felix drew closer to the hearth and looked up. She sniffed at the edges of the duvet, then ducked her head and walked away. Nevertheless, she kept on looking back at it, as did Jean. *Is the duvet secure?* Jean fretted. *Might Felix be able to dislodge it?*

Amid her worrying, Jean looked down at herself. Her pink dressing gown was pink no more. Her hands were pure filth. *I'm going to have to have a shower,* she thought. She was scared of going upstairs in case Felix imitated Harry Houdini again while she was gone, but she had no option. So Jean showered, and put her blackened clothes into the washing machine. Then, as the washer tumbled and hummed melodically, she and Felix finally settled in for the night.

When Jean sat down on the sofa in the living room, Felix

immediately jumped up into her lap for a cuddle. All was forgiven. Santa Claws was just the station cat once more.

After that, Jean and Felix had a lovely Christmas. Following her little escapade, Felix was no trouble at all; she didn't even cry at night. On Christmas Day, Jean gave her a treat of a little bit of Sainsbury's finest unsmoked salmon, which she sentimentally served up in a white china bowl that had once belonged to her children when they were babies: it had the letters of the alphabet painted on it in blue. Felix absolutely loved that salmon; she devoured the small amount Jean let her have and purred noisily for more.

Boxing Day was mostly spent with Felix gazing out at the garden through the tall French doors, miaowing every now and again as she stared morosely at the great outdoors. Jean felt a bit sorry for her in the end, so glum was her constant vigil. Felix seemed jealous of the neighbour's tabby cats who tumbled in the garden, and of the robin and the wood pigeons who flew about the trees.

Even when it grew dark, Felix maintained her watch by the window. Jean had some solar-powered fairy lights wound round her trees, and after the sun had set they came to life automatically and twinkled in the darkness. Perhaps they reminded Felix of the fairy lights wrapped around the stately columns of her home. Perhaps she was missing it.

She was certainly pleased to be back when Jean opened up the carrier the following day and Felix scampered out. She sniffed all around the team leaders' office and wandered over to Billy's garden. She carefully traced the route they walked together for the security checks and careered around the car park. She paced up and down the platforms, on patrol. But the man she was looking for wasn't there.

Billy was still not back at work.

27. The Hardest Goodbye

'Are you coming down t'meeting today if you're feeling all right?' Angie Hunte asked her long-time colleague on the phone.

'Maybe not today, Mrs H,' Billy replied in a hoarse whisper. 'But I'll be back soon. Don't you be messing about with any of my stuff, now! I know what you're like.'

Angie hung up, smiling despite herself at Mr Grumpy's words. She and Billy had worked together for so long now that they had the kind of friendship where they could rib each other and call each other out; Billy was forever telling her she'd messed up his recycling system by throwing something in the wrong bin, and she was forever telling him that he was in her office to hand over to her and not to inspect her rubbish!

Angie and Billy stayed in touch while he was off, and Angie kept him up to date with all the developments at the station, so that he'd be up to speed when he got back. The most significant of these was that Paul, the station manager, was moving on to pastures new; Andy Croughan would be fulfilling the role again until they found a permanent replacement.

So it was Andy that Billy telephoned when he had some news of his own to share. That sore throat of his wasn't getting any better – and it wasn't a cough or a cold or a minor infection.

It was cancer.

Andy felt stunned. Even though Billy had been off sick for

a while now, Andy had been convinced he would be back to work soon. And Billy, too, had been similarly convinced. In fact, *everyone* at the station had been – for it had only been a month or so since they'd seen him and none of them thought it could be anything so serious.

After that phone call, things moved very quickly. It was an aggressive form of the disease, and Billy's weight plummeted dramatically. His condition deteriorated so fast that Andy felt like he'd had no time to come to terms with the news of his colleague's illness before he received another call, this time from Billy's wife. She shared the news that suddenly, shockingly, on 31 March 2015, Billy had died.

Andy replaced the receiver slowly; his shock at the suddenness of Billy's passing almost visceral. Billy was gone. It was up to Andy to tell the team.

He tried to find them one by one. The nature of the railway meant that the team were always moving around when on shift, as transient as the trains themselves: there was always a customer to be served or a train to be caught; it would have been impossible to have had one big meeting to break the sad news to them all. So that morning, on Wednesday 1 April 2015, Andy found himself standing on the front steps of the station, trying to catch the team as they came in for their shifts. Never had he seen so many faces fall, so many tears blinked back, so many murmured words about 'waste' and 'loss'.

When Angie pulled up in the car park, she was already concerned. She'd tried phoning Billy and his wife, Val, to have a chat, but they hadn't come to the phone. *Something's wrong*, she had thought, as the telephone had rung on and on emptily in her ear, unanswered and unattended to.

She slammed her car door distractedly, thoughts full of Billy, and made her way to the station steps: the route she had walked so many times before with her colleague, as they handed over to each other from their shifts.

She almost stopped dead when she saw Andy standing on the steps. She knew, instantly, that something was wrong. She didn't know it was Billy, but as Andy spotted her and walked over with a concerned look on his face, she knew she wasn't going to like whatever it was he had to say.

Andy felt relieved, in a way, when he saw Angie standing at the bottom of the steps. He had wanted to catch her before she came into the station. He knew how close she and Billy had been, and he didn't know how she would take it. He'd sensed, perhaps, that it was best not to tell her in front of the team.

He took her arm and led her to one side to break the news.

When you've worked with somebody for the amount of years that Angie and Billy had worked together – longer than some marriages, all told – and when you've laughed and joked and moaned and said a lot of things to each other that only that other person ever knows, it leaves a big, big hole when they die. Although Angie knew he was sick, seriously sick, she'd never really believed that Billy would leave them. Well, you just don't think things like that. You put a brave face on, or even a grumpy face, just some face, whatever face you need to help you carry on, and then you graft and you continue and you get the job done. That's what Billy had always done. The garden and the art display and the environmental innovations hadn't come easy: he had grafted for them, just as he had done on the railway for the whole of his life.

Angie crumpled when she heard the news. That was what it was like. This strong woman, normally so bustling and busy, never fazed by anything, sank in on herself. So much so, she couldn't do her shift. Like Billy, she couldn't continue anymore. Not this time.

But, of course, in the end she had to carry on – without him. Maybe not that day, but in the days and weeks to follow, Angie and the rest of the team had to continue: making the announcements, checking the tickets, helping the customers, and much more. Their grief was bearable at home, but they found that as soon as they got past the ticket barriers, everything reminded them of Billy. His name was still on the rotas, his photo was still on the wall, his pigeon hole was still stuffed full of the memos he would never now read. And perhaps the biggest reminder of all was Felix.

She didn't understand what had happened to him. No longer did the silver people carrier swing into the car park for her to sit upon when Billy's shift came to an end. No matter how many times she weaved her way through the garden, Billy never once appeared in his overalls to dig amongst the soil, bending down to scratch behind her ears with a rough, weathered hand. There was no lap to sit on or ankles to follow around. There wasn't even much that smelled of him because, this being a workplace, personal items were confined to drawers and lockers, and even a clever cat like Felix couldn't unlock metal doors.

It wasn't a nice time for anyone at the station, but it was Angie who took Billy's loss hardest of all. She couldn't help the depth of her grief, which was unexpected and unprepared for: the hot tears that pricked suddenly at her eyes, the way her voice might abruptly start to wobble. Yet, as a team leader, her colleagues looked to her for answers – and she had to give them. Regardless of what had happened, Angie's job was to run things; that was what she was employed to do. When she left her office, she had to be ready with the solution to any problem thrown at her.

But inside her office . . . That was where she could let it out, if she needed to – and she did need to; she was only human, and sometimes emotions need to be shared. Yet being the boss, there was no colleague she could share these feelings with . . . No colleague but one.

'The grumpy old bugger's gone, Felix,' she told the cat. 'What are we going to do now?'

If she needed to, she could turn her chair towards the wall, to face away from the door with its glass window, so that nobody could see – except Felix. Felix was always there, and always listened, and always seemed to understand. Angie used to say to her what she was feeling, and Felix would look at her with so much compassion in those big green eyes of hers, and she would hop up onto Angie's lap, too, so that Angie could stroke her: long, loving, reassuring strokes that were as much for Angie's benefit as the cat's. Somehow, after a cuddle and a chat with Felix, Angie found she could pull herself together again. She could take a deep breath and go out once more onto the platforms, back on autopilot, back on remote, with a cheery smile and a can-do attitude, super-powered by a bit of hidden strength given to her by the station cat.

As for that station cat, she had to learn to live without Billy. But he had left her a legacy that became a favourite haunt. Every day, she would wander over to Billy's garden. If it was a happy day, she might meander through the catmint. If she was feeling playful, she might use the plants as camouflage for hunting pesky pigeons. But she had some days, too, when she wanted to be quiet, and then she would simply sit in the long grass, thinking her cat thoughts and watching the world go by. And if anyone dared approach her at that time when she really *wasn't* in the mood, she would fix them with a look that said, 'Go away!'

And only the foolish would ignore the glowering glare of the station's own Mrs Grumpy.

Billy's passing had a massive impact on the team of Huddersfield station – and beyond. When Gareth Hope learned of the news, he felt a real sense of loss. After all, Billy had a lot to answer for in Gareth's own life. Without Billy's fatherly intervention in his career, Gareth knew all too well that there was a very strong chance he'd still have been sitting at Huddersfield station at that very minute – with a cat upon his knee.

Yet he found that Billy hadn't entirely left him, for his words of wisdom still rattled around in his head from time to time: advice to last a lifetime. Billy would never be forgotten.

And Angie wanted to make certain of it. As 2015 drew on, she and the rest of the team decided that they wanted to commemorate Billy's incredible contribution to the station. There was no way they could allow somebody like Billy to pass on without marking it in some permanent, respectful way.

Whatever memorial they decided on, Angie was adamant that it had to be situated by Billy's garden, because that had been such a passion of his when he was alive. When she thought of him, she pictured him over there in his overalls, grumpily digging up dirt. The team elected to erect a memorial bench – and it was paid for by the company, who were more than happy to honour this most special employee.

The bench was due to arrive that summer. But Angie didn't want the bench to be delivered and be used right away. It was Billy's bench, in Billy's garden, and she wanted to do something significant to mark its arrival at the station where Billy had performed his life's work. She started to put a plan into action . . .

When the bench finally came, they found it had been damaged in transit. Maintenance man Dave Chin was called out to redo all the joints, which had been twisted. But he said it was a pleasure doing it. If they hadn't been done, and done properly, Billy would have shouted at them; that they knew. Mr Grumpy was still making his presence and his wishes felt, having been such an unforgettable character in life.

Dave measured out the garden and the bench and picked out a spot for it smack bang in the middle. It would sit just in front of the soil bed, perfectly positioned so that customers could enjoy the environment he'd created and spent so much time working on. And that environment was still being cared for beautifully. Though Billy's idea to invite the group with learning difficulties to maintain the garden alongside him hadn't come to fruition before he died, the Friends of Huddersfield Station, a local volunteer group, had taken it over – ensuring that Billy's legacy would live on.

Angie's plan to mark the bench's arrival was coming together, but at the time Dave put the bench up on the station it wasn't *quite* ready, so they covered the memorial with sheet plastic and yellow-and-black warning tape – to make sure no one could use it before the grand opening.

Then Angie made a phone call to Billy's wife.

'Val?' she said. 'Can you come down to the station on Monday, please? We've got a little something we'd like you to be here for.'

When Val arrived, she found a smart, pale wooden bench set before Billy's garden, with an enormous white ribbon tied around it. She found a shiny new gold plaque commemorating her husband attached to its side. And, unusually, she also found the booking-office windows closed, for everyone wanted to participate in the opening ceremony for Billy's bench, and the team had closed the serving windows as a mark of respect.

'Oh!' Val said, in surprise. 'I didn't expect all this.'

'Well,' said Angie. 'It's just how we feel about him. This is how we feel about Billy and this is what he meant to us. We're just showing you, is all.'

At 12 o'clock on 10 August 2015, Huddersfield station came to a standstill. Over on Platform 4, the team gathered in their uniforms and their hi-vis vests for a very special occasion in honour of a very special man. Angie said a few short words, then Val was invited to cut the white ribbon and Billy's bench was formally declared 'open'. It was a lovely occasion, with smiles and shared memories and laughs, and afterwards – as the station returned to its usual, busy self and the ticket windows reopened and the trains moved on – the party transferred to the back offices, where Angie had ordered cupcakes for Val and every member of the Huddersfield team. They were covered in Smarties and chocolate chips and colourful icing, and people helped themselves throughout the working day, and even into the night shift.

Felix loved the new bench, and would frequently wind her way around its four sturdy legs, just as she had once done with Billy himself. The bench was set in a spot where it caught the late afternoon sun, and weary travellers often rested upon it.

That sun sometimes glinted off its smart gold plaque, which read:

In memory of Billy
Station Team Leader – Huddersfield
14/02/1994 – 31/03/15   21 years' service
Will be remembered fondly and missed dearly at this station

And he certainly was remembered fondly. That was why, whenever Angie did her security checks on an early shift and walked past his bench, she'd always say, in her cheery way, 'Morning, Billy!'

But it was just the wind that answered now: 'Morning, Mrs H.'

28. A Helping Hand

With a hiss of its brakes, the train from Leeds pulled into Huddersfield station on a Monday morning in September 2015. Off stepped a nervous gentleman, self-consciously smoothing down the lapels of his smart navy jacket. He cleared his throat, then squared his shoulders and went to find the station manager. It was his first day in his new job. His name was Andrew McClements, and he was the new team leader, replacing Billy.

They were very big shoes to fill. As he was introduced to the team, perhaps Andrew sensed a certain surprise in his new colleagues' expressions as they covertly checked him out, in the way of all existing employees when they meet a new co-worker for the first time. For Andrew, who came from St Helens, near Liverpool, was not only very different in personality to Billy – he was friendly and laidback, with an easy smile and an approachable manner – but he was also more than forty years younger. Andrew was just twenty-two years old.

He was younger than even the youngest team leader by over a decade. He had worked at TPE for a couple of years already, selling tickets first at Warrington and more recently at Manchester airport. In the wake of Billy's sad passing, the team leader role at Huddersfield had been advertised, and Andrew felt incredibly lucky to have secured the position. It would provide a rare opportunity to get to grips with a genuinely hands-on operational role, and would also give him a really good flavour of what the railway was all about. Yet he also knew it was going to be one hell of a challenge.

He had been hired by Will, the new station manager who had joined earlier in 2015. Will was a sharp dresser – he always donned a smart suit – with close-cropped dark hair. He showed Andrew about the station with great energy, for he was one of those characters who was always running round effervescently – something that didn't gel too well at times with the presence of the railway cat. Will would often discover Felix sprawled in the middle of the concourse, sunbathing, just at the very moment he was darting across it. He would have to leap into the air to avoid treading on her, with a cry of, 'Come on, cat, get out of the way!' But his colleagues had also spotted him stroking her – with Felix sitting squarely on the station manager's own desk, as though she really did run the place – so it was clear that he was as susceptible to her many charms as everybody else.

Andrew at least didn't have the anxiety of meeting the Boss for the very first time that day. TPE ran its team training at Huddersfield station – there were bespoke training rooms located in the upstairs part of the staff-only area – so Andrew had encountered Felix once before, when he'd been attending a course there.

'Have you seen the cat?' the trainer had asked him.

'No, what cat?' he'd responded, surprised. Then he'd gone downstairs and found Felix asleep on top of the photocopier. She'd opened one green eye, a bit grumpy at having her catnap disturbed, but she'd obliged when he'd given her a bit of a pet and a cuddle, and then the pair had gone their separate ways.

By the time he'd landed the team leader job, though, Andrew knew a little bit more about her reputation. During her years at Huddersfield, Felix's fame had slowly been spreading. By now, everyone locally knew of her, and everyone within TPE did too. There were times at the station these days when a small crowd of people would form around her when she was spotted on duty, all wanting to pet her and give her treats. Her Majesty, on the whole, received them as any monarch might a group of eager courtiers.

But although he knew all about Felix's fame, she wasn't at the forefront of Andrew's mind when he started working at Huddersfield – to what would have been her great displeasure, had she known. He had bigger concerns than the station cat: he had an awful lot to learn.

There was the operational side of things: the nightly unit diagrams and shunt movements to manage. There was the night-shift work itself; Andrew had never worked nights before, and didn't know how he would find it. There was the finance: the team leaders had to balance thousands of pounds a night in cash and perform a lot of complex accounting. There was the line managing and the security checking . . . and so much more! He felt as if his head was going to explode as he tried to get to grips with it all. Moreover, as Angie Hunte had found before him, being a team leader meant you were dealing with it all on your own, for he didn't want to show any weakness to his team or to confess that he was struggling. He knew that he was young to be in this role and he felt some pressure to prove himself.

The other team leaders gave him invaluable advice during his induction period, and he learned as much as he could from them all. Time and again he realised just what big boots he had to fill, following in the footsteps of Billy. He felt quite apprehensive as he cleared out the old-timer's drawer and, eventually, commandeered his pigeon hole. By that time, at least, there was no longer a sadness in the air any time that Billy was mentioned. People were at the stage where they were openly and easily talking about him and recalling funny stories of the times they had once shared: 'Do you remember when Billy . . . '

Much as he might have wished he could, Andrew couldn't stay in training forever. The night finally came when he was left to run the station on his own.

He slid the big metal bolt across the front doors and walked through the silent station on his way back to the office. Felix accompanied him, and he absent-mindedly held the door open for her as the duo went into the office, his brain already ticking over everything he had to do in these long, quiet hours before sunrise. He decided he would start with the finance.

It wasn't long before he became thoroughly stressed out. The computer software wasn't doing what he wanted it to and the piles of cash before him just didn't balance. He didn't want to get it wrong and let everyone down – but it was like one of those nightmares where you realise your very worst dreams are coming true.

'Come on, come on,' he said aloud to himself. 'I just want to get through this.'

He ran his hands worriedly through his short dark hair and sighed deeply. Anxiety was building inside him, growing from a small seed in his stomach and sprouting all the way up to his shoulders, which felt tense and tight. *Think, think!* he told himself.

Felix was lying next to him on the desk. She gave a sleepy little yawn and stretched out, making herself comfortable. The slight movement caught Andrew's eye and he stared at her for a little bit as she dozed on the desk companionably. Her presence made him realise: *you are not alone.*

He would have felt like that, otherwise. He would have felt that no one was around to help him, and that he had this insurmountable mountain to climb all by himself. But a problem shared is a problem halved, and the simple fact of Felix being in the office with him made his troubles seem suddenly lighter and more manageable. She had a soothing presence, a calming, peaceful and companionable spirit, and he found himself taking deeper breaths, in rhythm with the lazy flicking of her tail. Suddenly, the mountain didn't seem quite so tough to climb after all.

As Andrew settled into the job, he found that Felix was always on hand whenever he needed support. He'd be getting worked up about the shunt movements – because if he got *that* wrong, it would result in massive, very public delays and an awful lot of money wasted – but Felix would usually be out and about on the platforms at that time, hunting down the fawn-coloured moths that were attracted by the station's bright lights. Seeing her pounce determinedly on her prey would fill him with determination too, and he'd turn back to the complicated diagram with a new sense of purpose. As he wrote reports, she'd lie on his lap, and he'd find himself typing with one hand and stroking her with the other. *Why is it taking me so long to write this?* he'd wonder.

In more ways than one, Felix was the answer.

Of course, the railway cat wasn't doing this entirely out of the goodness of her heart. It was a *quid pro quo*. Felix was a working cat – and she wanted paying for services rendered.

Andrew was cashing up one night in the office when he noticed Felix looking up at him from the floor and mewing.

'Just give me a few minutes, Felix,' he said, trying to keep track of the complex calculations in his head.

He went back to his money-counting. Gradually, Felix got closer and closer to him. She inched along the ground. She leapt lightly up onto the desk. She stood there for a little bit, miaowing, but when Andrew didn't respond she edged forwards once again . . . and again . . . and again, as though she was playing her own version of Grandmother's Footsteps. It finally got to the point where Andrew realised he couldn't see anything but Felix's fluffy face directly in front of his, completely obscuring his vision.

'All right, cat!' he said, giving in at last to her demands for attention. He scribbled down the figures he'd added up so far and gave her a bit of love.

'Right, then, that's enough for now,' he said, a few minutes later. 'I'll feed you just as soon as I've finished cashing up, OK?'

He picked up Felix and moved her to one side, then carried on with the accounting.

Well, Felix wasn't going to be so easily diverted as that. Patience wasn't part of her repertoire. The white-tipped paws came out. *Tap, tap, tap, tap, tap* . . . On his arm, on his shoulder, on his chest. Eventually, she sat straight up on her hind legs and put both front paws firmly on him, leaning her whole body against his. Her oh-so-persuasive pats seemed to be saying, 'I know it's a bit early for my supper and I know you're in the middle of something important, but I am really rather peckish!'

And when even *that* didn't work – 'I just need one more minute, Felix,' Andrew said pleadingly. 'Look: I'm on the last pile!' – she bent her head to his hand and gave it a gentle little nibble. Not with any aggression, and not to hurt him, but just to assert herself. 'Come on, laddie,' that nibble said. 'Enough messing about. I'm the Boss, and when I tell you I want something doing, you do it. Understood?'

'OK, OK!' Andrew said, hands in the air, surrendering. He left the money on the desk and stood up.

The moment Felix saw him move, she sprinted as fast as she could to the filing cabinet. Once, its uppermost drawer had held official documents and top secrets – now, it was the cat-food drawer. It belonged to Queen Felix, and the cat knew it well. In excitement, she leapt up on top of the cabinet and stared pointedly at her drawer until Andrew opened it.

Felix purred in approval: 'That's more like it.' Stiff as a board, ears to attention, she watched as he pulled out a pouch of 'Felix', then shadowed him into the kitchen. Only once he'd set her bowl down for her would she give him any peace. It was quite an example for the young team leader of how tenacity, commitment and determination could get results.

Yet it wasn't all work and no play. As Andrew and Felix bonded, he got to know her personality well and came to appreciate how playful she was. A favourite game during the night shift was 'hide and seek', especially amid the tourist-information leaflets in the lobby. The wooden holder that displayed them read 'Welcome to Yorkshire', but to Felix's mind it was more like 'Welcome to the Best Cat Playground *Ever*'. She would duck and dive behind the leaflets – and just when Andrew thought he'd caught her, she'd dart out and start a running race with him. He noticed, though, that as she legged it onto Platform 1 and he followed in her wake, as soon as she hit the yellow line she turned left and ran along it, never once crossing it. It was always safety first for the station cat.

Felix liked a bit of rough and tumble, too, playing hunting games and rugby with her soft mouse toys and the moths. Rugby league had been established not fifty paces from the station, in 1895 at the George Hotel in the square, and Felix seemed determined to honour that heritage in the way she enthusiastically rugby-tackled the brown bear that Andrew kicked for her and threw herself into all their games.

Everything at the station could be made into a game in Felix's mind – even if she didn't always intend it to be that way. She had a somewhat embarrassing episode shortly after Andrew started at the station that she *really* had to style out as intentional fun. The station was getting a new computer installed, and Felix was delighted to discover that – when the computer was still inside it – the brown cardboard box it came in made for a splendidly solid, comfortable location for a catnap. The box had arrived at the start of the week but the computer wasn't being installed till later on, so for the next five days or so Felix got into a regular routine of jumping onto the box and lazing about on top. She was always doing that with various items around the office; another favourite spot for a sleep became the (switched-off) paper shredder, on which she could only just fit; her tail and even her back legs would dangle down, but she professed to be comfortable.

By the end of the week, Felix knew all about that cardboard box – or so she thought. Safe as houses, she believed. But, unbeknown to her, Lisa Gannon, the IT manager, came in one day to set up the new equipment and took the computer out of its packaging – leaving the now-empty box in its usual place.

Lisa was working away when Felix came wandering into her workspace, strutting about with her customary confidence and poise. Up she leapt onto the supposedly sturdy cardboard surface . . . and fell straight through the open top into the empty box below.

Well, that was a surprise!

Felix quirkily stuck her head out of the top of the box, as though checking if anyone had noticed. Lisa was giggling away at her, so Felix brushed it off with a ruffled shake of her fluffy body. In fact, once she'd recovered her equilibrium and her dignity, she found the empty box made for a rather entertaining setting: she spent at least five minutes sitting happily in it, before jumping out and trotting off to find another adventure.

There was always one about at a station like Huddersfield. As the autumn nights grew colder, however, Andrew realised that some of Felix's adventures weren't merely for fun. A lot of the time, they were much more important than that.

One serious issue that railway stations regularly have to deal with is runaway children. Shockingly, 100,000 children in the UK run away from home every year – and many of them, having nowhere else to go in the cold, dark nights, are drawn towards railway stations where there will be light, and maybe food and company, and at least a roof over their heads when the rain is driving down outside. Even in the relatively short time that Andrew had worked at Huddersfield, it was plain it was an issue; the team encountered a runaway child in the station sometimes as often as once a month. They had a duty of care to them, of course, so they would step in and call the authorities, so that the children could be looked after and not slip through the net.

It was a particularly bitter Yorkshire night towards the end of November 2015 when Andrew clocked on for the night shift. Christmas was within touching distance and you knew it from the weather alone. Andrew blew on his hands as he patrolled the platform throughout the early hours of his shift, feeling very glad for the warmth of his thick winter coat.

He cast his eyes up and down the platforms. Used to the patterns of the trains, the team were always conscious of someone who seemed to have been around on the station for rather too long. Andrew's gaze settled on a young lad further along Platform 1, who had caught his eye earlier too. He'd been on the station for a long time now, so Andrew started walking towards him, wanting to see if he needed any help.

As he approached, he could see that the boy was shivering. He was wearing scruffy trackie bottoms and a T-shirt with a thin black coat over the top. Given the freezing temperature, Andrew would have expected him to be wearing a scarf, gloves and a hat, but there was nothing like that on the lad. His hands looked red raw from the cold.

'Are you all right there?' he asked him.

The boy shot him an anxious look and nodded, saying nothing. He was perhaps eleven or twelve years old.

'Where are you travelling to, then?' Andrew enquired. You did sometimes get kids travelling by themselves on the station, and he didn't want to jump to conclusions. But alarm bells were ringing for him – it wasn't far off 11 p.m. and the lad had been there too long. He had to find out more. 'Have you got a ticket?'

The boy shook his head. He seemed very shy.

'Are your parents meeting you here or at your destination?' Andrew went on delicately.

The boy looked as though he'd been thrown a lifeline. 'My mum's coming to get me,' he said hurriedly, perhaps thinking that his answer would buy him a little more time in the shelter of the station.

He had a strong southern accent and Andrew could tell instantly that he wasn't a local. Though he had a lovely manner about him and his reply seemed convincing, it was evident nonetheless that he was extremely vulnerable.

'OK, that's fine,' Andrew said slowly, not wanting to scare the boy off – he was safer by far here at the station than out on the streets and he didn't want the child to panic and run. 'Do you want to wait in the waiting room? Can I get you a drink?'

The boy nodded again, and Andrew took him into the waiting room and fetched him a hot drink from the back office. The lad clasped his hands around the warm cup eagerly, blowing on the steaming brew. As he drank his drink, Andrew tried to keep chatting with him in order to find out more about his background, asking him where he'd travelled from and similar queries. None of the boy's answers added up.

'My mum's coming to get me,' he kept saying, over and over, but it plainly wasn't true.

In the end, the boy realised that Andrew wasn't fooled and started opening up to him, explaining what had gone on. He'd recently been moved to a care home up north and had run away from it on impulse, without any kind of itinerary or plan. He obviously had a fair few issues and Andrew knew he'd have to call the police. Not wanting to alarm the boy, he told him he'd be right back and quietly slipped away to the office where he could make the call. He informed them of the situation, and they told him they would come and collect the boy – but they couldn't be there for half an hour or more. It was up to Andrew to try to keep him safe on the station.

To begin with, it wasn't too hard. The boy was a rail enthusiast, and when a freight train began to rumble by languorously, he asked if they could go out onto the platform and watch it pass. Andrew went with him, a bit concerned that the suggestion was just an excuse for the boy to leg it – but it wasn't. The train's lights lit up the child's face and for the first time since Andrew had met him he looked happy, watching the freight train pass.

But after its red taillights had disappeared into the darkness, the young lad and Andrew were left alone in the cold night, with the clock ticking by so slowly. The boy didn't know the police had been called, and Andrew wanted to keep him there until they showed up. Half an hour wasn't long at all in the grand scheme of things, but as each second ticked sluggishly by on the orange-digit display boards above their heads, it suddenly seemed like an eternity.

Andrew was just starting to panic when a brainwave hit him: *Felix*. If anyone could keep the boy safe, it was her. She was just having a wander about, so Andrew picked her up and placed her on the bench next to the boy.

'Have you met Felix?' he asked him brightly. 'She lives here on the station.'

The lad, who'd been staring glumly at the ground, looked up in surprise to find a black-and-white cat sitting next to him. Felix's fame hadn't spread down south and the boy didn't know that the station had its own cat. He stared in some astonishment at her, uncertain what to do next.

Felix sat very still on the bench, as though assessing the situation. Her tail, hanging off the back of the seat, flicked to the right, to the left, as she considered the child before her. Then, very slowly, as though conscious of his vulnerability, she stood up and edged towards him.

'Why don't you give her a treat?' Andrew asked the lad. He handed him some Dreamies. Felix sat down again at once, knowing the drill.

'Would you like one?' the child asked her hesitantly.

In response, she flickered and flashed her green eyes at him, almost as if she was rolling them and saying in affectionate amusement, 'Stupid question, my lad.'

A bit timidly, the boy extended an upturned hand towards her, the treat nestled in the middle of it. Felix very gently bent her head to his hand and took the treat from his palm with her rough pink tongue. She licked her lips afterwards, as though to say politely, 'Thank you so very much indeed.'

'Another?' the boy asked, warming up, taking pleasure in her pleasure.

Felix didn't need asking twice.

The two of them sat together on the bench, and Felix entertained that child as only she knew how. After the treats had been eaten, she happily let him pet and stroke her, sitting calmly by his side and never once showing the slightest grumpiness. In truth, she was simply doing her job as part of the customer-facing team of Huddersfield station – and doing it brilliantly. The boy was still stroking her when, thirty minutes later, Andrew saw two uniformed officers walk out onto the platform.

He went to meet them and together they cautiously approached the runaway. Now calm, he didn't flee – or lie. The police took a statement from both him and Andrew, then told the child that it was time for them to take him back to the care home.

The boy stood up bravely. Before leaving, he turned back to face the railway cat.

'See you, Felix,' he said, with a slight smile twitching at the edges of his lips. 'Goodbye.'

29. Felix the Facebooker

'Do you reckon it's Angie Hunte?' asked the gateline worker at Huddersfield station. 'Could she be the one who's set up this Facebook page for Felix?'

Chris Bamford, his colleague, shook his head. 'I don't reckon so,' he replied.

'Andrew McClements?'

'Nah.'

'What about Geoff?!'

'Are you having a laugh?'

Relations between the station cat and the crotchety team leader were famously still at an impasse.

'You know who my money's on?' said Chris. 'I reckon it's Martin.'

All eyes turned to the unassuming announcer, who was quietly making his way, head down, to the tiny announcer's office where he spent so much of his time during his shift. Ever since he had befriended Felix with that mouse-on-a-string toy when she first arrived at the station – her very first toy – he and Felix had remained close. Martin even kept a little bag of cat treats for her in his desk drawer.

'He's got the opportunity, hasn't he?' reasoned Chris. 'He's always in the back office. He could be on Facebook all the time and we'd never know.'

The gateline team assessed this possibility with the keen consideration of super sleuths. Ever since Chris had discovered that there was a Facebook page for 'Felix, the Huddersfield station cat' – it had come up on his recommended pages and he'd liked it instantly – he and his colleagues had been playing this guessing game, trying to work out who it was that had set it up. The page had been running since July 2015 and it was now December; it had a couple of hundred likes. As more and more of the team had discovered it through their personal Facebook accounts, tongues had started wagging on the concourse about who was actually running it. No one had the faintest clue – but the team were all convinced that it had to be a member of the team. Every day, Chris and his colleagues on the gateline tried to figure out who was maintaining the page and keeping it a secret. It was almost like *Cluedo*: 'I think it was Andy Croughan in the team leaders' office using a smartphone.'

The amount of thought they applied to it would have put CID to shame: psychological profiling, alibis, opportunity and more all came into play. When it came to Martin, the announcer's notorious quietness at work certainly made him enigmatic enough to be a prime candidate.

'It's got to be him!' exclaimed Chris.

But Martin was coming up for retirement in January 2016, and the others thought it highly unlikely that he'd be at the cutting edge of social media, creating a Facebook page for his feline friend, no matter how cosy the two of them might get in the announcer's office during Martin's long shifts. No: they had to think again.

As they investigated the page updates further, they stumbled upon a crucial piece of evidence: every single picture on the Facebook page appeared to have been taken around 6.30 a.m. Whoever was running the page *had* to be someone who was always on the platform at that time.

The conclusion was clear: it wasn't a colleague, it was a *commuter*.

Suddenly, every bleary-eyed customer who passed through

the gates was a suspect. With the commuters having season tickets, Chris and his colleagues barely saw each one for longer than ten seconds as the steady stream of early-morning customers flowed through the doors. It was hardly long enough to make an assessment. Most of them walked slowly, somewhat miserably: not yet woken up properly and none too pleased to be there, on their way to work. Others darted through the gates and ran at full tilt towards a train scheduled to depart. They clutched takeaway coffee cups and newspapers, and headphone cables trailed from their ears as they tried to tune out the reality of another working day. There were people in suits, overalls, uniforms and chemists' smocks; the cyclists arrived like new breeds of human, with orange Lycra skin and angular helmets reshaping their heads. It could be any one of them: it was like looking for a needle in a haystack.

Could it be the middle-aged woman in the windbreaker who always had a kind word for Felix? Or might it be the hipster who wore media glasses and moleskin shoes and brought the cat treats in a Tupperware box? There was a man with a full beard and long, greying hair who had potential; or what about the redhead with the art portfolio and the sketching pad? The options were literally endless; the mystery seemingly unsolvable.

They never did guess. In the end, a few members of the team messaged the page and offered to help support it by sending through some behind-the-scenes pictures of the station cat hard at work in the back offices, and a channel of communication was opened with the mystery Felix fan.

'Here,' Chris said to whoever it was. 'Make sure you introduce yourself next time you come through. We'll have a drink or something, get to know each other.'

And that was exactly what happened. It was an ordinary

morning, the day the mystery commuter finally walked up and introduced himself. Chris was busy assisting customers when he felt a polite tap on his shoulder at 6.30 a.m. He turned around to see a tall, bespectacled gentleman dressed in a dark-grey suit and carrying a black laptop bag.

'Hello,' he said, meekly. 'I'm Mark Allan. I run Felix's Facebook page.'

The mystery was solved.

Mark had been commuting from Huddersfield since the summer of 2014. He'd lived in Huddersfield all his life, nearly fifty-five years now, but he'd always driven to work before, being based all over West Yorkshire: Wakefield, Bradford, Leeds . . . But when he'd got a new job in an office in Manchester, he'd decided to get the train. Every day now, he caught the 6.40 a.m. service from Platform 1.

He hadn't noticed Felix at first. Many commuters didn't, being too engrossed in their smartphones or their *Metro*s to spot the railway cat. Mark himself was usually plugged into his headphones, dressed in his dark-grey suit, which, he thought, was the exact same shade as the skies above Huddersfield in winter.

It could be grim, commuting through the Yorkshire winter – but it felt a little like spring had come early at the start of 2015, when Mark had been introduced by the station team to a special little someone.

He'd been walking down the platform that morning, thinking it was just another day, when he'd seen one of the customer-service guys in a yellow hi-vis vest holding and stroking a cat. A cat? Mark did a double take. This must be the station cat. He was famous in Huddersfield (Mark thought she was a boy), but Mark had never seen him.

'Who's this, then?' he asked the attendant in a friendly

fashion, pulling the headphones out of his ears and engaging in conversation for once.

'This is Felix,' announced Glenn, introducing the cat.

'Hello there, Felix!' said Mark cheerily. He reached out a hand and gave Felix a nice stroke. She gazed at him thoughtfully from the safety of Glenn's arms. 'My, he's a grand-looking cat, isn't he? Very handsome.'

'Actually, she's a girl . . . '

And then the whole story of Felix the station cat was told to him: how she had come to be employed there, and how the team had nicknamed her 'the pest controller'. In reality, though Felix did still catch the odd mouse, leaving her 'presents' for Angie to find, the name was more of a joke than a job description. They didn't tell Felix that, of course.

Mark wasn't much of a cat lover, in all honesty. He'd never had cats himself and, frankly, everything he'd seen of cats' behaviour in his friends' houses made him think they were a bit of a nuisance. One moggy had completely shredded a mate's sofa just a month after they'd got it; *crikey*, he'd thought at the time, *my wife would go absolutely up the wall if that happened to us. It's bad enough having kids, but a cat? No, thanks.*

Nonetheless, there was something about the railway cat that he found rather endearing. The feeling wasn't necessarily mutual – Felix initially viewed him with suspicion, as she did most people she didn't know, but that was only because her very real experiences with 'stranger danger' had made her naturally cautious.

As the months passed and winter at last turned into spring, it became Mark's habit to walk down to the bike racks and the Head of Steam while he waited for his train; this was also Felix's favourite spot. The regular sight of the beautiful fluffy cat on a typically grey Yorkshire day – when it was so misty and cloudy you could see only a silhouette of the distant hills and none of the detail – cheered him greatly. So much so that one day he found himself snapping a couple of pictures of her on his smartphone.

Felix, as had become her way over the years, posed for them with the good-natured acceptance of a celebrity who is constantly being stopped and asked to be part of a selfie. She positioned her head handsomely and waited patiently for the shutter to close. As Mark travelled on the train to Manchester that morning, he casually flicked through the snaps he'd taken. She really was a fine-looking cat: that fluffy fur, those enigmatic green eyes, the striking white bib. He uploaded the images to his personal Facebook page – to say, simply, 'I see this cat at Huddersfield station' – and thought nothing more of it. But when he next logged in, he was astonished to see that the pictures had got *loads* of likes; more than he'd had before on any other photo.

Crikey, he'd thought, *there's something going on here.*

He'd imagined there must already be a Facebook page for Felix herself – she had been at the station for four years, after all, and within Huddersfield she was a bit of a superstar – yet when he'd searched for one in the early summer of 2015 nothing had come up. That surprised him. Other railway cats had blogs – Quaker, the Kirkby Stephen East moggy, had one called 'The Secret Life of a Station Cat' – and they were undeniably popular. In June 2015, meanwhile, there was enormous interest when Tama, the famous Japanese feline stationmaster, sadly passed away at the age of sixteen after years of dedicated service; she was so beloved that 3,000 people attended her funeral. With that level of interest in station cats it seemed only right that Felix should be on Facebook. Consequently, when Mark discovered she didn't yet have her own page, he decided to create one

It seemed a good idea in more ways than one, and for

Mark it personally meant a great deal. Mark's job was very finance-based and serious, and he thought that creating a Felix Facebook page could be a real laugh. He thought that it might provide him with a creative outlet, mild-mannered businessman that he was. Rather than spending those ten minutes in the morning while he waited for his train looking at his phone or reading the newspaper, he could do something with and for Felix instead. Something *fun*. Something colourful to brighten up the dark-grey shades of his regular life. He pulled his laptop towards him and began building the page.

The first priority was to decide what to call it. Should it be 'Felix, the Huddersfield cat' or just 'The Huddersfield train cat' or even 'The TransPennine Express cat'? In the end, he went with simplicity: 'Felix, the Huddersfield station cat'. It took about half an hour to set up the page, then he added the handful of photos he'd already taken . . . and that was it. Job done. So it was that on 2 July 2015, Felix became a Facebooker.

Mark didn't like to break the news to Felix, but she wasn't all that popular. Mark shared the page with his own Facebook friends and she got about fifty likes; then one hundred, as those friends shared it with their friends. But it was small-scale stuff.

That didn't matter one bit to Mark. As the summer of 2015 wore on, he found he fell in love with running the Facebook page for Felix. It gave a bit of a kick to his morning to come onto the platform and find out if she was there – and, if she was, to stage an impromptu photo shoot and have a bit of a play with her. He enjoyed coming up with ideas for what her posts might be and the more he got to know her, the easier it became to think of what she might 'say' if she was running the page herself. By September, being Felix's

Facebook manager had become a bit of a minor obsession. It had added so much to his life that Mark wanted to give something back to the cat at the centre of it all – so he started bringing in treats for her on his morning commute.

Mark didn't know that Felix favoured Dreamies. He just bought an 80p bag of a supermarket's own-brand treats – but Felix, as it turned out, wasn't fussy when it came to the calibre of her canapés.

The first morning he brought them in he greeted her with a scratch of the head, then got the treat bag out of his backpack. Immediately, Felix was up on her feet, gazing at him lovingly as though he was the most fascinating creature she had ever come across. She followed him eagerly to the metal bench where he normally sat and gobbled up the treats one by one; he gave her just a handful. They had a really nice time together before the 6.40 arrived and Mark ran to catch it.

The following day, the same thing happened: a head scratch, followed by a handful of treats on the bench. It wasn't long before Felix grasped that this was a fellow she really wanted to be with every morning. Mark would never forget the day he entered the station and started walking down the platform towards the Head of Steam, only to find Felix sitting waiting for him on their bench. She turned her head towards him as he approached. 'Welcome,' the flash of her green eyes seemed to say. 'Yes, you are blessed: *I* have deigned to wait for *you*.' She greeted him affectionately when he sat down and rubbed behind her pointed black ears. From that moment, a new routine was forged.

Every morning, the cat and the commuter rendezvoused at 6.30 a.m. by the Head of Steam. The team no longer wondered where the cat was at that time – for she was always with Mark. Sometimes she'd eat the treats from his hand; at other times he'd flick one off the seat of the bench with his finger to turn it into a game. Felix, delighted, would bound off the bench and be after it at once, enjoying the drama of the hunt. He got to know her well and learned how street-wise she was; not only about crossing the tracks, but also at staying out of the way if a delivery arrived for the pub or if a catering trolley was being noisily loaded onto a train. Felix pretty much waited for him every day without fail, but if for some reason she was kept away, he would leave the treats for her on the windowsill above the bike racks.

When he came back in the evening, those treats were always gone.

Sometimes, Felix would run to meet him when she saw him striding along the platform towards her. The pair would then walk side by side back to their bench: the best of friends. Despite his previous disinclination towards felines, Mark found himself softening. He hadn't especially liked cats before, it was true – but then he'd never met a cat like Felix.

As the pair grew closer, Mark staged more and more ambi-tious photo calls. One favourite was when he pulled his laptop out of its bag on the platform and opened it up for Felix to 'use'. With a treat placed upon the keyboard, she was more than happy to pose with the computer. Mark added an amusing caption to the image: 'Excuse me, can you press "ctrl, alt, delete" for me?'

Perhaps the funniest time, though, was when he brought a loaf of Warburtons in with him and asked Felix to pose next to it. The other commuters gave him strange looks as he crouched on the platform with a packet of bread and a cat – he looked like an absolute *lunatic* – but it was all in honour of his art. The caption read, with feeling: 'Felix: the best thing since sliced bread.'

Come 31 October, he was having great fun with apps and posted an image of Felix where she was surrounded by cartoon ghosts in celebration of Halloween. He was getting a brilliant response to his posts, and by the time the team started joining in too, just before Christmas (Glenn and his girlfriend Teresa became heavily involved), the page was up to nearly 500 likes. Mark couldn't believe it: this was beyond his wildest dreams! Never had he thought the page would become so popular.

Felix, had you asked her, would never have had any doubt. Day after day she showed her character and spirit. Andy Croughan was astonished one night shift when she escorted him to the takeaway shop: she sat outside and waited for him to order, before walking companionably back with him to the station, as though they were a couple who had just nipped out for fish and chips. Michael Ryan got a shock when a passer-by tapped him on his arm as he was walking through Huddersfield town centre one afternoon and said, 'Excuse me, is that your cat?' He looked round in surprise to find Felix walking neatly behind him; she'd been following him for five minutes ever since he'd left work, looking for all the world like a feline soldier on a passing-out parade. She was so far from home that Michael turned right around and walked all the way back again, Felix following meekly till she was home.

Sometimes, she playfully harked back to the days of her kittenhood. Andrew McClements was standing chatting with Dale, one of the customer-service team, one day when he saw a sudden look of surprise – and pain – cross his colleague's face. Felix had decided to climb up his back, as she used to do with Gareth Hope when she was a tiny kitten.

But she wasn't a tiny kitten now – and Felix's claws were

not forgiving once the whole adult weight of the cat was channelled through them. Despite Dale's shock and involuntary wiggle, she valiantly climbed right the way up to his shoulder and even placed her paws upon his balding head. But it was all a bit wobbly and she didn't stay up there very long before she executed a dramatic gymnastics-style dismount.

Another time she tried that trick, however, she found a much more willing accomplice. Adam Carter, a young blond man who worked in customer service, was doing a night shift one early morning in the winter of 2015 when it happened. He and Felix had just opened up the main doors so that customers could gain access for one of the night services. The *Metro* had already been delivered so Adam grabbed a copy and started reading it.

Felix clambered all over him while he did so. She sat on his shoulder for a while, sticking her nose into the news, as though she was a curious fellow commuter straining to see the article in his paper. Then she seemed to think, *I wonder*... Hesitantly, she made the final ascent onto Adam's head. This time, she managed to get her balance just right and became terribly comfy up there, perched on Adam's hair like a live version of a Russian *shapka* hat. She was too big to get her tail up there too, so this hung rather obviously all the way down the side of Adam's face. It would occasionally tickle his nose as Felix wagged it in pleasure at having successfully returned to one of her all-time favourite perches. At four and a half years old, she was very heavy, but it was a pleasant weight and Adam didn't mind it; he thought it was quite funny.

The cat and the customer-service assistant were discovered sitting like that in the ghost-town lobby when some customers came onto the concourse.

'Morning!' Adam said to them cheerily, speaking from a face full of cat tail.

The customers looked over at them. There was a bit of a pause, and then they seemed to think, *Forget it*... 'Morning,' they merely said gruffly in response. Another eight customers came through the gates, and not one of them blinked an eye.

After all, it was only the station cat – and everyone knew Huddersfield had one of those.

To Queen Felix's dismay, though her fame had grown, people were perhaps becoming a little bit *used* to her. In December 2015, Felix was *not* the star of the TPE Christmas card from headquarters. They chose a child's drawing instead; can you imagine?

Angie was spitting feathers, and if Felix had ever managed to catch any of those pesky pigeons she would have been too. When Angie opened the envelope that held the Christmas card and pulled it out, Felix was sitting alongside her at her desk. As they saw what was on it – and that it wasn't Felix – the two girls looked at each other levelly in mutual disapprobation.

'Yeah, I understand, Felix,' Angie said in agreement, easily reading the disapproval in the cat's haughty emerald eyes. 'It should be *you*, Felix. Don't worry – I'll have words.'

Angie talked to *everybody* about the shocking fact that Felix wasn't on the card – she even complained to one of the managers. 'Where's our Felix? We can't have a Christmas card without our Felix!' she cried passionately.

But, of course, nothing was done. The railway cat was old hat. Just as Billy had once warned Gareth, she'd been in the same job too long. 'You've got to move on,' Billy had told the young announcer in his gruff old voice. 'If you don't move every three or four years, people will think you've given up, and they'll never think of offering you another job.'

The pest controller had been at Huddersfield for nearly five years now. Was it too late for Felix to land a promotion? Maybe the station cat wasn't destined for greatness after all . . .

30. One Night in January

Andrew McClements tore at the Amazon packaging surrounding his parcel, and sniggered a little bit when he saw what was inside. But, when he heard the door open behind him, he quickly shoved the package into his desk drawer: *nothing to see here.*

It was one of the other team leaders, Geoff.

'I'm heading off now,' he said. 'You'll be all right?'

'I'll be fine,' replied Andrew confidently. It was 29 January 2016 and by now he was an old hand at running the night shift on his own – if not quite an old-timer. 'Have you seen Felix, by the way?' he asked, keeping his voice light, as though he wasn't all that interested.

'Not since I sent her packing earlier,' Geoff replied curtly. 'But you know what that cat is like: she'll be back.' He looked rather gloomy at the idea. 'Night, then.'

'Night, Geoff.'

Andrew waited until he was gone, then checked on the package in his desk drawer once again. He couldn't wait for this night shift to begin.

A few hours later, in the early hours of 30 January, Andrew once again rolled open his drawer and pulled out the brown cardboard packaging. Felix was sitting on the desk with him and she sniffed with interest at the unfamiliar smells carried on the package which had travelled through the mail.

'Guess what, Felix?' Andrew said to her brightly. 'This is for you.'

Her head jerked upwards and she fixed him with those big green eyes. 'For me?' they seemed to say.

Andrew reached a hand inside the package and pulled out a tiny, pet-sized, yellow hi-vis vest – just like those worn by the human members of the team on the platforms of Huddersfield station, but this one was especially for Felix.

The fluffy cat bent her head to the luminous fabric and examined it quizzically. It had long been apparent to the team that Felix recognised their bright jackets – now, she was getting one of her very own.

Andrew had told no one that he'd ordered it. It was a surprise for them all and he'd kept it completely secret, even after the vest had arrived, as he wasn't quite sure how Felix would react to it. She could be a diva, after all. She'd never worn any sort of clothing before and Angie Hunte had told him that, although Felix looked absolutely fabulous in her purple glittery collar and wore it quite happily once it was on, she could be a little madam when the team or the groomers tried to get it on or off her. He feared that the temperamental terror might well throw a strop when asked to model her new uniform, so Andrew wanted to introduce Felix to it privately to give her time to get used to it. He wasn't sure quite how much convincing she might need to wear it.

But Felix seemed delighted with his gift as she gave it a thorough investigation, twitching her enormously long white whiskers. The jacket lay flat upon the desk, its two hi-vis stripes catching the office light from time to time, as she sniffed at it and prodded it with a curious paw. It wasn't made specifically for cats, but pets in general; it had an adjustable Velcro strap so that dogs, cats and all sorts of creatures could wear it safely.

Ordering it had been Andrew's idea alone. As he'd settled

into Huddersfield station, over the passing months he'd come to realise just how much Felix was an essential part of the team. She was very much considered a member of the team and he knew from his own personal experiences with her what a very special contribution she made to the station. But even though she spent hours and hours of her life out on the platforms with her human colleagues – patrolling or sitting up at the customer-information desk – she wasn't properly equipped for the job. How was it fair, when she did her duty so diligently, that she didn't have her own uniform? If she truly was a member of staff – which she undoubtedly was – Andrew thought she deserved her own hi-vis vest, just like her colleagues. He had searched online and found one easily. With a click of a button, Felix's hi-vis vest was on its way.

The cat finished her sensory exploration of the jacket and sat down on her hind legs, looking pleased as punch. Her right ear twitched backwards as she heard Andrew rustling a second package.

'More?' her fluffy face seemed to say. 'For me?'

There *was* more. Much more. For the team at Huddersfield didn't only wear yellow hi-vis vests as they went about their work: they wore company-issued name tags showing their job titles. These were official TransPennine Express ID badges that came direct from head office. In Andrew's opinion, it was rather unfair that Felix had to work without one.

So, in secret, he had emailed headquarters at Bridgewater House in Manchester.

'Can we have a name badge for Felix, please?' he'd written, and waited with bated breath for their response.

Well, they'd thought he was nuts – absolutely nuts. But they agreed to make one anyway. Andrew had been delighted with it when it arrived. It was exactly like the formal badges he and Angie and the other team members wore, totally proper: a silver metal badge with a smooth white front and a safety pin on the back. Felix's name was written in clear black letters in the middle of it, while the formal Trans-Pennine Express logo was positioned artfully in the top-right corner. It looked even more splendid than Andrew had imagined.

'All right, we'll do it!' HQ had emailed him. 'What job title do you want on it?'

Now, forget 'To be or not to be?' – *that* was the question. From what Andrew had observed, Felix did way more customer-service work than actual mouse-catching – so should her badge reflect that massive contribution she made every day to the commuters and customers of Huddersfield?

But no – it didn't seem quite right to give her the same job title as everyone else.

Felix, as befitted her feline form, was ordinarily termed 'the pest controller' by colleagues – it was what she had been called by the team ever since Angie had filled in her very first disbursement form for Felix's food: *Pest controller needs nourishment* . . . It was a long-standing joke.

Yet that didn't seem quite right either. 'Pest controller' seemed a bit too ordinary for Queen Felix. The cat clearly thought she ran the station – and according to the hierarchy chart that had hung in the office for many years, she *did*. 'Pest controller' didn't recognise her many years of experience, for she now outranked in years of service many of the newer members of the team; after all, she'd been there longer than Chris Bamford and Andrew himself. She needed a job title which rewarded that service and her extensive expertise, and which also recognised her own regal sense of superiority over the station. What could it be?

As Andrew pulled the metal badge from the package and formally presented it to Felix, there were three neatly typed words written below her name.

SENIOR PEST CONTROLLER

Felix had been promoted.

Andrew felt rather too self-conscious to say 'Congratulations!' as he handed it over, but Felix looked thrilled nonetheless. She sniffed enthusiastically at the badge to begin with – though, admittedly, her eagerness soon faded once she realised it wasn't a badge-shaped treat.

Andrew took the badge back from her curious twitching whiskers and securely fastened it to the chest of the hi-vis vest.

'So, how about it then, Felix?' he asked her. 'Shall we give this a go?'

The cat inclined her head against his proffered hand. He gave her ears a good scratch to encourage her, and then picked up the station cat's new uniform.

'I'm going to put it on you, now,' he told her, like a practised dresser working backstage at the New York Ballet, reassuring his charge during a quick change. He opened up the jacket and placed it across Felix's fluffy black back. She looked up at him enquiringly as he did so, as though to say, 'What *are* you doing?'

The jacket had two Velcro straps – one for under the belly and one for around the chest. As Andrew fastened them, he chattered away in a friendly fashion to Felix, stroking and reassuring her, but in truth she didn't seem to need it. She appeared curious more than anything else, and once it was on she didn't mind it at all.

In fact, she seemed quite happy.

Released from Andrew's hands, the railway cat promptly

had a walk about the desk wearing her brand-new uniform, rather as we humans do when we're trying on new shoes.

'Well, don't you look smart,' said Andrew proudly.

And she did. The luminous jacket glowed brightly against her dark fur, while the neat fastening around her chest made her look somehow pulled in and puffed up, like a proud peacock. Her long white whiskers skated along the edge of the jacket, and as Felix put her best foot forward on the desk, she looked as well turned out as any child might on their very first day of school.

Felix seemed to enjoy her new official get-up. In pride of place on the left-hand side of her chest was her name badge bearing her new job title. Andrew didn't want to miss the opportunity to record this momentous milestone in Felix's career so, while she happily strutted about on the desk, he slipped out of his chair and started taking pictures.

Snap! Felix prowling past the blank screen of a computer.

Snap! Felix pausing on the edge of the desk, as though conducting a shoot on a clifftop, her fur blowing in the breeze. She stared expertly into the middle distance as Andrew moved and clicked around her.

He took shot after shot. She looked brilliant! He couldn't believe how well it had all come together. For about five minutes, Andrew and Felix were hard at work on their modelling shoot. Andrew took as many photos as he could, trying to get the best one possible. It was about 4 a.m. and the rest of the station was completely deserted and still – except for this hive of activity in the team leaders' office. The perfect shot came when Andrew was crouched down awkwardly and looking up at the senior pest controller from below, as she posed nobly on the end of the desk. Taking the shot from below somehow emphasised her stature now that she was a senior member of staff.

He glanced at his smartphone after he had taken it. *That was a great photo* – Felix looked so professional! Her smart new name badge was clearly visible in shot, as was the vest. Most importantly of all, Felix's face was a picture: she wore a very serious expression, as though she were about to head out onto the platforms right that minute and begin her diligent duty. She had one paw slightly forwards, taking a step: ready, as always, for action.

'You look great, Felix,' Andrew said with feeling. Gently, he eased her out of the outfit and tucked it away in his drawer again.

Felix shook her fur – for it had been flattened a bit by the jacket and she needed to puff it out again for the golden-girl glamourpuss look that she favoured. Then she jumped down off the desk and wandered away, thinking no more of it.

But Andrew's work wasn't yet done. Chuckling a bit to himself, he went through the pictures and pulled out that money shot. He attached it to an email addressed to all the team at Huddersfield station and wrote in jest:

Date: 30/01/2016
Time: 04.42
Subject: Felix's new uniform

Hi all,

Below are some pictures of Felix in her new uniform, please make sure this is worn at all times; regardless of any injuries you may sustain when attempting to dress her.

Of course, Felix was *never* actually going to wear the uniform on duty – she was too much of a diva for that. It was all part of the joke. But the *real* joke was going to be that picture. His colleagues had known nothing of his plan to get Felix a hi-vis vest – let alone an official name badge too – and Andrew couldn't wait for their reaction. If it was anything like his own, this was going to go down brilliantly.

And it did. All that day throughout Huddersfield station there were guffaws and giggles as team members opened up the email and saw Felix kitted out in her brand-new uniform.

'I thought it was brilliant!' exclaimed Angie. 'Super! Wonderful!'

Everyone thought it was really cute – and a *lot* of fun. Andrew also got quite a few cheeky emails back, telling him he was mad because of what he'd done and the lengths to which he'd gone to do it: absolutely *mad*.

And there was another email that came through, too: from a colleague asking if he'd mind if they sent the image to Mark Allan, for him to upload to Felix's Facebook page.

Felix's popularity on Facebook had been steadily growing. Only the day before, 29 January 2016, she'd hit a new milestone: 1,000 likes on Facebook. Mark and the team members helping him with the page had started adding videos as well as photographs to the site and that had perhaps encouraged more people to start following the feline. The railway cat had spent Christmas with Glenn and Teresa that year (they'd gone to town, buying Felix her own stocking full of cat-friendly presents and treats) and they'd uploaded a festive video of her playing with a bauble on their tree, tapping it repeatedly with her paw in transfixed fascination. Things like that enamoured Felix to her growing legion of Facebook fans, and the team involved with the page thought that Andrew's image of the station cat in her hi-vis vest and name badge would go down a real treat.

'Yeah, sure,' Andrew said casually when they asked him. 'No problem at all.'

At 5.54 p.m. on 30 January 2016, Felix changed her profile picture on Facebook to the hi-vis vest shot.

No one at the station knew it, but life would never be the same again.

31. Felix Is Famous

Andrew McClements was walking into the station concourse for his shift when he noticed a couple of the gateline team nudging each other as they looked at him.

'Andrew,' they called out. 'That picture of Felix is gathering some steam online.'

Yeah, Andrew thought sarcastically, *of course it is.* He knew the Facebook page had got a few more likes since the profile picture had been changed; a couple of days afterwards, Felix had been up to 1,266 fans, which Andrew assumed must be what the team were referring to. He supposed it was pretty special – it had taken Felix seven months to reach 1,000 likes, so to get a quarter of that in just a few days was great. The ever-loyal *Huddersfield Examiner* had run a piece on Felix's promotion ('Felix the Huddersfield station cat gets a purr-motion' read the headline) and even the online website Mashable had run a story on it: 'I'm famous!' posted Felix jokily on Facebook as she shared the link. But whether all that counted as 'gathering steam', Andrew doubted.

He headed into the team leaders' office and sat down, his mind running over all the tasks ahead of him that day. Working at the station was a relentless job in many ways: the services ran day in, day out, twenty-four hours a day, seven days a week. No wonder Felix took so many catnaps.

Just then, his work phone rang. 'Hello?' he answered.

'Andrew McClements?'

'That's right.'

'I'm ringing from head office at Bridgewater House. I work

in the communications department,' said the caller. 'I'll cut straight to the point: what's going on with that cat of yours?'

They must have heard about the Examiner *article,* Andrew thought. 'I didn't realise you would have heard about this,' he said in confusion, slightly unsure as to why the communications department for the whole of TransPennine Express was getting involved with such a local piece of PR.

He heard a laugh down the telephone. 'I think you should check Facebook,' said the caller.

Andrew drew his keyboard towards him and tapped out a few commands. Up came the familiar blue branding of the social-media site. As Andrew entered his log-in details, he still felt puzzled. Surely this wasn't big enough for head office's involvement?

Then he saw it. On the menu at the side of the page, listing the top trending news items, he spotted a familiar fluffy black face. 'Huddersfield, UK/Cat gets promoted to senior pest controller' read the associated link. It was right at the top of the list: the number-one trending item on Facebook! Reeling in amazement, Andrew clicked on the link. A second page opened up – with an awful lot of links to an awful lot of news outlets.

Felix was famous.

And the media wanted more. The phone kept ringing . . . and ringing . . . and ringing. The *Daily Mail* wanted a quote; they would be sending a photographer. National newspaper after national newspaper dialled the Huddersfield station number – and soon the broadcast media jumped on the bandwagon too. It all felt a little out of control, but Andrew hadn't been put in the position of team leader for nothing. He hoped, if the station and TPE could respond to this quickly enough, that it would be a real opportunity for Felix. If he could give the media what they needed, then he felt that he could work *with* them – rather than everyone being swept away in this unexpected maelstrom of media attention.

Although this sort of thing was completely out of his comfort zone, he stepped up to the plate to address the avalanche of incoming reporters, all desperate for information on the now nationally famous station cat. Assisting him in dealing with the media were Chris Bamford on the gateline and Andy Croughan, the man who had been so closely involved in bringing Felix to the station in the first place – and who had just been appointed as Huddersfield station manager following Will's departure in January.

They were just in time. Even as the trio started giving interviews and quotes to a sea of reporters on the phone, things started snowballing online. The Mashable article was shared nearly 3,000 times; Felix went up to 4,000 fans on Facebook ... then 10,000 ... then 20,000. Mark Allan watched the rising numbers with astonishment – and learned to turn his email notifications off pretty damn quick! After the *Daily Mail* article was published, it was shared nearly 30,000 times – which brought even more likes to the Facebook page. It was totally unbelievable; none of them had ever seen anything like it.

And then Andrew got a call from ITV. National TV. *Gulp.*

Although Andrew and the others were nervous about the media attention, the cat at the centre of it all seemed unperturbed. As one of her colleagues told Buzzfeed, 'Well, the fame hasn't quite gone to her head. As with most cats, they already think the world revolves around them.'

As the station started filling up with cameramen and photographers and journalists jumping off the train from London (via Wakefield Westgate), many team members found themselves doing peculiar limbo movements in order to stay out of shot. They might work with a suddenly famous station cat, but that didn't mean they wanted to become famous themselves. But for Chris and Andrew, who had agreed to do the ITV interview together, there was no choice but to appear in front of the cameras.

'Let's split it between us,' Chris had said to his colleague, as they nervously waited for the camera crew to turn up. 'If we do that, we've got each other's backs.'

But even with that reassurance, Andrew still felt apprehensive as he went to collect Felix for her big moment in front of the TV cameras. Although Chris and Andrew would be the ones doing the speaking, they didn't kid themselves: it was Felix everybody was here to see.

She was hanging about the office, not up to much; totally unaware of her impending media stardom.

'The ITV people are here, Felix,' Andrew told her shakily. He knew she couldn't understand the words, but he was speaking to calm himself as much as her. He opened his drawer and pulled out the hi-vis vest with Felix's name badge pinned on it. All the media wanted Felix to be wearing her uniform in shot – she just looked so cute in it. 'Time to get dressed.'

Felix stood patiently as he pulled on the little jacket and made sure she looked smart; but then, how could Felix the railway cat ever look anything but beautiful? As though picking up on Andrew's tension, however, there was a bit of uncertainty in her eyes as he fastened it around her and then picked her up to carry her outside to face the cameras.

Not everyone could pick up Felix; Mrs Grumpy wouldn't countenance such an intrusion on her personal space from any Tom, Dick or Harry. But Andrew had been watching the master, Dave Chin, at work, and one day he'd decided to try it, since he and Felix were buddies by then. He'd followed Dave's tips – 'Be confident, be quick' – and she'd turned out to be very comfortable sitting in his arms. That was why it was Andrew who carried her out to meet her admirers. The ITV people had asked him to hold her steady in his arms while he simultaneously spoke to the camera.

What a request! As if he didn't have enough to worry about. How did that saying go? 'Never work with animals or children.' Felix was famously Miss Independent; Andrew knew that she would stay in his arms only if she wanted to. He could imagine the drama if she leapt out of his hold and scarpered. The young team leader only hoped that the theatrical diva he knew was inside her would rise to the occasion today – and bask in the limelight as she always had.

'Come on, then, Felix,' he said. 'Let's do this.'

Felix blinked back at him. She was facing forwards in his arms – all the better for the cameras to capture those enormous emerald eyes of hers – and her white-tipped toes dangled down. Andrew gave her a big firm stroke on her fluffy black head. Did she have any idea what was coming?

Together, they stepped out of the back office and onto Platform 1. There were cameras *everywhere*. Felix looked with interest at them, and Andrew could tell she was a bit unsure, but they both drew strength from being together. He kept talking to her and stroking her, and she gradually relaxed in his arms as Andrew and Chris answered the questions posed to them.

And, once she'd relaxed, Felix was able to enjoy the centre-stage position she had always relished since her very first day at the station. She was a very comfortable cat nestled in Andrew's arms in the hi-vis vest, and even the clicking of the photographers' cameras – for there were people taking pictures as well as filming – did not bother her: used both to the noise of the trains and the smartphones of strangers, she didn't even flinch.

After the interview section of the filming was over, both photographers and cameramen wanted to capture some footage of Felix running free on the platform. Like a singer mid-set during a stadium show, Felix disappeared back inside at this juncture with her official dresser, Andrew, in order to take off her jacket. Despite what her growing number of Facebook fans might *like* to think, Felix didn't actually wear her hi-vis when she was running about; the team always took it off before they let her loose.

Once she was attired solely in her birthday suit and her glitzy purple collar, Andrew, like a bodyguard extraordinaire, escorted her back outside to the little lobby between the customer-information point and the lost-property office. Here, he set her down on the floor.

Felix sniffed the air cautiously. The crowd that had congregated on Platform 1 had swelled even further since she and Andrew had popped back into the office, as the customers too wanted to see the famous railway cat in action. There was now a massive crowd of people gathered in a circle surrounding the doorway, and so many cameras and phones on display that it was as if a mini electronics store had suddenly been set up slap bang in the middle of Huddersfield station.

Felix paused in the doorway, as though making her public wait, upping their anticipation. Only once she was ready did Andrew take in his hand one of the Dreamies treats he'd brought out with him, and throw it far from the doorway, out onto the platform.

Years of training for this moment stood Felix in good stead. She knew what to do when someone threw a treat for her – oh yes she did. Out she bounded from the lobby with impressive athletic grace, darting after the treat, and as the station cat confidently cantered along the platform, the air was filled with the *click-click-clicking* sound of the cameras. It was like a celebrity arriving on the red carpet – which, of course, she was.

Once on her walkabout, Felix gave the cameras what they were waiting for. She walked this way; she walked that way; she sat on command; she wagged her tail – then she drew out from her bag of tricks the one star turn that had them all gasping in acclaim: Felix stood up on her hind legs and caught a treat between her two front paws. Felix had always had showbiz in her spirit and she certainly gave the reporters something to write home about.

Naturally enough, her brilliant performance led to more and more admirers – and more and more media interest. She had 30,000 Facebook fans; 40,000; 50,000 . . . People couldn't keep up. It went on for weeks, the station team tripping over the BBC and the *Telegraph* as they tried to keep the station running smoothly. It was surreal and it led to a couple of really mad weeks for all at Huddersfield station.

Andrew thought the live radio interviews were the worst. At least ITV had been a pre-record, so if he made a mistake the crew could stop filming and he could start over again. But he found himself sitting in his office, listening down the line to BBC Radio 5 Live and hearing, 'And we're now joined by Andrew from TransPennine Express who's going to tell us all about Felix the cat,' and then suddenly he was live on national radio.

In between the filming and the photos and the live radio interviews, the media continued to call up, asking for quotations, so he and Felix and Chris were giving soundbites, both visual and audio, to the assorted press. Felix had never done so many photo shoots in her life. Just as the traditional media interest started to die down, the internet media caught up:

another wave of Felix-focused stories from The LAD Bible and others followed.

And amid all this liking and sharing and tweeting and reporting, something incredible happened.

Felix's fame went global. And she didn't just hop across to France on a booze cruise – she went properly international: jet-setting-superstar *global*.

The first Felix's family knew of it was when some of her Facebook fans started posting foreign media clippings of her on her page, saying that that was how they had discovered her. Following the coverage of her well-deserved promotion in the UK press, she hit the headlines in Taiwan, the Netherlands, Hong Kong and many other places. Andrew was bowled over when he learned that the ITV footage featuring Felix, Chris and him had been re-used by an American broadcaster – Felix the railway cat was on *Good Morning America*! Australia joined the party, as well as Japan and China. Felix was a bona fide international icon, with fans in France, Germany, Italy, Canada, Brazil, Mexico, Argentina, Lithuania, Estonia . . . The list went on and on – and then on!

The staff at Huddersfield had always known she was special, but this was something else. Angie Hunte thought it was absolutely super. 'To me, she's always been famous,' she said proudly. 'But, you know, it doesn't matter how global she goes, she's still my kitten, my baby.'

It was Dave Chin who summed it up in a nutshell: 'She's just a little star.'

And her new, worldwide fans seemed to agree with him. With all this happening in February, Felix was soon the flattered recipient of many Valentine's Day cards. Perhaps it was just as well that the stray black cat, her 'boyfriend', had not been seen on the station for a while, for he might not have been able to control his jealousy at this flood of not-so-secret admirers. But the love-themed billets-doux were only the start of Felix's fan mail. As the year drew on the team found their mail bags becoming full of post for Felix.

Angie couldn't believe it when all this stuff started arriving. Felix had letters from Canada, America, France . . . Her fans were sending her all sorts. Somebody even sent some catnip from Ireland.

Parcel after parcel after parcel was brought to the station mailbox by the local Huddersfield postman. They were simply addressed to: 'Felix, the Huddersfield station cat'. The global superstar was sent gourmet suppers and laser toys, cat bowls with her name on them and heart-shaped dishes, posh turquoise collars printed with pink cupcakes – and even a supersized cat-treats tin from America. She was mailed a bumper pack of goodies from her favourite food brand 'Felix', as well as sardines from John West. She was even contacted by the famous Battersea Dogs & Cats Home, who gave her a special branded bowl.

That was the one that got Angie. 'Wow' was all she could say as she stood in the office, reading the message from the celebrated rescue centre.

Other cats 'wrote' to her to inform her of their vermin-catching capabilities, as though Felix was a pest-controlling cat idol in the feline world; one resented the 'intervention by human' that had decreased his tally to only three mice and one sparrow. Many told her how much they admired her work at Huddersfield, and she was showered with congratulations on her promotion. Letters were signed by humans and cats, dogs and rabbits, the 'x' of affectionate kisses often accompanied by the sketch of a pawprint too. Lots of children took the time to draw her colourful pictures, while others sent her postcards from their holidays.

Perhaps the most special letters, however, came from

other station cats. It seemed there was a collegiate feeling among the members of this railway kitty club. Felix received correspondence from Batman and Metro-Miez, German station cats from Cuxhaven near Hamburg who sent her 'signed' pictures, as well as from Jojo, the Southend Victoria station cat. Jojo, another black-and-white moggy, kindly sent Felix some treats and told the Huddersfield cat how she had the British Transport Police, who cared for Jojo down in Essex, wrapped around her piebald paws. Felix knew *that* feeling well . . .

So many gifts and offerings arrived that Felix's filing-cabinet drawer in the team leaders' office became absolutely chocka. There was far too much for one cat to consume in one lifetime; too much even for those with nine lives. As the Royal Family did before her, Queen Felix found that it was best to donate some of the thoughtful offerings to local cat rescue centres, where other cats less fortunate than she would be able to benefit from her fans' incredible generosity.

That didn't mean she wasn't grateful. Felix had been well brought up by her family and the station team made sure to photograph her with the myriad gifts upon receipt, so that she could post special 'thank you' messages on Facebook and people would know that their presents and letters had reached her safely. Felix looked by turns happy, curious, hungry and bored in the assorted snaps.

For that Facebook page, Mark's creativity was showing no bounds as he catered to the legion of fans following Felix. With tens of thousands of admirers posting and inter-acting with the railway cat online it became a major job keeping up with all the correspondence – and that was before he thought about new ideas for posts. Nonetheless, Mark was absolutely in his element. He'd hoped that the page would become a creative outlet for him; he'd never expected this. Felix really had changed his life.

Andrew got more involved with the page, working alongside Mark and filming amusing videos of Felix playing on the night shift to entertain her fans. The cat watched in fascination one evening as he edited a movie of her onscreen in the office.

'What *are* you thinking?' Andrew asked her, genuinely wondering. Felix's green eyes never left the screen as the TV version of herself bounded and jumped and ran on the monitor. The flesh-and-blood Felix was obsessed with it. Andrew couldn't decipher her enigmatic expression, but as she sat beside him in the office she became transfixed by her own moving image.

Of course, she wasn't the only one. With demand so high for the Facebook page, there was an enormous appetite for new footage of Felix. Mark was so diligent about updating the page that he even logged in on holiday, replying to fans and adding images from the stockpile he had created.

'Are you checking that Felix page again?' asked his wife in dry amusement. 'There are three people in this marriage: me, you and Felix!'

Mark's affection for Felix was by now immense. 'I didn't expect that I'd become attached to a cat,' he said in wonder. 'But I have.'

As the Facebook friend numbers soared, Mark, Andrew and the others grew more advanced with their media-making, adding soundtracks to videos and editing Felix's funny little actions in time to the music. Her early promise jiggling along the platforms on jazz nights had flourished, making her a proper dancing queen at last. One of Mark's favourite mini-films was when he added the *Chariots of Fire* theme to a slow-motion recording of Felix chasing pigeons on the platform. It went down really well.

The pigeons now became characters who teased her online (as they did in Felix's real life), always just out of reach of her hunting claws, with 'Percy Pigeon' getting a starring role in the Facebook posts as her nemesis. And Luther, Felix's brother, was also introduced to her fans: Mark sketched the contrast between Felix's busy, exciting life on the railway and her sibling's apparently tranquil domestic routine with an owner.

Fact can be stranger than fiction, though, for Luther had recently had an adventure of his own. He'd disappeared for five weeks but come back safely; his family thought he must have got locked in a barn. However, there must have been some sand in there, because when he came back to them the short-haired black-and-white cat had sand between his toes. The running joke was that he'd been away on his holidays.

Felix herself was the lead joke on April Fools' Day for the *Huddersfield Examiner*. The town was shocked to read the headline: 'Devastation as Felix the Huddersfield Station Cat is poached to move to Leeds Station'. It caused outcry. Facebook user Gavin Hudson even commented: 'This is bigger transfer news than Messi and Ronaldo swapping teams!'

The relief was plain on everybody's faces when it was revealed to be a harmless prank. No one could imagine Huddersfield without her.

'She's part of the fixtures and fittings here,' her colleague Michael Ryan said affectionately.

Except, you know, way more glamorous . . .

And it was glamour a go-go as Felix turned five on 17 May 2016. She received birthday messages from across the globe – and a very special gift indeed.

For Felix the famous Facebooker now had more than

60,000 Facebook fans. In time, that number would grow to far more than that. No wonder she looked so pleased with herself these days: the spitting image of the cat who got the cream (*and* the salmon *and* the prawns).

But there were some at the station who were not as pleased as Felix. While many of her colleagues thought her international fame was cool, others considered it a load of nonsense. They couldn't believe the world had reacted in this way to her. To them – so they said – this social-media 'icon' was just a lazy cat who sat in the station and got in everyone's way.

Team leader Geoff was one of those who thought her popularity very strange indeed. He still shouted at her to get out of the office whenever he saw her appear. It was just a cat at the end of the day; why were people so interested?

Her many thousands of adoring Facebook fans could tell him that.

32. Back to Work

'Oh my God, it's her! It's her! It's Felix!'

Felix almost raised an eyebrow as she heard the excited voices. But she didn't flinch or flee: this was a regular occurrence by now. She was sat on duty at the customer-information point, and the eager tourists crowded round her, smartphones out to take selfies with the famous railway cat.

In the light of Felix's celebrity, Huddersfield station had suddenly become a key destination for her tens of thousands of fans.

They travelled for miles – Andy Croughan had met people from China, Germany and Canada who had come to see her. It was the same at home. English fans altered their travel plans so they could alight at Huddersfield in the hope of catching a few minutes with Felix; regular commuters came that little bit earlier in the mornings just to have some fun. Though people never fought over her, the team sometimes noticed looks of disappointment crossing people's faces if Felix was already holding court with someone else when they walked by. At other times, especially if Felix was in a playful mood, whole crowds would gather around her as though she was a street performer in Covent Garden who had painted herself blue from top to tail.

That was the magic of the railway cat.

The team got a big kick out of seeing how happy customers were to meet her. Felix brightened people's days. It could be a family walking through: a mum now with a beaming grin, her seven-year-old daughter skipping out of the station as she held her dad's hand and chattered away about the beautiful cat. Or a young couple in their early twenties – a redhead in Doc Marten boots with her long-haired boyfriend – who might sit right down on the floor to feed the cat a treat. People would literally lie on the floor and clamber over benches and bikes to be near her. Others couldn't believe their eyes.

'Is Felix real?' Andrew was asked by two girls from New Zealand one day.

'What do you mean?' he asked, somewhat taken aback.

'Well, we've seen all the pictures, but it's hard to believe something like that,' they said doubtfully, as they chatted with him at the booking-office window. 'Is it real? Is it all real?'

Andrew had just finished feeding Felix, so he knew she was nearby. He brought her out to show the girls that, yes, the station cat was definitely real. Their faces were a picture.

'She *does* exist!' they exclaimed in wonder.

Though Felix was happy to accommodate all this attention when she was on duty – 'She handles it well,' said Angie Hunte proudly, 'she handles everything well' – Felix was not, of course, just a celebrity. She was a railway cat: she had a job to do and platforms to patrol – and all-important catnaps to have. Her social-media fame hadn't curtailed her independent explorations, nor changed the way she wrote her own rota for the day. Inevitably, on some occasions when excited fans turned up at the station Felix, sadly, wasn't there to greet them.

Wanting to avoid any disappointment to her many admirers, she took to warning people of her busy schedule on Facebook, asking them to leave a five- or six-hour timeframe for their visit to Huddersfield if they *really* wanted to see her, in case she wasn't on duty when they first called by.

She hoped they would understand. After all, she was a cat, not a showgirl. She didn't appear on demand – what cat would?

Luckily, most cat lovers knew that all too well. In fact, the unpredictability of whether Felix would be on duty or not made the joy of actually meeting her all the greater.

'Finally!' a lady cried aloud on the platform one morning when Angie was on shift. 'I've finally seen Felix, the Huddersfield station cat!'

The best things come to those who wait.

Gradually, life returned to normal for Felix – well, as normal as life ever gets when you're a senior pest controller with thousands of adoring Facebook fans. She settled back into her routine of helping the team leaders with the night shift and the morning rush, but she still chose to avoid the evening crushes and especially the rowdy customers from the Friday night Ale Trail. Once again, she took to settling in her favourite spot on the customer-information desk. It was a great little location, for not only did she have a prime view, she was also right by the door to the back offices, which meant any and every team member who went by could give her a stroke or a pat on the head as they passed – and they all did. It was as if they couldn't resist her; but it had been that way from the start.

In the summer, Felix got involved in a charity fun run, wearing a GPS tracker on her purple collar to measure out her own 5k race; she raised more than £5,200 for a children's charity. She was also present for the opening of Huddersfield's new first-class lounge, and had a special grooming session to keep her cool in the summer heat. Her fans often paid attention to her grooming on Facebook – even commenting if her travels across the train tracks had left her with dirty feet – so Angie tried hard to make sure her baby always looked in tip-top shape.

Felix and Mark Allan still met regularly at 6.30 a.m. by the Head of Steam each working day. Mark was always pleased to see her, and was not ashamed to say it. It had become part of his morning routine, as well as Felix's.

So fixed was that routine that when Mark went off on holiday for a week, he felt very weird indeed on his last day before his vacation. *Felix doesn't know I'm going away on holiday,* he thought sadly.

Indeed, it was a very sad Felix the following day: Chris Bamford looked out to see her sitting in her usual chair on the metal bench, looking hopefully up towards the station entrance, but the tall man in the dark-grey suit never came. She waited every single day of that week for him. Chris felt so sorry for her that he went down to see her himself.

'He's not coming,' he said helplessly. 'I don't know how to tell you.'

He gave her a few treats and they kept her going until Mark got back. When Chris looked down towards the Head of Steam on the day he returned, the routine was back up and running: the cat and the commuter were sitting side by side on the bench, Mark's face lit up by a smile as he laughed at her playful antics.

So Felix continued to do what she had always done best: touch people's hearts.

There came a warm day when Andrew McClements was out on duty. It was a Saturday, a day when the station was always full of people travelling to Manchester or Leeds for the weekend. It was very busy, about lunchtime, when he noticed a mother with a five-year-old son battling towards him on the platform. He approached, closing the distance to help them out.

'Hello, there!' he said in a friendly fashion to the boy.

But the child stared pointedly at the floor and refused to make eye contact with him.

'Hello,' his mother said. She wafted a hand around her face, which was framed by her blonde hair, gently fanning herself; it was a scorching day, and even in her cool summer dress she looked a little harried and hot. 'I was wondering,' she went on, anxiously. 'I understand if we can't, but can we see Felix, please? My son *really* likes Felix.'

Andrew glanced at the child again. 'Oh, do you?' he said jovially; but once again the child said nothing. He stood unmoving by his mother's side, his eyes boring holes into the ground. He seemed *really* shy – or perhaps, Andrew realised, it was something else.

'It would mean a lot to us,' his mother said, speaking for her son again.

'Let me see if I can find her,' Andrew replied.

He fought his way through the daytrippers waiting on the platform and nipped into the back office to see if Felix was around. He really wanted to find her because it seemed to him that the child deserved this special treat of meeting her.

It had occurred to Andrew that perhaps the boy had autism. Maybe, just maybe, Felix could make his day.

Felix had just woken up from a beautiful sleep in the shower room and was more than happy to accompany Andrew back along the platform. 'If you need me, I'm here,' her merry walk seemed to say. The two of them made their way back to the mother and her son.

As soon as the station cat loomed into view, the child raised his head.

'FELIX!' he yelled exuberantly – the first thing Andrew had heard him say. 'Felix, Felix, Felix!'

He started flapping his arms and grinning wildly. Andrew had never seen anyone so excited in all his life. The boy became incredibly animated and flapped his way over to the cat. 'Felix, Felix, Felix!' he kept saying, over and over and over again, as if in that one word were all the words in the world: love, hope, happiness.

His mum watched him with the purest, happiest smile on her face. She looked at Andrew above her child's head and mouthed, 'Thank you.' She was so grateful that they'd got to meet the cat.

As for Felix, she stopped where she stood and waited for the boy to come to her. She fixed her big green eyes on him thoughtfully. Felix had an uncanny knack of reading people. She seemed to know instinctively who could be trusted and who posed a threat; who was after some play-time or who warranted a glaring look; and who just needed some understanding.

She blinked up at the boy as he stared obsessively back at her, still flapping a little, unable to control his limbs in his overwhelming excitement. As she stared at him, looking deep into his eyes, it was as though she was making a special, personal connection with him. The child reached out a still-flapping hand and patted her gently.

'Felix,' he said again.

She sat down next to him, wrapping her big fluffy tail around herself and settling in for a nice, long cuddle.

'Felix,' he said again as he stroked her, squatting down on the platform. His animation eased into a profound calm. *'Felix.'*

Epilogue

'Hiya, Felix,' says Andrew McClements in the summer of 2016. 'Did you miss me?'

He bends down to stroke her fluffy black head as she winds familiarly in and out of his legs. She doesn't answer his question, but she might well be pining for him. For Andrew no longer works at Huddersfield station – he has been promoted to head office.

In his opinion, although he has lots of people to thank for that promotion, Felix is especially deserving of his gratitude. In stepping up to the plate when the railway cat became an international icon, he impressed HQ with his initiative – and left the station in June. He still returns regularly to Huddersfield as part of his new job, though, and it is always a pleasure to see Felix, not least because he always wants to say 'thank you'.

'I owe Felix quite a bit for my career,' he acknowledges gratefully. Like so many others before him, his life has been bettered by the railway cat.

One other such person – and another regular visitor – is Gareth Hope. If ever he is going through Huddersfield he always jumps off the train to say 'hello' to his not-so-little-anymore black-and-white cat. It's the first thing he does the moment his feet touch the platform: rush off to see her and find out how she's been. As he and his cat catch up on their news, he is glad to see that she hasn't been spoiled by her global fame. She is still the same little cat.

Gareth could barely believe it when Felix became so

internationally renowned – but he also allows himself a wry smile about her success. What was it he'd written on his 'pros and cons' list in the days when he'd been trying so hard to convince Paul to get a station cat? Is he allowed to feel at least a *little* smug? After all, he'd told them years before that a station moggy would be 'good PR'.

Though it's nice to go back and visit, Gareth has never regretted moving on. Billy had been right about that – as he had been right about so many other things too. Even now, Gareth is looking to the future. He has a bright idea about a station duck . . .

The visitors Felix attracts to the station aren't all ex-colleagues or Facebook fans. Every now and again, her family come wandering through to say hello too.

'My relationship with Felix now is that Felix is a railway cat,' says Chris Briscoe, her 'grandfather', honestly. 'Whether she remembers me or not now, I don't know; I only go up three or four times a year. But I'll always give her a scratch behind the ears when I'm at Huddersfield.'

If you go down to Huddersfield station today, Felix, the railway cat, may well be there on the platform. She sits and watches the trains go by, soothed by the ebb and flow of their tide, seeming to enjoy the choreography of the carriages: the way the separate services come in, pause, and then split in opposite directions once more, simultaneously travelling north and south.

Sometimes, Felix's own life seems like those separating services: so many people she has met along the way have moved on with the tides of the trains. Gareth, Andrew, Paul, Martin . . . and never forgetting Billy. But other people are always there, as solid as the sand beneath her feet. People like Dave Chin and Jean Randall; Angela Dunn and Angie Hunte. And even Geoff, the crotchety team leader.

There's something about Geoff. Is he *really* as crotchety as he seems?

The team leaders' office door has a big glass window in it: when the door is closed, anyone can wander by and look right in, and the person in the office wouldn't know they were watching. So Geoff probably didn't realise that Chris Bamford came to knock upon his door one afternoon – but he did. Chris pauses outside, his fist raised ready to knock, when he suddenly lowers his hand silently, a slow smile spreading across his face. In the office is Geoff – and he is petting Felix the cat.

'Geoff claims not to like Felix,' says Michael Ryan, 'but everyone knows he loves her more than he lets on.' And Felix knows it too.

'We've *all* grown to love her,' adds Rachel Stockton, who'd named Felix all those years ago. 'We'd all be heartbroken if anything happened to her.'

The team wouldn't be the only ones. Felix has touched the lives of so many customers too – not least that of Mark Allan, the man who runs her famous Facebook page. So successful has it become that he's actually been given his own official pass by TransPennine Express. His lanyard reads: 'Personal Assistant to the Senior Pest Controller'.

He still doesn't want a cat though: 'Felix is the only girl for me.'

That's as it is for Angie Hunte, too. 'She's always been special,' she says. 'I love her to bits. I can't imagine being without her. She's grown with me from a baby and from the first day I held her.'

And how very, *very* much that kitten has grown in the years that have followed. From being just a playful ball of fluff in the palm of Angie's hand to becoming the senior pest controller, Felix has had quite a journey. Yet, somehow, she has taken it all in her confident, supermodel-strutting stride. She's an independent lass at heart, is Felix, and that spirit has always seen her through her many adventures.

The TransPennine Express passenger charter reads: 'We are proud of our staff and you can expect to be greeted with a warm welcome and receive exceptional customer service.' And Felix, the railway cat, is certainly an exemplary employee.

So look out for her, next time you're there. She might be hiding by the bike racks, or on duty at the desk. She might be over by Billy's garden, or sprawled right across your path. Obviously, *you'll* be the one stepping round *her*. Remember: she is Queen Felix, after all. 'She does whatever she wants,' says Chris – and that's as it should be. For Felix is a station cat; she's part of history.

For her family of colleagues – who are really more like friends – her fame has not changed her. That lively, playful, disdainful and loving cat they see every day is still just as much a part of the team as always. Five years on, Felix continues to make it a pleasure for them to come to work, whether their alarm is going off at 4.45 a.m. or they are facing a night shift with its long, but no longer lonely, hours.

'I think everyone likes Felix,' says her colleague Adam Carter. 'Having her around makes the place seem a little more homely and friendly; it makes it a nicer place to work. She's a symbol of that.'

'She's Felix,' Angela Dunn says simply. 'What would we do without Felix?'

Acknowledgements

This book would have been impossible to write without the generous support of the team at Huddersfield station. Angie Hunte, truly a Felix favourite, was especially and repeatedly helpful – and it was a genuine pleasure to see the joy in Felix's fluffy body as she scampered along the platform with Angie and came out from her hidey-holes the moment she heard her voice. Gareth Hope made a special trip to Huddersfield to contribute to this book, and also kindly dug out documents and photographs to assist with the writing. Special thanks also to Andrew McClements, Andy Croughan, Angela Dunn, Chris Bamford, Dave Chin, Mark Allan, Alan Hind and Jean Randall for generously giving up significant time for interviews; and to Chris and Joanne Briscoe for taking the time to recall Felix's first eight weeks as a kitten in their home. I am also grateful to Pauline for looking after me during the night shift at Huddersfield station, and to all those other members of the team who kindly filled in surveys, sent photographs, replied to emails or shared anecdotes: Adam Carter, Amanda/Chrissy, Christine, Craig, Dave Rooney, Jon Ironmonger, Liam, Louise Jacobs, Michael Ryan, Rachel Stockton and Sam Dyson.

At Penguin Books, a massive thank you to editor Fiona Crosby for brilliantly spotting Felix's literary potential and for making this book happen. Thanks to all at TPE for letting Felix tell her story, especially Sarah Ford, Jack Kempf, Sarah Cunningham, Lisa Gannon, Catherine Unsworth. Last, but by no means least, thanks to Beth Gribble for identifying the plants in Billy's garden, and to my husband Duncan for all his support.

The following books, newspapers and websites were consulted in order to bring Felix's story to life:

Books:

A Century of Huddersfield: Events, People and Places over the Last 100 Years by Brian Haigh and Susan Gillooley (Sutton Publishing, 2000)
Golden Years of Huddersfield: Local Nostalgic Photographs from the 1940s, 50s and 60s by Diane Harpwood and Phil Holland (True North Books, 1998)
Huddersfield: Home Town Memories by Melvyn Briggs and John Watson (The Derby Books Publishing Company Ltd, 2011)

Newspapers:

Daily Mail, Guardian, Huddersfield Examiner.

Websites:

bbc.co.uk/news, bluecross.org.uk, buzzfeed.com, districtdavesforum.co.uk, factretriever.com/cat-facts, Felix's Facebook page, manchesterandsalfordrspca.org.uk, mentalfloss.com, purr-n-fur.org.uk [an especially brilliant resource on the history of station cats], rspca.org.uk, vets-now.com.

Photos:

Photo section images provided by Andrew McClements, Gareth Hope, Al Richardson, TransPennine Express, and the Felix the Huddersfield Station Cat Facebook page.

Finally, thank you to Felix, the Huddersfield station cat.